*THE*
FOURTH
LION

# *THE* FOURTH LION

## ESSAYS FOR GOPALKRISHNA GANDHI

EDITED BY
VENU MADHAV GOVINDU
SRINATH RAGHAVAN

ALEPH

ALEPH

ALEPH BOOK COMPANY
An independent publishing firm
promoted by *Rupa Publications India*

First published in India in 2021
by Aleph Book Company
7/16 Ansari Road, Daryaganj
New Delhi 110002

This edition © Aleph Book Company 2021

Copyright for individual essays vests in the respective contributors.

All rights reserved.

The authors have asserted their moral rights.

The views and opinions expressed in this book are those of the respective authors and the facts are as reported by them, which have been verified to the extent possible, and the publisher is not in any way liable for the same.

The publisher has used its best endeavours to ensure that URLs for external websites referred to in this book are correct and active at the time of going to press. However, the publisher has no responsibility for the websites and can make no guarantee that a site will remain live or that the content is or will remain appropriate.

No part of this publication may be reproduced, transmitted, or stored in a retrieval system, in any form or by any means, without permission in writing from Aleph Book Company.

ISBN: 978-93-90652-32-7

Printed at Parksons Graphics Pvt. Ltd., Mumbai.

This book is sold subject to the condition that it shall not, by way of trade or otherwise, be lent, resold, hired out, or otherwise circulated without the publisher's prior consent in any form of binding or cover other than that in which it is published.

# CONTENTS

*Preface*   ix

## Section I
## Literature and Culture

1. In Love with Myself?   3
   T. M. KRISHNA
2. As the Conch Sounds   11
   NIRUPAMA MENON RAO
3. 'The Waters of that Other Ocean': Vedanta and a Single Man   21
   KESHAVA GUHA
4. At Home in Two Worlds   33
   MARIA AURORA COUTO
5. A Study in 'Creative Compassion'   42
   JAYANTHA DHANAPALA AND TISSA JAYATILAKA
6. *Gandhi, My Father*: A Creation in Conflict   51
   FEROZ ABBAS KHAN

## Section II
## History

7. 'Pa Rishi': Gandhi's Constructive Critiques of Parsi Culture and Society   57
   DINYAR PATEL
8. Intimate Enemies: Rajaji and Kamaraj   68
   A. R. VENKATACHALAPATHY
9. Jhinu Kantvu: To Spin a Fine Yarn   80
   TRIDIP SUHRUD
10. Harold Laski and Indian Independence   89
    ISAAC KRAMNICK

11. Ashoka and Gandhi 101
    UPINDER SINGH
12. Tracking a Prime Minister's Travels to Ajanta and Ellora 111
    NAYANJOT LAHIRI
13. Pacifist, Anarchist, Satirist, and Historian of the Water Closet 127
    VENU MADHAV GOVINDU

## Section III
## The Environment

14. Grasslands Lost in the Woods 143
    JANAKI LENIN
15. On Birdsong and Human Well-being 155
    VIVEK MENON
16. The Environment: A Renegotiation with Ourselves 164
    SOPAN JOSHI
17. A Message from Versova 177
    ERIK SOLHEIM
18. 'Capitalism' through an Asian Lens 185
    AMITAV GHOSH

## Section IV
## Politics and Public Affairs

19. The Roots of 'Hyper-Nationalism' 191
    PRABHAT PATNAIK
20. With Borrowed Eyes: A View of India's Future 202
    RAJMOHAN GANDHI
21. Bengal: A Short History of a Long Decline 212
    RUDRANGSHU MUKHERJEE
22. Norway's Role in Peacebuilding and Conflict Resolution 220
    JON WESTBORG
23. Thinking About Politics in India 231
    GOPAL GURU

## Section V
## Memoirs

| | |
|---|---|
| 24. Getting to Know Gopal<br>RAMACHANDRA GUHA | 243 |
| 25. An Island of Sanity<br>ELINOR SISULU | 253 |
| 26. Making Truth Powerful<br>ARUNA ROY | 264 |
| *Publications of Gopalkrishna Gandhi* | 275 |
| *Notes on the Contributors* | 277 |

PREFACE

Administration, diplomacy, governance—Gopalkrishna Gandhi has served in these domains of statecraft with distinction for over four decades. His writings too have spanned diverse genres, embodying deep scholarship as well as a profound understanding of politics and history, literature and culture. Respected for his statesmanship and judgement, admired for his learning and craft, Gopalkrishna— known to many as Gopal—is also an exemplar of a fading ideal of our republic, one that placed ethics and the pursuit of the common good at the core of our public life. Most notable and important, however, is his ineffable warmth and compassion.

Born on 22 April 1945, Gopalkrishna Gandhi was the youngest of the four children of Lakshmi and Devadas Gandhi. After studying English Literature at St Stephen's College in Delhi, he joined the Indian Administrative Service in 1968. Serving in the Tamil Nadu cadre, he held various positions, including the editorship of the *Gazetteers* of Tamil Nadu in which capacity he produced the first gazetteer of the district of Pudukkottai. His most important contribution to the state, however, pertained to a crucial yet under-appreciated facet of its modern history and politics—migration.

During the colonial era, a large number of Tamils had migrated to Ceylon (present-day Sri Lanka), primarily to labour in the tea gardens. Following the independence of India and Ceylon, the fate of these workers and their descendants became a major political question. In 1964, the two countries signed an accord, whereby India was to accept and rehabilitate more than half-a-million 'plantation' Tamils. Gopal worked on this difficult and sensitive process, initially as Tamil Nadu's director of rehabilitation and then in the Indian High Commission's office in the Sri Lankan city of Kandy. After this stint abroad, he served in various capacities including as secretary to the Governor of Tamil Nadu and with R. Venkataraman during the latter's terms as the vice president and president of India.

In 1992, Gopalkrishna Gandhi took voluntary retirement from the administrative services and set out for his first diplomatic assignment—as the founding director of the Nehru Centre in London, an institution that would become prominent in India's cultural outreach. In 1996, he was appointed India's high commissioner to South Africa and Lesotho. The following year, he was recalled to serve as secretary to the newly elected president of India, K. R. Narayanan. Diplomatic and gubernatorial assignments followed: as India's high commissioner to Sri Lanka (2000–2002), the ambassador to Norway and Iceland (2002–2004), and as the governor of West Bengal from 2004 to 2009. In 2017, he unsuccessfully contested the election for vice president of India with the support of diverse opposition parties.

Honoured with a number of awards as well as doctoral degrees from universities in India, Sri Lanka, and South Africa, he is currently a distinguished professor at Ashoka University. The sheer range of his professional activity and contributions attest his extraordinary public life. However, encompassing Gopal's career in a conventional, if glittering, arc barely explains his significance as a public figure.

As with so many of his generation—born as he was at the cusp of India's Independence—Gopal's life has been shaped by the paradigmatic values of what we may call, by way of shorthand, the Gandhi-Nehru era. This was perhaps doubly so owing to his lineage: his paternal and maternal grandfathers were Mohandas Gandhi and Chakravarti Rajagopalachari. He is at once a product and an exemplar of that endangered 'idea of India'. Gopal's sensibility is suffused with the ethos of Bharat and Hindustan.

In his formative years, Gopal also had the examples of his older siblings—each of whom chose a different path and achieved distinction in their endeavours. Tara Gandhi Bhattacharjee has worked on khadi, craft, women's issues, and steered a number of organizations. Rajmohan Gandhi is well known as a fearless editor, peace activist, and greatly admired historian of modern India, and biographer of many stalwarts of the freedom struggle. The late Ramchandra Gandhi distinguished himself as a profoundly original philosopher and thinker.

While he has mostly worked outside the formal portals of academe, the range and depth of Gopal's knowledge of India's past and present is formidable. If his deep understanding of the mechanics of government, constitutional principles, and contemporary political history was honed by decades of experience in significant positions, his scholarship extends into social, cultural, and ethical realms as well. While he has produced numerous excellent volumes centred on Mahatma Gandhi, they provide only a glimpse of Gopal's masterly understanding of the era of our freedom movement. His unerring command of the sources on our founding figures and his insights on modern Indian history has informed the work of many scholars.

Gopal's engagement with the life and legacy of Gandhi is an ongoing exercise and too extensive to consider in detail here. For the most part, his method has been to carefully assemble the historical record and allow it to speak for itself. The apparent simplicity of this approach masks a lifetime of learning and contemplation on the life of the Mahatma and its meaning. Here, we may mention two of his volumes as illustrating his method. Though Gandhi has been studied from a myriad of perspectives, in *The Oxford India Gandhi,* Gopal opens up new dimensions of understanding. By a careful excavation of Gandhi's own writings, utterances, and other authentic sources, he gets to the essence below the encrustations of the 'plaster-saint image of Mahatma Gandhi'. The result is an intimate portrait of the man known as Mohandas—a living, breathing individual, passionate, full of vitality, and with his share of foibles and failures.

While the Indian experience is at the centre of Gopal's oeuvre, he is also attentive to the wider sweep of history. Take, for instance, his attention to the affinities between India's anti-colonial history and the struggle against apartheid in South Africa. This is not only due to the obvious connection of the Mahatma with South Africa, but also to independent India's role in the long struggle against apartheid. Of significance in this context is the volume of Mahatma Gandhi's writings on South Africa since his return to India (*Gandhi and South Africa: 1914–1948*), which Gopal edited with that champion of the global anti-apartheid campaign and doyen of Gandhian studies, the late E. S. Reddy.

A 'regular writer of occasional pieces', by his own account, Gopal has also used the essay for wide-ranging explorations into the history and culture of modern India. Thus, he writes with evocative understanding on the lives of personalities as different as the Carnatic vocalist M. S. Subbulakshmi and the Mahatma's devoted secretary and biographer, Pyarelal—two of the individuals featured in a delightful collection of pen-portraits, *Of a Certain Age: Twenty Life-Sketches*. Exceptionally alive to the rhythm and cadence of languages, his prose conveys mood and emotion as well as argument and evidence. Consider this excerpt from a newspaper article on the hymn 'Abide with Me' played during Beating Retreat at the culmination of India's Republic Day celebrations:

> The winter sun dips behind Raisina Hill. It seems not to want to go, but cannot linger. And as it goes, it swathes the house of India's President atop that hill with a halo of golden twilight. The North and South Blocks beside it, similarly, turn bronze. These are lights from the sky. Nature's illuminings, not tawdry emissions from bulbs and tubes held by wires. Stately camels from the Bikaner Camel Corps of the Border Security Force line the red sandstone ramparts, standing silhouetted along the slopes rock still. Full-maned horses from the 61st Cavalry stand motionless with their statuesque Sowars. All in fact is still, all quiet in expectation of a musical experience that goes beyond music to life, to the theatre where life itself stands still—in the complete uncertainty of the next moment, the next fraction of the second. In other words, in the great pulsation of war.

('What Abide with Me means to India', *Hindustan Times*, 22 January 2020.)

Or, in a different register, the unalloyed delight of the bala-Gopal that all of us who once were children can share: 'Chhoti invariably let me have the fifth and final cheese ball with the last swipe of ketchup. Heaven lay in that final crumb and lick. And Chhoti was that heaven's very angel.' ('Supernumerary' in *Remembered Childhood: Essays in Honour of André Betéille*, edited by Malavika Karlekar and Rudrangshu Mukherjee.)

◆

As a student of English and a diplomat, Gopal is at home in the world. But he is equally at ease with the linguistic and cultural diversity of India. In an era when bilingualism is a rarity, Gopal is multilingual not only in the spoken sense, but in his literary abilities as well. This has afforded him access to the cultural lode encoded in several languages and their literary corpora. If Tamil and Gujarati were spoken in his natal home in Delhi, Hindustani was the language spoken outside.

Gopal has published translations using all these languages. He completed the English translation of Manu Gandhi's Gujarati volume on the last days of Kasturba and Mohandas Gandhi, *End of an Epoch*, at the mature age of seventeen. More recently, he has rendered into English the canonical Tamil text *Tirukkural*. Notably, he has also translated, from English to Hindustani, Vikram Seth's *A Suitable Boy*. The translation drew acclaim for its ring of authenticity and some debate as well.

In his literary endeavours, Gopal has consistently explored and reflected on the ethical dilemmas that people wrestle with in their private and public lives. His 1985 novel, *Saranam* (republished as *Refuge*), based on his time in Kandy, looks at the lives of the plantation labourers but also dwells on the wider human predicament. His play, *Dara Shukoh*, highlights an intriguing what-if of Indian history: What if Dara, more open to the diversity of religions and cultures of India, had succeeded to the Mughal throne instead of Aurangzeb? We may note that *Dara Shukoh* was published in 1993, soon after the demolition of the Babri Masjid.

Soft-spoken and affable, Gopal has a sense of humour. But he is also a man of quiet conviction. This was highlighted by his recent book, *Abolishing the Death Penalty* (2016), where he went against the grain of Indian public opinion to unequivocally state his position against capital punishment. The book needs to be read and discussed more widely, for it reflects on a difficult question with moral clarity.

Gopal's self-effacement and natural restraint suited him well for administrative and diplomatic positions. But a different facet of his personality was also visible during his term as the governor of West Bengal. While courteous and measured, he infused meaning into the office of the governor and insisted on staying true to his responsibilities as a custodian of constitutional values. Additionally, instead of limiting himself to the confines of Raj Bhavan and official propriety, he reached out to the people of the state. Owing to Gopal's comportment in office and public engagement, he earned both popularity and respect. While the office of governor is often seen as a moribund institution and associated with political intrigue on many an occasion, Gopal's tenure suggested the healthy possibilities inherent in this position.

In the past decade, Gopal has written regularly in the media and spoken from public fora. As a commentator on public affairs, he has voiced the concerns of many Indians on matters of public morality and our rapidly changing social and political mores. He has also written and spoken as a concerned citizen on the environmental challenges that we confront. Here, Gopal has benefited from the presence of an in-house expert, his wife, the ornithologist Tara Gandhi who has been closely associated with a number of biodiversity conservation programmes and has written or edited a series of important books on the subject. Gopal also connects the environmental crisis with the politics of our times. As he argued in the 2019 edition of *The Oxford India Gandhi*, 'The misuse of political power in our times is matched by the misuse of technological and commercial power over resources. If we need a politically ethical future, we need an ecologically ethical future as well.' Gopal has often dwelt on the metaphor of the lions on the Ashoka pillar. In particular, he draws our attention to *the fourth lion* that is present but not visible. Gopal refers to this liminal but vital presence as Zameer-e-Hind or the 'conscience of India'. In his own quiet way, Gopal has given voice to Zameer-e-Hind and has reminded us that our voices count too.

This volume is offered as a festschrift to Gopalkrishna Gandhi to celebrate his seventy-fifth birthday in 2020. The essays are organized into thematic sections—Literature and Culture, History, the Environment, Politics and Public Affairs—each of which speaks to issues that have long interested and concerned Gopal. The final section presents more personal reflections, though the personal and the public have always been intertwined in Gopal's life.

We thank Isha Banerji, Pujitha Krishnan, David Davidar and others at Aleph Book Company for shepherding this volume to its published form. We are very thankful to all the writers featured in this volume for their essays (originally written in 2019). We regret that Professor Isaac Kramnick passed away in late 2019 and remain grateful for his contribution. The diverse backgrounds, nationalities, and generations of the contributors are, we hope, representative of the wider community that shares their respect, admiration, and affection for Gopalkrishna Gandhi.

Venu Madhav Govindu and Srinath Raghavan

# SECTION I

## LITERATURE AND CULTURE

# 1

## IN LOVE WITH MYSELF?

### T. M. KRISHNA

Reflecting on oneself can be a frightening thought, let alone an exercise. It necessitates objectivity and critical thinking that expose vulnerabilities buried deep within our mind. Unless we are prepared for what it entails, retrieving these vulnerabilities can trigger a state of emotional loneliness or vacuum. On the other hand, when engaged in a robust and caring manner, we can stumble upon a moment of surprise, revelation, and a chance to start anew. I do not mean reflection of a superfluous nature, which refers to the nuts and bolts, functionalities, and mechanics of survival. Such questions deal with improving oneself, mastering techniques, and polishing rough edges. Not unlike a market-related reassessment; they help in redesigning and turning oneself into a better product or whatever we might be selling. In today's time, even this has been outsourced to self-help books and online lectures.

Even in a serious and sincere engagement with the self, there is a limiting element: the focal point in the questioning still remains 'me'. The discovery revolves around the target who is the reason, subject, influencer, and influenced. I concede that the self can never be removed from such an endeavour, but as long as it remains the nodal point of reflection, it is an insurmountable obstacle. Looking at something that we are involved in objectively is possible even if 'me' remains the source of the perspective. But we have to cross this boundary for the ability to turn back and observe ourselves. This dispassionate externalization goes far beyond clinical objectivity. And I use the word dispassionate with great care. Being dispassionate is not a synthetic or plastic state. It is the ability to feel not as oneself but as the feeling itself. This, then, allows us to enter the heart of anyone and gives us the ability to receive limitlessly.

The 'I' will always refuse to question the critical fundamentals that it believes secure the individual and protect its being. These 'no-entry' zones remain unchanged because the 'I' fears its identity will be sacrificed and what it trusts shattered. There is within each one of us a propensity to believe, accept, and follow unquestioningly. Once something is accepted and followed, the next step is to lock it up in an iron safe and throw away the key. What if we were to break open that safe? Will there be anything of us left?

In this essay, I am going to attempt to remove myself from being the keystone and try to discover the music, questioning my own non-negotiables. But am I then going to speak from the point of view of the receivers—the 'others' in this interaction? Let us try something more complicated; an uncharted territory. Can the conversation come from the intersection, the object that binds us, brings us together, that we share, the music itself? What if we give that object of experience—Carnatic music—a 'self'? As much as this self is a product of the minds on and offstage, can she (I am already giving her gender identity) still have thoughts about me? This is anthropomorphism, maybe just a game I am playing to justify myself. But let me try and, if I fail, then you, the reader, should recognize it; this will then give you an insight into how distant we are from being honest to ourselves.

◆

I don't want to read Krishna's ramble on why he wants to write as me. I'm tired of his assumption that he knows me well enough to pontificate to the world where I come from, how I look, and what I feel. He has also confirmed my gender. How does he know I am feminine? Does this arise from his own postmodern need to stand apart from the musical crowd as a feminist? We live in times when people inform us of their 'gender pronouns' yet Krishna is stuck in a different era, so much for his progressiveness! For the record, I have watched him long enough; he is as problematic as every other man! He wants to drive home the point that I have been moulded and projected by men, their listening and handling. They have used conniving stratagems to design me.

There is no doubt that I too am a product of a male chauvinistic society, but who isn't? Men are also a construction of the same space. Their sense of manhood is entirely twisted and, from time immemorial, they have used it to govern and control society. In such a scenario what does Krishna expect me to be? I cannot be any different and hence he should stop picking on me. I have always had to play the game. If I want to survive, I have to let men present me in the manner that gives them at least a superficial feeling of dominance. For the record, female musicians are just as male chauvinistic and hence I am pandering to both sexes. But I am no fool; within every musical expression I have planted a possibility of sexual fluidity.

Men have categorized ragas as male and female. This was done by giving them gender-specific names or cataloguing them in a certain manner. Even when ragas are segregated according to the time of the day—morning, afternoon, and evening—the male–female differentiation is subliminally evoked. But I am clever. I have let this happen and allowed them that sense of achievement. They feel they have figured me out, encapsulated these beautiful ragas in a few verses in manuscripts and conquered me with their renditions. Then I play my game.

Take, for example, Raga Shankarabharanam. The name refers to the ornaments of Shiva. And the moment the artist or listener recognizes Shankarabharanam, they instinctively associate the name and sound with every Shiva temple they know of: his varied forms, the linga, the Nayanmars, Muttusvami Dikshitar's emotional connection with him…the list is endless. I can do nothing about this, because human beings have physically, poetically, architecturally, and religiously given it this identity. So my work is behind the scenes. I made sure that Dikshitar, Tyagaraja, Syama Sastri, Papanasam Sivan, and the Oduvars heard me in their mind's ear in a manner that smudged these conscious associations. They did not hear me as male or through the images associated with that word. I flowed like a river; when they followed every branch, inlet, and main channel that finally headed towards the delta, the name and image vanished. It was an aural scape that they saw, touched, and internalized. This was the Shankarabharanam that they put into the composition.

It was not easy even for these geniuses. They struggled and grappled with gender obviousness. But once they dived deep, all divisions vanished. Every time a serious musician sings this raga, he or she begins with images but soon Shiva disappears. Neither does Parvathi control. They will, of course, come and go. What else can you expect from the human mind that is filled with generational layers of information? But in the experiential non-textual and textual presentations of the raga, I have subverted male sexuality. Even in its most forceful phrases, the singer and listener are not sure if Shankarabharanam is masculine, feminine, or fluid. Their mental mapping algorithm fails. In this failure exists Shankarabharanam. I did not stop there; I went a step further. I gifted this raga to an unsurpassable woman, M. S. Subbulakshmi. Now Shankarabharanam is her ornament, not Shiva's.

At times it is also important to blur experience. I consciously imbued Bilahari with an unmistakable sensuality that these conditioned human beings only associate with the female gender. In parallel, I convinced Tyagaraja and Dikshitar to create robust, adrenalin-filled pieces in the same raga. Now they are all confused: is Bilahari the sensual female or the aggressive male? I hope you are listening as I am making a point here. I am not this or that; I am every shade of gender. I send out so many different understated signals through raga, text, tala, and laya that allow human beings to come in contact with those shades of themselves that they deny. Even if they do not realize it, this happens.

But what am I saying? At one end of the spectrum, there are those who claim that words are placeholders or coat stands for ragas and talas to conjure a myriad of emotional experiences. At the other end are people who would swear I am a tool of religious propagation. Hindu dharma is at the very core of who I am. Krishna seems to be prevaricating. He began by saying that words are not useless or meaningless but they have potent meaning that lie beyond semantics. Words have sonic thrust is what he seemed to be conveying. Then, all of a sudden, this man decided that I need to be speaking for and to many people, the marginalized, other faiths, about conflicts, and respond to the realities of today. He sang the poromboke song and brought Perumal Murugan's poems into my fold and now he is bending backwards to give Ashoka's edicts musical shape! He has said this is strategy and that, at some point, he hopes this diversification will lead to the disappearance of the necessity that lyrics should be of only one sort. He hopes to equalize ideas, which, in turn, move us closer to purely acoustic associations. The meaning of meaning itself being expanded.

Honestly, this is utterly utopian. How does he expect a species that comprehends life only through words to sincerely commit to something beyond it? And, worse, accept it as a search for meaning? Even if they know this exists and experience the unfathomable in me beyond their urgency for meaning, they thrive on the semantics. This gives them superior legitimacy, cogency, and concreteness. They will never be able to move away from this understanding.

Lyrics, which are part of my being, are most definitely uniquely placed. Words in me are not socio-religious tools for any kind of propaganda. Neither are they entirely sans linguistic meaning. I try very hard to keep lyrics in a state of flux or tension: are they the meaning or not? I want to keep wondering. I offer both but not obsessively. It is essential for me to crosswire emotional triggers and I use this in such a manner that musicians and listeners swing between both realities. At times they delve into memory, belief, and relationships. On other occasions, they are weeping but do not know why. They move from one to the other and somewhere in between; in limbo, just lost. I want them to remain lost for as long as possible, but that is so hard to do. Their cultural conditioning pulls them back into fixations.

People who want to deny linguistic meaning entirely try their very best to deny its appearance. They feel this is a lower aesthetic experience and are disturbed by its powerful impact on them. There were times in the past when I felt Krishna was torturing himself to push away the impact of a word on him. But he has come some way now and is able to just let it happen without judgement. I hope he realizes at some point of time that he does not need to reconcile this perceived conflict. Tyagaraja filled his lyrics with meaning and took them beyond it. He was not stuck in one or the other. Even if what he said may not have always been acceptable or appropriate, I can live with that because I know that he also felt something beyond and offered that to everyone.

It is in this emotional elasticity that you can discover life. Life's wonderment lies in the abstract and tactile. By teaching human beings to feel in multiplicity, I am hoping they become a whole. I wish musicians and audiences will allow me to just be and do what I do, not exploit me for their personal agenda.

There is one thing on which I have no disagreement with Krishna. I want to fly far beyond the social and religious boundaries drawn around me. I am trapped and do not know how to break free. I want people from the entire spectrum of society to embrace me and celebrate my sound. But I am also to blame for the present state of affairs. I took refuge within just one community: Brahmins. There is no doubt they truly nurtured me and showed me dimensions I did not know existed. But I was also being opportunistic. I consciously stayed within their quarters and did not allow anyone from 'outside' to enter. I was so in love with myself that I negated and trivialized all the music that flourished outside. To further secure this exalted status, I made myself even more incomprehensible. I made musicians stop thinking of me as an aural being. I became a construct, a complicated exercise. Consequently, musicians are unable to experience my true self. Sometimes they come very close but turn their backs because they want to display their virtuosity. The virtuosity that I convinced them was me!

Today, I am jealous of the music that is heard beyond my jurisdiction. There, everyone just drowns in exhilaration.

Unfortunately, I have made that so much more difficult for those close to me.

My greatest crime was unquestioningly watching the devadasis and their music die. It happened right before my eyes; their voices and selves were destroyed and thrown by the wayside. Look at what I did just now. I thanked the Brahmins but forgot that it was the devadasis who sang lullabies when I was a child, protected me when my home and temple were under attack and untiringly shared my legacy with every new generation. I was them and they were me. But once I found a more socially respectable and acceptable safe haven, I left them to fend for themselves. I went to the extent of wiping out their perspective of me from the memories of people. And along with them I also owe the nadasvaram community an apology. They were collateral damage in my path to 'modernization'.

Finally, let me go where Krishna began his reformation drive; by deconstructing my exterior, the performance. He got one thing right; I am not limited by any form of performative structure. But he tried proclaiming an idea of non-form, or at least that is how it sounded. For all of you to experience my beauty, I need a communicable form. The question that Krishna was probably trying to ask was: can there be many frameworks? Yes! Most certainly there can be. What remains unclear even now is what will be the foundational basis for these different versions of me.

Krishna has attempted presentations with aesthetic continuity that are exciting. At times they have been interesting and sensible. At times it felt like I had to dance to his whims and fancies. He has pushed me around too much and too often. Every time he gets on stage, I don a new avatar. When it takes a while for me to gather my bearings and cater to his demands, how can he expect the listener to come in without apprehension or confusion? They are bound to misinterpret what he does and think he is maligning me. Unfortunately, he is always in a hurry; he really needs to pause. Right now, Krishna is still able to remain eclectic and offer new insights. What happens when he exhausts himself? Will he get stuck? Will he concretize me like they did about 100 years ago into another so-called successful format?

It is very difficult being an intangible, abstract idea. I do not have material form and you cannot hold me physically. In your mind, you can enslave me without cuffs and in my desperation to remain valid I just obey. But I use all my inherent resources to influence your thought and emotions. I am a sound that comes and vanishes in a jiffy, only to remain alive in your heart. But I am also a specific sound—the Carnatic sound—a designation that gives me certain attributes and responsibilities. I am specific but my work is expansive. I have to influence those who draw strength from whatever I am to open their minds to the larger world. I know this means I will metamorphosize and is possibly why I am nervous. I do not know what lies ahead in such a future and hence I am passive-aggressive and defensive. I hope I will learn and change because I understand it is essential that I rub shoulders with everyone.

Be patient with me, give me some time.

2

AS THE CONCH SOUNDS

NIRUPAMA MENON RAO

For a brief period in my early diplomatic life, I was concerned with men and women whose voices were scarcely heard, 'a people known only to themselves', as Kamaladevi Chattopadhyay once wrote—the dispossessed plantation labourers who worked in the 'hill country', that area of Sri Lanka known as the central highlands. It was this that led me to Gopalkrishna Gandhi who, as a serving diplomat in Kandy, Sri Lanka, was working on similar issues. I must confess to being in tremendous awe of him because of his lineage: someone who, as an infant, had been held in the Mahatma's arms, a much loved grandchild. Over the years, my respect for Gopal and his humanism has only grown, and he has become a cherished friend.

The year was 1981. Black July 1983, when the island erupted in ethnic riots spewing indescribable hatred of a majority for a minority, loomed large in the future. But encountering the people of the tea country meant coming face to face with years of 'sounding silence from silence' as elucidated in the opening chapter of Gopal's moving novel, *Refuge* (*Saranam*) (Penguin: 1987). Velu, a stateless individual, with no citizenship to call his own, tossed to and fro between the two nations, India and Sri Lanka, sounds the morning conch that calls the estate lines to work and order. As my reading eye beheld Velu, the fleeting image of Beethoven's physical state of deafness settling into the inner recesses of his being crossed my mind. With the elan of a maestro, as the author describes him, Velu raises the conch ceremoniously above his head, takes a deep breath and then, from the hollows of his lungs, breathes 'into the spiral hollows of the conch a gust of life which suffused the estate. Pooum! Poooummm!' But even as that sound resonates through the estate lines, the hum inside his head tunes out human voices and stretches into infinity. Before long, 'Velu was in the zone of complete soundlessness'. Soundlessness. That is the ultimate end-state. Tranquillity settles on Velu. Witnessing life 'on the estate with an almost perpetual smile in his eyes and on his conch-kissed lips', soundlessness seems the sole legacy he is left with.

I wonder how Velu, if he were a crystal gazer, would have surveyed life, situated in the midst of the landscape of 'yuttam' or war, in his country of birth, thirty years down the line. His conch shell would have sounded over the lagoon of Mullaitivu and lapsed into the hum of seabirds hovering over the bodies of women and children in the water. The landscape of soundlessness is deafening, indeed. Yuttam, as the Sri Lankan writer Sharika Thiranagama explains, is a chronicle of one nation polarized by numerous narratives, all surrounding the civil war, giving it a 'thickness, an agency' which is central to this day, twelve years after the end of the conflict. Who, then, picks conch shells from the sea of the dead, the missing, and unaccounted for, how do you make sense of soundlessness? The deafness of Velu, the soundlessness at the end of war and conflict, calls out for empathy, altruism, and benediction to heal the wounds, to reaffirm the meaning of our existence, and to make life fluid again.

The musician and conductor Daniel Barenboim while delivering the BBC Reith Lectures in 2006, spoke of how sound does not live in this world. It evaporates; it is ephemeral. In his words, it has 'a permanent, constant, unavoidable relation with silence. The first note comes out of the silence that precedes it.' Music begins in silence, it interrupts the silence. It is sound that marks our beginning, as we are born from our mothers' wombs, it is not vision. The ear is functional from the forty-fifth day of life in embryo. And it is sound that connects to our emotions, deep in our bodies.

The conch in most Asian cultures is a call to worship and a manifestation of the divine. It is a thrilling call, not to order, but to joy, worship, and human connectedness. It is a musical instrument. Music in essence, determines 'the standard of human existence' (Barenboim). Despite the darkening skies, it speaks to us, of optimism and the language of continuous dialogue. It teaches us to float in this world, despite the tug of downward current. It will not allow us to be passive about our future; it reaffirms that we can coexist in lands of opposing narratives. It combines transparency and strength with power, showing us how everything is connected. The music on the Golden Record sent by Carl Sagan into space in 1977 encapsulates the basic message of music as the soundtrack of our humanity. Even if any extra-terrestrial being has not heard it yet, think of the way it binds us to strangers, little men and little women, who recognize its universality and its inner voice. I cannot imagine a human soul that will not reach for the light celestial on hearing Surshri Kesarbai Kerkar's voice on the record:

*Jaatkahan ho, akeli gori, jaanenapaiyyon,*

(Where do you go alone, girl, do your feet not know)

*Kesar rang ke math bhaye hoy, Hori khelat Kanha re,*

(The fields are coloured saffron, Krishna plays Holi, there I go)

Here is a song in Raag Bhairavi, immortalized alongside Chuck Berry, Mozart, and Bach, now more than twelve billion miles away from earth, on the spacecraft *Voyager*, headed for Sirius, the brightest star in the sky. The soundless universe, we would like to think, allows the music to go on and on, escaping our planet's orbit, into galactic oblivion.

Perhaps one understands what Susan Sontag meant when she said that music like this is the most perfect, the most pure, and the most sensual of the arts. The sound penetrates into the core of the body, generating passion, pathos, or joy as the circumstances demand (Sontag, *Reborn: Journals and Notebooks, 1947-63*). Or, one recalls Edna St Vincent Millay, who wrote as a twenty-eight-year-old, 'I can whistle almost the whole of the Fifth Symphony

(Beethoven), all four movements and, with it, I have solaced many a whining hour to sleep. It answers all my questions, the noble, mighty thing, it is "green pastures and still waters" to my soul' (St Vincent Millay, *Letters*).

Beethoven, who belongs not just to his motherland, but to the world, wrote music that espoused the cause of human fraternity. His work rises from the confluence of both emotion and intellect, connecting the head, the heart, and the stomach—a strong, authentic, unqualified utterance like a 'gushing spring which leaps from the inaccessible depths of the mountain' (Romain Rolland). I visualize him in early nineteenth-century Vienna, sounding an imagined conch shell, a call to rally around the cause of human emancipation from naked power and domination. His music is rich with so many gathered voices. Like the Tamil labourers on the Lankan tea estates in *Refuge*, he is best known only to himself, but with all the voices held within him, captured in his creative soul. He has no friend; he lives alone but his heart embraces all. In his words, he exists, 'To do all the good one can, To love liberty above everything, And even if it be for a kingdom, Never to betray truth' (*Album-leaf*, 1792).

Deafness had begun to assail him from his late teens, with his ears humming continually. He was miserable and bereft, 'my situation is terrible.... I feel the most miserable of all God's creatures'. Resignation, that sorry refuge, seemed all that was left to him. But he would wage a war against destiny, not allowing it to overcome him completely, taking 'fate by the throat', as he wrote in a letter to a friend. As the effects of the French Revolution began to permeate Europe, he was filled with empathy for revolutionary, republican ideas. He became an upholder of unlimited liberty, of national independence, of universal suffrage as a proper basis of human happiness. Perhaps it is an inordinate share of physical suffering, as he endured, that makes for beautiful art with healing powers. It also prepares the soul for the joy in his culminating the Ninth Symphony, which descends from the skies, soothing the sorrowful soul with tenderness, taking possession of us, in a wonderful ode.

He reminds one of Subramania Bharathi here, as the latter's creative muse overflows with joy for all living creatures (Beethoven: 'alle menschen werden brüder'—all men will be brothers) and he (Bharathi) says, 'Therefore men of the world, make love and lead exuberant lives' meaning divine love, human love, love of nature, and love of freedom. This is sound without fear or encumbrance, the ultimate soul-force of liberation finding expression.

Tagore called it 'the surplus in man'—our ability to idealize, to move beyond the surface, to create our own profoundly personal visions. He speaks of the 'God of humanity', seeking spiritual antecedents in Persia, Sufism, and in Wordsworth. The passages which describe Tagore's intense joy on experiencing nature recall Beethoven's own words of the beauty of the Rhine and its shores, of the body drinking in overflowing light and peace. He evokes the image of the Bauls, the minstrels of Bengal who declare the divinity of Man, 'and express for him an intense feeling of love'. This is music that expresses determination, the sense of the individual battling the dreary desert sands of habit and hierarchy, and also overflows with joy and affirmation. It finds a voice in the famous 'Ekla Cholo Re' (Walk Alone), a favourite of Mahatma Gandhi, a song of resistance but also of solidarity. 'Ekla Cholo Re' was a song centrally associated with Gandhi's resistance against colonial rule, combining the spirit of dissent with the joy of striving and overcoming all odds. Similarly, Tagore was able to render 'Jana Gana Mana', our national anthem, as the ultimate ode to pluralism, harmony, and the worship of the divine as the dispenser of the destiny of Bharatvarsha. This is an example of music preaching the 'Religion of Man'.

◆

Rajmohan Gandhi, the Mahatma's grandson and Gopal's older brother, has spoken of his grandfather's fondness for music. In December 1931, Mahatma Gandhi returned to India via Switzerland where he spent a few days at the villa of the French writer Romain Rolland. The account of Rolland's sister, Madeleine, describes the spinning wheel and evening prayers (extracts from the Gita, ancient Sanskrit hymns, and 'a canticle' of Rama and Shiva, intoned by 'the warm, grave voice' of Gandhi's disciple, Mira Behn (Madeleine Slade), as Rolland himself wrote) against the background of the Savoy Alps, Lake Leman, and the glaciers of the Dent du Midi. There are references to the young musician who, at dawn, plays the violin below the windows of Gandhi's room and how, on the eve of his departure, a choir from Villeneuve sings the celebrated 'Ranz des Vaches' (Calling the Herd), the song which is almost a national anthem in Switzerland, arousing patriotic love and homesickness, and which moved Henry David Thoreau to recall 'woods where the wood thrush forever sings'.

On the last day of his visit, the Mahatma requested Rolland to play on the piano an andante movement of the Fifth Symphony of Beethoven and 'Les Champs Elysées' by Gluck. This had some significance, since Mira Behn passionately loved the music of Beethoven and it was through Beethoven that she had met Rolland in 1923, before Rolland introduced her to Gandhi. It was thus apposite that Beethoven's music was played as 'Gandhi knew that it was through Beethoven that Mira had known Romain Rolland and, that it was to Beethoven therefore that he owed his faithful disciple' (Madeleine Rolland).

Mira Behn was profoundly moved by the music but when Rolland asked Gandhi for his reaction, the latter replied with 'a little laugh, both candid and mischievous', 'It must be beautiful because you tell me so.' For Mira and Rolland this lack of acknowledgement could not have been easy to accept. For Rolland, Beethoven and his music embodied an 'oceanic sensibility' that was close to spiritual faith, and for Mira, the music was the ultimate medium that was the vehicle for her deepest emotions, at the core of her earthly existence.

Gandhi's reaction may have been summary and insensitive to his two friends but in the scheme of his commitments to a life dedicated to struggle against the British, there was little time to probe the depths of Beethoven and his genius. That he was curious to hear something of his music reveals a globally aware sensibility, open to cultural influences of non-Indian origin and not spurning an understanding of them. He did not claim any special knowledge of Beethoven or his music, which explains his reaction to Rolland's question about whether he had liked what he had heard. But he was a lifelong voyager across seas, always open to ideas from across the world. The image of the first four notes—three short and one long—of the Fifth Symphony being associated with the 'V' for victory sign which in Morse Code is dot-dot-dot-dash, or three short clicks and one long, as a symbol of victory and freedom against fascism during World War II, would have ignited his interest.

Perhaps he was also, like Tolstoy, not attracted to classicism in music but instead, taken with the folk traditions marked by songs laden with sincerity, simplicity, and joy. 'All folk art will educate and unite men, will make them understand the joy of unity outside the barriers raised by life' (Tolstoy, *What is Art?*). The bhajans sung at Gandhi's prayer meetings were infused with the popular wisdom of the common people and the joy of unity with the divine. He termed the voice of M. S. Subbulakshmi as 'exceedingly sweet' as she sang the Meera Bhajan, 'Hari Tuma Haro' and was quoted by Sardar Vallabhbhai Patel as saying, 'To sing a bhajan is one thing; to sing it by losing oneself in God is quite different'. Rolland was also to note that the Mahatma was 'very sensitive to the religious chants of his country which somewhat resemble the most beautiful of our Gregorian melodies', and that they exchanged ideas on art 'from which he does not separate his conception of truth, nor from his conception of truth that of joy, which he thinks truth should bring'. (Rolland in a letter to an American friend in 1931). Gandhi's was thus an oceanic sensibility as deep as Beethoven's. In effect, 'the seeker after truth hath a heart tender as the lotus, and hard as granite'. The one western opera that has as its theme the life of Gandhi, 'Satyagraha' by Philip Glass, visualizes him as standing before the rich and the powerful in the 'white robe of simpleness' (Tagore), his persona imbued by the freedom of the soul, reminding the world that what is huge is not great and pride is not everlasting.

Gandhi would have rallied to the words of Martin Luther King, Jr. when he said that the human ability to create had produced songs of sorrow and joy that have helped us cope with times of happiness and tragedy. Putting the hardest realities of life to music enabled the creation of a new hope and a 'sense of triumph'. King saw much of the power of the Civil Rights Movement in the United States coming from music, 'It has strengthened us with its sweet rhythms when courage began to fail. It has calmed us with its rich harmonies when spirits were down. Everybody longs for meaning. Everybody needs to love and be loved. Everybody needs to clap hands and be happy. Everybody longs for faith.' It is this clapping of hands, and longing for faith, that saw the traditional chorus 'I'll Overcome Someday' or 'I Will Overcome' evolve into the signature anthem of the civil rights movement, 'We Shall Overcome', which did not spread by commercial recording or sheet music sales, but merely by word of mouth, as did the songs of our freedom movement.

This raises the question: to what extent should musicians reflect on the world or the national situation of their day? Most composers over the last few centuries have provided commentaries on the state of their societies and politics through their music. This is both in the music of war and of peace. Benjamin Britten's 'War Requiem' is a repository of his pacifism, of his commitment not to destroy another life, although the question may be raised, is great art, poetry, and music enough to ensure the prevention of war? Perhaps the answer rests with Wilfred Owen, who wrote shortly before his death in World War I:

> Above all I am not concerned with Poetry.
> My subject is War, and the pity of War.
> The Poetry is in the pity.

And, the best definition of humanism is expressed in Gandhi's love for the timeless bhajan sung in his prayer meetings:

Vaishnava jana to tene kahiye
Je pir paraee jane re
(Call only that man a true
Vaishnav who is sensitive
To the pain of others)

Displacement, forced migration, drowned refugee children dressed in their Sunday best on sandy beaches—these are the leitmotifs of our times. The music has died for them. Have we globalized indifference, as Pope Francis said in 2015? Closer home, I see hunger of the heart, body, and the mind. This makes, as one of our most distinguished civil servants said long ago, a cultural renaissance for India most essential—not the culture of consumerism, but a culture of humanism. A cultural renaissance with pluralism at its centre, that pluralism which has accounted for the survival of India over millennia (P. N. Haksar, 1992). It is what Gandhi would have elected for.

Music provides humanism with an ideal vehicle; it is a natural vector for unifying and giving voice to the unknown, unsung men and women who escape the attention of the more privileged among us. I can visualize the Mahatma embracing such a concept—as he would have this song from Sri Lanka's tea gardens by the bard C. V. Velupillai:

*From time to time*
*From the highway*
*I shall strike*
*Upon my harp*
*And sing my song*

*... My men*
*They lie dust under dust*
*Beneath the tea*
*No wild weed flowers*
*Or memories taken*

*...(And of the women)*
*Fieldwards drawn they go;*
*Baskets flung across*
*Their leaf-shaped eyes;*

*Their star centres*
*Scan the flushing rows*
*And deft fingers clip*
*Two leaves and a bud*
*Two leaves and a bud*

*Peacock gay sarees*
*And amber soft jackets*
*Of dark green and yellow*
*Their old ties renew.*
*The vermilion hue*
*Pencilled on the brow,*
*Flower's red on lips*
*They leave them neat*
*They leave them sweet.*

And so the conch sounds and the music flows.

3

## 'THE WATERS OF THAT OTHER OCEAN'
### VEDANTA AND A SINGLE MAN

KESHAVA GUHA

'I suppose that most novelists have considered, at one time or another, the project of writing a religious novel.' This is the opening sentence of 'The Problem of the Religious Novel', an essay that Christopher Isherwood wrote in 1946, at the midpoint of his own life and career as a novelist, in which he sets out an agenda for a hypothetical book about conversion and sainthood. On the basis of the five works of fiction he had published up to that point, Isherwood was an unlikely novelist of religion. Nor is he conceived as such today—even though, from his conversion to Vedanta in the early 1940s, religion came to dominate his work and life. Isherwood's posthumous reputation rests solely on three novels, *Mr Norris Changes Trains* (1935), *Goodbye to Berlin* (1939), and *A Single Man* (1964). The first two, set in decadent Weimar Berlin, are wholly secular. The third is seen as a pioneering gay novel—which it is—and as little else.

In this essay I argue that religion, in the form of Vedanta, is every bit as central to *A Single Man* as sexuality. Vedanta is the key to the novel—the only way to truly make sense of it. Isherwood's relationship to Vedanta transformed his fictional technique, in ways that most Western admirers of *A Single Man* have been blind to.

### Vedanta as the Key

The action of *A Single Man* is contained within a single day. This structure was inspired in part by *Mrs Dalloway*. The 'single man' of the title is George, 'Geo' to his friends, a middle-aged Englishman who teaches literature at a college in southern California. He has recently been bereaved; his partner, Jim, first leaves him in a doomed attempt at heterosexuality and is then killed in a car crash.

The novel begins with George waking up and ends with him going to sleep, and perhaps dying in his sleep. While the influence of Vedanta is evident throughout, it is most obvious in this architecture of the day and life cycle, and in the questions of identity and consciousness that inevitably follow from waking and resting.

'Waking up begins with saying *am* and *now*. That which has awoken then lies for a while staring...down into itself until it has recognized *I*.... *Here* comes next.' This is from the opening paragraph. A few sentences later, we learn that 'now' is a 'cold reminder', that this it or I feel a 'sickish shrinking' from the day ahead and soon we learn why: 'Jim is dead. Is dead.' For almost three pages, however, *it* remains *it*, until it has washed and shaved, and begins to recall that 'It knows its name. It is called George.... By the time it has gotten dressed it has become *he*; has become already more or less George; though not still the whole George they demand and are prepared to recognize.'

This reading of the nature of identity, and its implications for fictional narrative are rooted in Vedanta. A conventional novel would simply give us *he*, *I*, George, from the first sentence. But to Isherwood, self-identity is not a given, but a function—of wakefulness, activity, and, perhaps, above all, other people.

From here on, George goes through his day as George, seemingly in the manner of the protagonist of a secular, realist novel. He goes to teach his class; spends plenty of time in pleasant erotic fantasies; visits an old friend (Charlotte, a fellow English émigré), and a former enemy (Doris, whom Jim briefly left him for, now dying in hospital); gets thoroughly drunk in the company of a student whom, with abortive sexual optimism, he invites home. He goes to bed, in drunken half-sleep, wakes up an hour or so later— crucially, this period is not presented as true sleep or waking—to find the student, Kenny, gone. And then we find him, truly 'asleep on this bed and snoring quite loud'.

The reader knows they are coming to the end of the day and the novel, but it is easy to miss that the entity asleep is described not as George, but as 'this body known as George's body'. What follows, however, is a total departure from the realist narrative. It is also very likely the most direct distillation of Hindu philosophy in all of English-language fiction. The body is known as George; by now, we think we know George.

But *is* all of George altogether present here?

Up the coast a few miles north, in a lava reef under the cliffs, there are a lot of rock pools. You can visit them when the tide is out. Each pool is separate and different, and you can, if you are fanciful, give them names—such as George, Charlotte, Kenny, Mrs Strunk. Just as George and the others are thought of, for convenience, as individual entities, so you may think of a rock pool as an entity; though, of course, it is not. The waters of its consciousness—so to speak—are swarming with hunted anxieties, grim-jawed greeds, dartingly vivid intuitions, old crusty-shelled rock-gripping obstinacies, deep-down sparkling undiscovered secrets, ominous protean organisms motioning mysteriously, perhaps warningly, towards the surface light. How can such a variety of creatures coexist at all? Because they have to. The rocks of the pool hold their world together. And, throughout the day of the ebb tide, they know no other.

But that long day ends at last; yields to the night-time of the flood. And, just as the waters of the ocean come flooding, darkening over the pools, so over George and the others in sleep come the waters of that other ocean; that consciousness which is no one in particular but which contains everyone and everything, past, present and future, and extends unbroken beyond the uttermost stars. We may surely suppose that, in the darkness of the full flood, some of these creatures are lifted from their pools to drift far out over the deep waters.... Can they tell us, in any manner, about their journey? Is there, indeed, anything for them to tell—except that the waters of the ocean are not really other than the waters of the pool?

Here is the essence of Vedanta, and thus of Isherwood's worldview and of *A Single Man*, which is why it must be quoted in full. Isherwood was introduced to Vedanta and to Swami Prabhavananda—a Bengali member of the Ramakrishna Order who had moved to California to promote his philosophy—by his friend Gerald Heard. He was attracted to it for a number of reasons: unlike the Anglicanism he loathed, it had no personal God or notion of 'sin', no proscription against homosexuality; its belief in the essential oneness of all life provided a spiritual basis for his pacifism; and he was immediately fond of the Swami, who wore Western clothes and was thus 'not off-puttingly Eastern and exotic', and 'was a chain-smoker, a habit which suggested both worldliness and an encouraging dash of human frailty'. Isherwood's philosophical views were often shaped by personal affinities.

But, above all, it was Vedanta's conception of identity and the self that appealed to Isherwood: its distinction between the apparent self of daily life with its belief in its own individuality and its stubborn anxieties and attachments, and a real self that is but a part of that universal consciousness. Vedanta in practice— through meditation—is the pursuit of self-knowledge through the dissolution of the apparent individual self. Isherwood is sometimes characterized as a narcissist, but he had always longed to shed his individual identity. All of this is on display in *A Single Man* and summarized in the dichotomy between the rock pools and 'the waters of that other ocean' to which we all return in sleep, and can strive to reach during the day.

Of course, the words 'Vedanta' or 'Hinduism' aren't present. The only Sanskrit reference in the novel is a comic play on the word 'Om', and there are a number of other comic misdirections, seeming attempts to foreground George's secularism: 'we most of us lose our sense of proportion in the presence of a nun', 'He looks out over Los Angeles like a sad Jewish prophet of doom, as he takes a leak'. Throughout the novel moments of spiritual or philosophical weight are followed by comic release of this sort. There was and is very little overlap between the readers of Isherwood's fiction and of his religious non-fiction (collaborative translations of Hindu texts and summaries of Vedanta for a Western audience). But the particular metaphor he uses here comes straight from his philosophical writing, and resolves all doubt over whether *A Single Man* should be read as a Hindu novel. In *An Approach to Vedanta*, written and published before *A Single Man*, he describes the difference between the real and apparent self: 'There is a part of myself which, being infinite, has access to the infinite—as the sea water in a bay has access to the sea because it *is* the sea.'

Once one recognizes the novel's Vedantic opening and climax, Vedanta becomes a kind of key to much else that at a first reading may seem only mildly out of place in a secular work. These can be stray words or phrases—Jim's corpse described as 'leavings', rather than remains; 'life-energy' rather than life or energy; George's journey 'deep down into himself', or the repeated use of 'fellow-creature' to refer to fellow humans.

But there are also repeated themes and motifs that make coherent sense when viewed through the Vedantic prism. George's habit of stepping outside himself, viewing his own body or speech as if it isn't *I, George*, moving or talking; the many reflections on the nature of individual and group identities; and the interest in the relationship between 'The Past', 'The Future', and 'Now', and in cycles of loss and rebirth. George goes to sleep at the end of the novel committed only to Now: 'Jim is in the Past...he will have to forget, if he wants to go on living. Jim is death...George clings only to Now. It is now that he must find another Jim. Now that he must love. Now that he must live—'. Even W. H. Auden, one of the novel's great admirers, was appalled by the idea of 'a new Jim'. But Auden was ignorant, indeed dismissive, of Vedanta and its manifestation in *A Single Man*.

## Sympathy and Universality

Vedanta is much more than a 'subject' or theme of *A Single Man*. It is also a profound influence on Isherwood's novelistic technique: both in the ways that he adapted his technique to accommodate Vedanta in this particular novel and, more broadly, in the manner of his development as a novelist after his conversion, exemplified by *A Single Man* but not limited to it. In some senses Vedanta radically changed Isherwood's method; in others, it reinforced his existing instincts.

Take the three novels almost universally acknowledged to be Isherwood's most important and accomplished—*Mr Norris Changes Trains*, *Goodbye to Berlin*, and *A Single Man*. The first two, set in Berlin but written after his departure from Germany, precede his conversion, and were written by an atheist with few fixed moral or political convictions. *A Single Man* was written by someone who had spent two decades engaging with Vedanta and, although he continued to have periods of doubt, was both a committed believer and as deep a scholar as it is possible to be without any knowledge of Sanskrit.

One of the principal differences between Isherwood the novelist of Berlin and of Vedanta is his treatment of character. *Mr Norris Changes Trains* is written with a shocking, near-total absence of sympathy. Its indelible characters are almost all grotesque; it is consistently and sometimes outrageously funny, but the humour is underpinned by a worldview that approaches nihilism. Isherwood, not usually prone to self-criticism, grew to bitterly regret this. 'What repels me now about *Mr Norris* is its heartlessness', he wrote in 1956. 'It is a heartless fairy-story about a real city in which real human beings were suffering the miseries of political violence and near-starvation.'

*Goodbye to Berlin*, its successor, has a softer tone, with moments of genuine tragedy not played for laughs. But it was only with *Prater Violet*, published in 1945 and the first novel written after Isherwood's conversion, that he begins to write characters with warmth and sympathy. *Prater Violet* is a satire based on Isherwood's experiences as a screenwriter: its central character, the Austrian film director Friedrich Bergmann, would have been a pure figure of fun in the Berlin novels. Here the comedy is humaized by the narrator's regard for Bergmann as an essentially noble guru-type.

*A Single Man* takes this move towards sympathy much further; every character is written sympathetically, not simply those whom George likes. Early in the novel we meet his neighbours, beginning with Mrs Strunk, an annoyingly conventional woman and, we will see, a homophobe. But our first encounter with her is written in a tone wholly out of place with Isherwood's earlier work: 'Mrs Strunk, sweet-natured though she is—grown wearily gentle from toiling around the house at her chores; gently melancholy from regretting her singing days on radio, all given up in order to bear Mr Strunk five boys and two girls.'

Later, George goes to visit his former rival, Doris. His anger and hatred towards her have faded in the face of grief at Jim's death, and now the image of her own decline. He sits with her, 'holding her hand, he feels less embarrassed by her sickness; for the gesture means, *we are on the same road, I shall follow you soon*. He is thus excused from having to ask those ghastly sickroom questions, how are you? How's it going? How do you feel?' Here again we see the novel's characteristic expansion of sympathy—George's, and Isherwood's—and also its suppression of Vedantic universality, the way in which George's brief feeling of oneness yields so quickly to comic whining.

Technically, *A Single Man* required two great departures from Isherwood's early novels. The first is of point of view. Isherwood's *Goodbye to Berlin* and *Prater Violet* are rather under appreciated for their formal inventiveness: they are narrated by a fictional character called Christopher Isherwood (or William Bradshaw; his despised full name being Christopher William Bradshaw-Isherwood), who is, by his own famous description in *Goodbye to Berlin*, a 'camera', recording the action of other lives rather than his own. It is a narrative mode that anticipates much postmodernist fiction and twenty-first-century auto-fiction.

In *A Single Man*, Isherwood switches to a third-person voice, outwardly more conventional but hugely ambitious in its moves between free, indirect style (for George); a sort of cinematic mode that pans in and out of various scenes and characters (Mrs Strunk, as above, or the descriptions of parts of Los Angeles); those descriptions of George's body and movement that feel external to George, and what might be called 'the point of view of the universe', the God-like omniscience—God in the Vedantic sense—of the rock pools and the other ocean, the only voice capable of delivering the novel's spiritual climax.

Along with this new narrative form comes a new approach to the construction of his principal character. All Isherwood's fiction, the familiar charge goes, is autobiography (some would add: all his autobiography is fiction). But the Berlin novels are remarkable for how little we actually learn of the Isherwood-figure—of his background, his appetites, and above all, his emotional life. *Prater Violet* gives us a little more, but only that.

George, to a large degree, *is* Isherwood—he never denied it. He has all the 'dartingly vivid intuitions' and 'greeds' and 'obstinacies' of the rock pool. He is full to bursting with individuality. Perhaps counterintuitively, this approach depends upon the versatility of the third person. The omniscient third person allows for anything: for Mrs Strunk to be written sympathetically, even though George feels no sympathy, for us to see George from the inside and the outside, for Isherwood to turn the camera inwards.

But surely does this make *A Single Man* less of a Hindu novel? If the essence of Vedanta is the impersonal universal consciousness, how can the beating heart of this novel be George, not just 'that which is called George' but undeniably human George? If anything, this division only makes the novel's reading of Vedanta more moving and complete: the life not of a saint but of an ordinary person, the waters of the pool *and* the ocean. The religious novel at its most effective needs both. *A Single Man* takes the great strengths of Isherwood's early work: limpid prose, photographic perception, and humour—while adding moral weight and sympathy, and subtracting nihilism.

**A Religious Novel without Religion?**

Vedanta in *A Single Man* is, as Flaubert believed a novelist should be in their work: 'like God in the universe, present everywhere and visible nowhere'. Invisible, that is, if the reader isn't looking, or is unwilling or unable to see. This has been a persistent quality among Isherwood's Western readers, including, or even especially, those drawn to his literary gifts. Ever since his initial conversion, his engagement with Vedanta and its influence on his fiction have been met with bemusement, contempt, or both.

In California in 1943, Isherwood knew his English contemporaries might struggle to understand. 'Are you still reading, or have you fallen under the table in a dead faint?' he wrote to his oldest friend, Edward Upward, in a letter explaining his adoption of 'Yoga adapted to the needs of the West'. Upward's reply was 'a model of charity towards an attitude one can't understand'. Their correspondence was suspended for several years.

Others were rather less charitable. 'How he does go on about God?' complained E. M. Forster. Auden, who had returned to the High Church Anglicanism of his family, thought the whole thing risible. In 1938, Somerset Maugham had said of Isherwood to Virginia Woolf: 'That young man holds the future of the English novel in his hands.' Isherwood's Californian life and novels led Maugham to lament that he had 'thrown it all away'.

This attitude can be explained, perhaps, by sheer ignorance, a reflexive hostility to all religion, or lazy associations between California and silly fads. Yet it endures, half a century later, in assessments of Isherwood by distinguished British writers and critics. Reviewing Peter Parker's biography—which contains a diligent if unsympathetic account of Isherwood's Vedanta years— John Sutherland derisively describes Isherwood as succumbing to 'the Eastern mysticism of the tinsel town gurus'. Alan Hollinghurst characterizes his religious exploration as 'an extended dim comedy of misapplied energy.... The overall impression is one of fruitless mortification.' While Vedanta 'obviously matters a great deal to him', writes Michael Wood, 'he can't often make it sound like anything but hokum.'

Few judgements can be as sweeping or dismissive as Allan Massie's: 'His commitment to Eastern mysticism and his Swami Prabhavananda...did him no good as a writer.' This was written in an essay that celebrates Isherwood's early fiction and acknowledges *Prater Violet* and *A Single Man*—books that, as we have seen, bear deeply the imprint of Vedanta—as 'two good novellas'.

Among critics, only Edmund White, one of Isherwood's most perceptive readers, has consistently argued for the importance of Vedanta to *A Single Man*: '[It] is a Hindu book without the Hinduism. You can really only understand it if you understand Vedanta.' But it is White's other characterization of the novel, as 'the founding text of modern gay literature', that is quoted. Isherwood is simply not understood to be an important religious novelist.

The trajectory of Isherwood's life and fiction and the nature of his achievement in *A Single Man* bear comparison with the most prominent English novelists of his generation: Evelyn Waugh and Graham Greene (all three born within twelve months of each other). Waugh and Greene converted to Catholicism in their twenties, and Catholicism grew to define a great deal of their fiction. In both cases, their religious novels have been taken very seriously as such, their faith recognized as the source of moral and spiritual weight and intensity.

The comparison with Waugh is especially relevant. Waugh's early satires, from the years immediately before and after his conversion—*Decline and Fall*, *Vile Bodies* and *Black Mischief*—are, like *Mr Norris Changes Trains*, essentially nihilist, the comedy depending upon a gallery of grotesques. The difference between these books and *Brideshead Revisited* or the *Sword of Honour* trilogy is easily diagnosed as having a religious source. But the difference between the Berlin novels and *A Single Man* is just as marked;

why is it so difficult for readers who acknowledge the achievement of *A Single Man* to take it seriously as a work of religious fiction?

This failure is part of a broader denial of seriousness to Isherwood's engagement with Vedanta, one in which even his biographers are complicit. Sometimes it stems from pure, forgivable ignorance; sometimes from regret that a brilliant young English writer went American. Isherwood's reputation in Britain never quite recovered from his emigration. Waugh thought of Isherwood and Auden as disgraceful cowards, caricaturing them as 'Parsnip and Pimpernel', poets who move to America to escape the war, in *Put out More Flags* (1942). But in many assessments of Isherwood, from Auden and Maugham to the present, it is difficult to deny a Western condescension towards Eastern religion as a proper subject for literary fiction.

Isherwood helped encourage a secular or non-Vedanta reading of *A Single Man*, both within the novel and without. His overtly Hindu novel, *A Meeting by the River*, was widely judged a failure, fuelling easy dismissals of the influence of his religion on his fiction. And *A Single Man* itself, even as it draws directly from his writings on Vedanta, never admits to being a Hindu novel; not even in Isherwood's published diaries.

This stands in particular contrast to something the novel is rather better known for. It was the first time that Isherwood had written an explicit account of homosexual life and love, with moving exuberance and freedom. Reviews of the novel, particularly in the United States, were ridden with horror at its frank sexuality. In his diaries, Isherwood wrote of the novel's reception: 'I spoke the truth, and now let them swallow it or not as they see fit. That's a very good feeling, and this is the first time that I have really felt it.' Speaking its name, for among the first times in English fiction; there is no euphemism in *A Single Man*, no concealment, when it comes to sexuality. Only to religion.

Isherwood's diaries do offer one clue as to why: he regrets that 'atheistical idiots', by which he means a number of his friends and contemporaries, are totally unable of comprehending his biography of Ramakrishna. He may have anticipated, correctly, that any overt references to Vedanta would doom *A Single Man*.

But the same subtlety that has made the role of Vedanta in *A Single Man* so easy to miss is integral to its success as a religious novel. *A Single Man* suggests that the most effective novel of Hinduism will deal not with a saint who embodies true consciousness, but with a person through whom the novelist can depict both the power and variety of individual life and the nature of universal consciousness. If anything, the fact that George does not appear to identify as any sort of Hindu, or even as one having read Vedanta—only heightens the effect. Unlike, say, Catholicism, Vedanta is unconcerned with the identity of the believer as believer. A Hindu novel does not need to be about a Hindu.

4

## AT HOME IN TWO WORLDS

MARIA AURORA COUTO

For the last twenty years I have lived in Aldona, one of the two largest villages in Goa, situated on the right side of the track since it is not in the coastal belt. This has ensured that our village is less invaded by builders, that I am surrounded by an expanse of green, and that the din of casinos, beach revelry, heavy metal music, is a distant rumble even though it disturbs. My late husband, Alban Couto, was born in this rambling house. His career took us to Patna, Goa, Delhi, London, Chennai, and back to Goa. Hence we have been blessed by friends spread across cities and countries. Since our return to Goa, the conversations with visiting friends echo a constant refrain: is Goa still a liberal space?

My life in Goa and in Dharwar, both liberal spaces as all of India once was, has led me to connect Gopal Gandhi and Girish Karnad. When the latter passed I wrote, 'Knowing him, as a friend and through his work, helped me grow beyond my Goan Catholic identity, helped me understand the depth and richness of Indian culture which is under threat today.' Memories of life in Dharwar and Goa are the coordinates and the source of tranquillity that have sustained me. I have been trying to get used to the gradual communalization of a once-inclusive Goan society, never mind the despoilment of its countryside, the corruption, and the impoverishment of its way of life. However, the shot that rang out in Dharwar, killing Kannada scholar M. M. Kalburgi, was a horror—a nightmarish awakening. It rang out in spaces which, we, those of us who grew up there, treasured as havens of peace, security, and friendship. Girish Karnad commented at the funeral that what had happened was not part of Kannada culture.

I had the benefit of exposure to and direct experience of the educated elite both in Goa and in Dharwar, a well-known centre of education in North Karnataka, popular with students from the neighbouring districts.

In addition, Dharwar was a cultural centre, home to Kannada writers and Hindustani classical musicians, the most eminent among them being Gangubai Hangal and Mallikarjun Mansur. These cultural influences enriched my life in a variety of ways. Most of my later life has been in urban areas as a teacher of English Literature and the wife of a senior civil servant. My Catholicism encompassed respect for the faiths of communities around me, and religious experience was not divisive.

On the other hand, my parents as well as the community converted to Catholicism in Goa, living in a society created by 450 years of Portuguese colonialism, were cut off from all links with what I would broadly define as the matrix of Indian culture. However, local traditions of worship, food, and language were incorporated within the changed ethos after the upheaval of the Inquisition. Religion and, up to a point, links with the Marathi language sustained the cultural mooring of the Hindu community. I benefited from growing up free from the less porous boundaries between the two communities in Goa. This was the case as a student in Dharwar and more so later.

Hence, now in my eighties, I look back on a life comforted and inspired within the embrace of Indian culture. In Delhi I was exposed to an abundance of cultural programmes, deepening my sense of what Gopal has described as India's 'plural soul'. Its expanse and depth enclosed my religion, a sensibility shaped by Konkani and English, inflected by Portuguese and Kannada, drawing from sources both Indian and European. It was a process which took me to Patna, Rajgir, Nalanda, Bodh Gaya, Vishnu Pad temple, reading in the Patna University Library, and mesmerized by the *Timur Nama*, *Shah Nama*, *Padshah Nama*, some autographs of Mughal emperors and princes, as also the book of military accounts of Maharaja Ranjit Singh in the Khuda Baksh Library. I listened to A. L. Basham speak about Sita's home much before the controversies of today.

My eldest child, born in Patna on the eve of Holi and blessed by the festive exuberance, was watched by two grandmothers—one clad in a sari, the other in a dress—conversing and praying in Konkani and Portuguese, surrounded by Bhojpuri- and Hindi-speaking staff who switched to English when necessary. The grandmothers had witnessed the child being blessed, a tika placed on the forehead. My mother, transplanted from a closed, Konkani- and Portuguese-speaking society to a Kannada-, Marathi-, English-speaking environment in Dharwar, was at ease despite the novelty of it all—the culture, the language, the energy, and excitement of a festival splashed its colour and joyfulness on her grandson.

Later, Gopal, as the first director of the Nehru Centre in London, and Girish Karnad who followed him, exposed audiences to the rich liberal traditions of India. I was fortunate to have attended most of the programmes from 1992 to 1994. So much of it was new and so central to a deeper understanding of who we are. There were some connections with the Raj. For instance, Mary Lutyens took us through the raising of the Rashtrapati Bhavan and her memories of Annie Besant; Radha Burnier spoke on the Theosophical Society; we admired her exquisite beauty in *The River*, her clarity, and scholarship speaking at a memorial to Achyut Patwardhan. I was dazzled by the sheer variety of the programmes.

There was art, music—Hindustani and Carnatic; theatre—Ebrahim Alkazi and Habib Tanvir; dance, including a tribute to Balasaraswati listening to her speeches on Bharatanatyam, politics—Jyoti Basu on the Permanent Settlement in Bengal, E. P. Thompson on Tagore, Rasheeduddin Khan on the challenges of building a federal policy and a plural society in India; a meeting at which several speakers shared the trauma of the demolition of the Babri Masjid; a talk on Bhakti as dissent—an examination of Alvar, a group of mystics from South India; the impact of Sufism on India. There was architecture, anthropology, Jewish history in Cochin and Calcutta, and environment with Medha Patkar speaking on the tribal world of India.

◆

Goa is often held up as an example of communal harmony despite its violent past in the early decades of Portuguese colonization. Our great poet, Bakibab Borkar, called it an original form of being—unique, incomparable humanism. Vegdench munxaponn... it is difficult to translate the first word.... Perhaps distinctive, exceptional, influenced by Buddhism, Sufism and, dare I say it, Christianity? D. D. Kosambi does say somewhere that Christianity humanized the stratified Sanskritic tradition.

'Conversion divided the community, but we were together at work; we shared a professional life and from it came intimacy, perhaps superficial yet humane,' said the ninety-year-old lawyer, the late Atmaram Xembu Poi Palondikar. 'We were together, tilling fields, fishing, labour which involved sweat and sometimes hunger for the whole community irrespective of religion,' says Pundalik Naik, a well-known Konkani writer. We share a history and a cultural bond which has survived.

Christianity added dimensions of culture but it is Portuguese law that has contributed to the uniqueness of Goan society, to the personality of Goans. Women are more confident and independent; there is a sense of equality and respect—much of it due to the European influences of philosophy and law which appealed to Aurobindo and Rabindranath Tagore. Both of them felt that unlike the Utilitarians, the European school referred to the very basis of humanism, the moral and ethical context as distinct from the motivation of self-interest.

Pombaline laws are a high point in our colonial history. In the mid-eighteenth century, the Marquez de Pombal, influenced by the ideals of the Enlightenment, introduced a humanist modernity throughout the Portuguese empire with a revolutionary law of equality without distinction of race, creed, or caste. His *Law of Equality* (1761) and *Instructions* (1774) provided the converts the rights of citizenship and representation which were extended to all Goans in 1910 when the Republic was established in Portugal.

Pombal upheld customary usages and institutions in Goa, reduced anti-Hindu discrimination, promoted education and tolerance, and abolished the colour bar. As a fruit of the Pombaline vision, Goa is the only state in India today to have a uniform civil code, which ensures women equal rights of succession, property, and inheritance. He annexed through treaties the area known as New Conquests which, along with the Old Conquests, comprises what we now know as Goa.

The missionaries who came to Goa were European, not just Portuguese—the main educationists were Jesuits who bridged the transition from religion to culture. They were products of the Renaissance and later of the Enlightenment. They achieved eminence as educators, evangelists, explorers, diplomats, administrators, government advisers, and technicians. They were required to develop a broad liberal culture in addition to theology and their education embraced science and technology. The first printing press in Asia was started in Goa in 1556.

These revolutionary laws along with education in the early centuries of conversion created an enlightened elite and a scintillating life of the mind. Although the elite were the first group influenced by early modernity, it was absorbed by the landless Catholic population and later identical groups in the Hindu population which have made Goa what it is. These laws have been cited for the elimination of gender oppression and the confidence of Goan women (which has been misrepresented after Goa became a tourist destination).

Perhaps it is because of this major difference between the two colonial powers that the intelligentsia in Goa was Europeanized in a very different sense from the elite in British India. The Portuguese did not seem to underline the Orientalist kind of othering that is associated with the British empire. The Goans wanted self-determination in matters of administration of resources, planning, and development of infrastructure.

Descriptions of Goa take into account the Portuguese cultural influence which undoubtedly is the strongest; yet ours is a layered history, a complex culture which I hesitate to define or even describe. A field study of ancient Goan culture and history reveals traces of the influences and vestiges of the Kadamba, Vijayanagar, and Bahmani period as well as interactions across the seas when Govapuri was a busy trading centre, with a brisk trade in horses. Though it failed to put an end to caste, conversion did blunt the edge of pollution which was, in many ways, transferred to the converted—who were regarded as beef-eating outcastes until, perhaps, the mid-twentieth century. Portuguese law had limited application. It helped resolve conflict, enabled registration of births, deaths, compulsory registration of marriages, and the sense of being protected by the state. Citizenship given to Catholics in the mid-eighteenth century and subsequently to all Goans in 1910 with the formation of the Republic in Portugal created a sense of self, of individuality, a characteristic that is palpable in daily intercourse with Goans.

By the late eighteenth century, Goa was almost entirely a Catholic space before the annexation. There was a slow movement of the Hindu population, perhaps first by the landed who then prospered as traders. Some of these trading houses later loaned money to the impoverished colonial power. Catholic and Hindu elites in time enjoyed immense prestige with titles conferred such as Viscount, Baron, and Commendador and Moço Fidalgo, one of the higher grades of nobility. Hindu elites were powerful in the economic life of the territory but also in the control of temples accorded by Regulamento das Mazanias (1886). This law governing the management of the temple and its properties gave immense power to the Brahmins. In pre-colonial times, the deity and the temple belonged to all; however, with Mazania Law the deity belonged to all but the temple and its properties were solely controlled by the mahajans, unlike in the rest of the country. A strong movement is rising among worshippers in some temples to repeal this law.

Unlike the British whose policies of enumerating caste made the system perhaps more rigid, the Portuguese did not take caste into account. The Dalit population of Goa which was about 2 per cent has risen today with an increase in the number of migrant labourers. Although the hierarchy remained and is reflected in the distribution of spaces in the village, the late Dadu Mandrekar, who led an Ambedkarite group in Goa, told me that Dalit women were employed inside Catholic homes, including in the kitchen and for taking care of children. Interacting with the Catholic society reduced humiliation and enhanced self-esteem. Although we adhere to caste and there is a perception among new arrivals who have set up second homes in Goa that caste identity is strong here, there are no caste atrocities. There is dominance and exclusion but there is no widespread caste violence and the communities live in harmony.

Goan/Indian culture and its entrenchment of the caste system, though alive, was perhaps also leavened by the communidade/gaunkari system—a unique and ancient system of collective land ownership—gramasanstha/gaunkari—which has preserved the sense of belonging to a village—though heavily compromised by Portuguese interference and out-migration of our people. It is responsible for the Goans' deep sense of self as rooted in land and its imagery. Economic life connected with the communidade system created a sense of community even if these were the upper classes of the caste system, and the needs of the rest were attended to.

The Republic of 1910 which separated church and state brought dramatic changes within the Hindu community, especially among the elite who had maintained their stronghold on trade and commerce. They availed of Portuguese education, were inducted into government service and professional life—lawyers and doctors, some of whom were employed in Mozambique and Angola. The move forward was dramatic. A community long repressed marched into the modern age due to the tireless efforts of social reformers. Perhaps I should say in conclusion that there was oppression of various kinds, and celebration of various kinds, which created resilience and vibrancy, a strong sense of individuality and possessiveness. We quarrel about scripts, for instance, and in these quarrels, issues of religion and caste come into play. The Feast of St Francis Xavier and the preceding nine-day novena draw pilgrims from various parts of the country, many of whom walk long distances. The tradition to pray at the shrine is alive and vibrant among the Hindu community in Goa. Anwesha Singbal, who won a Sahitya Akademi Award for poetry in 2016, concluded her speech at the prize-giving ceremony saying that Christmas in Goa is not complete without Hindus as is Chovoth or Ganesh Chaturthi, without Christians.

If Goans were the first people—for good or ill—to interact with the West, it is also true that with the humanism which European culture brought came the spirit of modernity and freedom of the mind. Jawaharlal Nehru wrote about the two Englands that came to India: the England of feudal structures and exploitation but also the England of Shakespeare and Milton. So did D. D. Kosambi more specifically about Goa. To Shakespeare and Milton he added John Bunyan's *Pilgrim's Progress*, mindful perhaps of the Christian spirit of sacrifice, struggle, and compassion that does survive despite the repression, exploitation, and betrayal of Christ's teachings that accompanied it.

Despite political instability for two decades or more, and early attempts to force Goa's merger into Maharashtra where it would languish as a taluka or district at best, the cultural strength of what politicians of all stripes describe as Goemkarponn, its uniqueness, remains due in equal parts perhaps to its landscape of undulating land, the sea, rivers, hillocks, paddy fields, coconut palms alongside mango and cashew groves, and our history. Both these created a Goan identity which has resisted the recent attempts of assimilation.

Nehru made it clear when he visited Goa in 1963, 'I have felt for a long time that Goa had a distinctive personality, and it would be a pity if anything were done to take away that personality. It may be that gradually time and other factors will bring about changes, but it is not for the government to enforce changes that will affect

Goa's personality. Goa can develop as it likes within the framework of India and thus add to the richness of India. It would be wrong to direct your energy to anything but the task of building up Goa, building up India and thus bequeath a great heritage.' In *The Discovery of India* he tried to understand and communicate the meaning of Bharat Mata, this vast land, a country in which 'each part differed from the other and yet was India' where parts varied yet made up a rich and great whole.

Knowing Gopal, reading some of his work, being exposed to the rich traditions that make us what we are, has deepened my sense of who I am.

5

# A STUDY IN 'CREATIVE COMPASSION'

JAYANTHA DHANAPALA AND TISSA JAYATILAKA

Over centuries, India and Sri Lanka have been locked in a geopolitical context which has engendered deep and indelible influences as well as tension and resentment. Inevitably, perhaps, Sri Lankan attitudes to Indian diplomats range from hypersensitivity to patronizing tones and generosity to reciprocal sincerity. Overall, this stems from a basic ambiguity towards India. Although it is the fount and source of the deeply spiritual legacy of Buddhism that shapes Sri Lankan culture, historically, India is also the source of destructive invasions which have left behind a segment of the population in Sri Lanka that continues to face difficulties in their total integration.

With Gopalkrishna Gandhi as the assistant high commissioner in Kandy (a post once held by a former president of India, V. V. Giri) and later high commissioner in Colombo, the chemistry was just right. A trained diplomat with solid professionalism, Gandhi came through with a sincere personal bonding enriched by his cultural and aesthetic interests.

Exceptionally, a man is born in a newly liberated colony with millennia of rich history and culture combining the paternal lineage of Mahatma Gandhi—the undisputed Father of modern India and apostle of peace and non-violence globally—and the maternal lineage of C. Rajagopalachari, the last (Indian) governor general of India. This extraordinary and unique gene pool would have been ideal for a political career had Gopalkrishna Gandhi chosen to pursue one. But he decided to serve India in other ways.

Tissa first met Gopal, Tara, and their two young daughters

when Gopal was serving as the assistant high commissioner in Kandy (1978-82). Of greater significance than any official interaction was the personal. Gopal, like all good South Asian neighbours, welcomed us to his home. I have a vivid memory of him carrying his young daughter on his shoulders as he strolled down Piachaud Gardens with his family. It speaks of a man whose centre has always been, despite his formidable intellect, his heart rather than his head.

This essay looks at some aspects of the man Gopal, as can be glimpsed through his novel, *Refuge*, which is based on the lives of the Plantation Tamils of Sri Lanka, as they were commonly referred to. In the author's note, he describes the years spent in Kandy:

> I was working on the rehabilitation of 'Indian' Tamils repatriating to the land of their origin in terms of the Indo-Ceylon Agreement of 1964, under which 5,25,000 persons with their 'natural increase' were to repatriate to India, leaving 300,000 with their 'natural increase' to stay back.

The use of apostrophes by the author is a clue to his opinion on this matter. The Plantation Tamils were and are referred to as 'Indian' Tamils in a bid to differentiate them from the Ceylon Tamils who had been domiciled in Sri Lanka for many centuries. The Plantation Tamils, on the other hand, had lived in Sri Lanka for about a hundred years or so. By the time the repatriation programme was formulated and put into effect, those who had originally been inveigled by the British colonial masters into coming over to Sri Lanka to work on the plantations were no more. Their descendants, the 'Indian' Tamils, who continued to live and work on the plantations, had been born on Sri Lankan soil, many of whom had never even visited India, which was considered their natural home by the governments of the two countries. Hence, the use of apostrophes underscores the irony of referring to these dwellers in a no man's land as 'Indian'. Even the use of apostrophes for the phrase 'natural increase' tells us what Gopal thought of such a cold and unfeeling manner of referring to people.

Gopal may have been a bureaucrat and a diplomat but his sympathies clearly lay with these stateless, powerless people who had become pawns in the game of power politics and regional alliances. One can deduce that it is not his DNA or bloodline that defines him as the grandson of Mahatma Gandhi and C. Rajagopalachari, but the fellow feeling he exhibits towards the marginalized members of the society. Commenting on speeches made by his paternal grandfather on the Mahatma's visit to Sri Lanka in 1927, Gopal Gandhi remarked:

> They show a creative compassion for the disadvantaged and a desire to cement the bonds between the two communities.

He added that it was his grandfather's 'creative compassion' which had made the greatest impression on him. On another occasion, in an address delivered by him at the Bernard Soysa Centenary Commemoration Oration in Colombo in 2014, he said:

> I pay tribute to Bernard Soysa as one who held offices, one whom offices did not hold; as one who held fast to socialism, but whom socialist politics did not hold in chains, as one who held esteem but whom esteem did not hold hostage. Bernard Soysa had status but he had something else of greater moment, namely, stature, the stature of an intellect twinned to public purpose and un-twinned from sectarian bias, parochial pinch-heartedness and, generally, from that common malady in politics everywhere—sheer, shameless self-advancement.

In speaking of Soysa, Gopal revealed the virtues he held dear and important. How and why we choose our heroes reveals more about ourselves than perhaps even the heroes themselves. Gopal's words afford us insight into the ideals and values he lives by. Instead of being a 'head-in-the-clouds' idealist, out of touch with reality, he is in fact acutely aware of the gulf between idealism and reality, between thought and action. A little further on in the same speech, he says:

> We should not...romanticise the Left. If the Left has had, very elevatingly, its high moments, it continues very energetically, to have its low moments; 'low' not in the sense of moments when it has been beaten—others have those too—but in the sense of slipping below its own ideals, its ethic, and knowing it has done so.

This tension between the 'highs' and the 'lows' of existence is what Gopal portrays with 'creative compassion' in his novel, *Refuge*. In the author's note, he quotes a former US ambassador to Colombo who wrote in his memoirs:

> The estate bungalows are roomy, surrounded by really lovely gardens. Servants are plentiful and relatively cheap. Social life is mainly limited to the local club—consisting of tennis courts and a bar. There, at weekends, the planters gather for bridge, gossip, drink, billiards and tennis. Somerset Maugham might not find the makings of a great novel immediately but the pressures of life in the small tea communities of Ceylon are apparent.

This is perhaps the abiding image of the plantations that a visitor might see and experience. To those passing by, the labourers and tea pluckers add colour to the picturesque image created by the green and mountainous terrain, but are invisible as individuals. But Gopal, tasked with repatriating a large number of these Plantation Tamils to India, viewed them as individuals and wrote:

> Great numbers of these estate workers met me every day in preparation for their journey to a motherland they hardly knew. Most of them had been born on their estates in the central highlands of Sri Lanka and knew little of the world outside. They viewed their prospective journey with unconcealed trepidation.

And thus was born his novel, which traces the lives of a family of Plantation Tamils who are brought into contact and sometimes in conflict with other members of the closed community; the Periadorai who wields absolute power over their lives and could upend their lives with a single command; the men down the pecking order who interpret the Periadorai's commands, sometimes according to their will and caprice; the Sinhalese villagers who live on the periphery of the estate and whose lives occasionally intersected with those of the Plantation Tamils; as well as other colourful figures like the deaf mute who blows the conch to summon the workers, the trade union activist who ironically becomes romantically involved with the Periadorai, the compassionate Italian Catholic priest, the wise Buddhist priest, the piano-playing Burgher doctor and his wife, and so on.

The main action of the novel is set in Craigavon Estate, where the scenic beauty of the landscape is described in lyrical prose. However, the author's focus shifts quickly to the lines, where the workers are housed:

> The lines on Craigavon Estate were typical of tea and rubber plantations on the island. They had ten rooms on one side and ten on the other, back to back. Twenty families therefore lived on each line. The walls and floors were earthen, the roofing of zinc sheets.

Gopal's criticism is implicit in these lines. It is not targeted towards Sri Lanka's failure as much as it targets the failure of humanity. In this failure he includes his own nation, for in his Bernard Soysa commemoration oration, he says:

> Anyone in Sri Lanka could ask me, 'who are you to be saying these things, lecturing to us? What about....

And he goes on to cite many instances where India had failed its people and humanity. If there is criticism, then it is criticism that is directed both outwards and inwards. In his portrayal, Nimal Rupasinghe, the young Oxford-educated Periadorai of Craigavon Estate, is a figure who struggles to reconcile his liberal education with the demands of the job. Birth, education, and circumstances have placed Rupasinghe in a position where he must align himself with the masters and not the servants, earn profits for his employers rather than seek to improve the lives of the workers—something he envisages will adversely affect the profit margin, his raison d'etre as the Periadorai. At the same time he is not as callous as his fellow planters, to whom the labourer is mere chattel to be exploited, if necessary, so that they could rise in their chosen career path.

On the other side of the invisible divide are people like Dr Baptist and his wife, Constance, the two priests—one Catholic and the other Buddhist—the mother of a Periadorai, Sujata Tilakaratne and, of course, the trade union activist, Martha Abeyesekere. When Dr Baptist is enlisted by the Italian Catholic priest, Father Giovanni, to host a piano recital to collect funds to repair the roof of an estate's schoolroom, these two segments of upper-class society are brought together to satisfy their thirst for society, culture, and entertainment. While Rupasinghe's refined education and training draw him to people like the Baptists, Father Giovanni, and the Austrian Buddhist monk, Venerable Seevali, he is discomfited by the implied criticism of the living conditions of those under his care and that of the government. At the same time, he is not comfortable in the company of his fellow planters either, whom he secretly despises. At a crossroads, Rupasinghe is forced to choose his path when a cholera epidemic sweeps through the line rooms of nearby Cork Estate. Unfortunately, instead of seeking medical help for those affected, the Periadorai of Cork Estate decides to cordon off the affected lines, permitting no one to enter or leave. Outraged on hearing this, Dr Baptist makes arrangements at the hospital to care for the affected patients. However, the intemperate and righteously angry doctor also shoots off a letter to the Periadorai of Cork Estate, accusing him of 'criminal negligence in not having contained the epidemic on the very first day and in not informing the health authorities himself'. Fuming, he rushes to confront and threaten the hospital clerk who was extorting money from sick patients.

Dr Baptist's actions, though justifiable, earn him some implacable and dangerous enemies. The humiliated clerk and his cronies in several estates, who were bent on making money out of this crisis, plot to get rid of the meddlesome doctor by writing an anonymous letter to the director of Health Services complaining about the doctor's violent behaviour towards the corrupt clerk, naturally omitting to mention the reason for such behaviour. It also earns him the ire of the Periadorais of the estates, who feel he has no business in interfering or commenting on the administration of their estates. They too form an alliance against the doctor and the Periadorai of Cork Estate writes a letter of complaint to the director of Health Services—though his letter is not anonymous and correctly spelt!

And what was Nimal's position on all of this? He had met the doctor and his wife at the piano recital and wished to get to know them better. After rubbing shoulders with his fellow Periadorais at the club, he had learned to despise them. However, circumstances had aligned him with the Periadorais instead. At a crucial moment, he places the doctor's letter of warning regarding the goings-on in the estates alongside the letter of complaint from the Periadorai of Cork Estate. To address the subtle criticism directed at the Periadorais in the doctor's letter, he decides to hear their point of view. But the choice does not sit easy on his conscience and these words from Eliot's *Murder in the Cathedral* keep echoing in his mind:

> Where is Becket, the traitor to the King?
> Where is Becket, the meddling priest?

The implications are clear—great men are often at odds with those in authority when they are guided by their conscience. And though Nimal has chosen to align himself with those in authority, there is an uneasy awareness that Dr Baptist might be a great man after all, who probably will be sacrificed so that the Periadorais can continue to do as they had always done. Having taken sides against the 'enemy', he goes out of his way to avoid the Baptists when he sees them.

Gandhi makes it apparent that it is no easy matter to choose between right and wrong. Sensitive individuals like Nimal choose wrong at great cost to their own sense of self and well-being. Nimal is feted by his fellow Periadorais when he turns up at the club and is unanimously chosen to be the leader of the group. But the more he upholds the status quo and his eventual success becomes apparent, the more he loses his grip on the situation. Eventually, he resigns and leaves for Colombo. There he does nothing, seeming to brood within his home, drinking, and resorting to taking drugs. For a short period, he embarks on a love affair with the trade unionist, Martha Abeysekere, but after an encounter with an old friend from Oxford at a seminar, Nimal realizes how far he has moved from the ideals he held dear in those early years. The novel ends on a tragic note with Nimal dying due to suicide.

The novel makes clear the creative tension that exists between right and wrong action. Though not obvious and clearly apparent, it can be sensed deep within. Nimal made the wrong choice partly because of the circumstances of his birth and position. There is thus no facile judgement of the choice he makes. Even Dr Baptist could have made a different choice and handled the corrupt clerk and the Periadorais somewhat differently—and thus avoided being more or less dismissed from his position. Persuaded by the Buddhist priest, Venerable Seevali, to let go of his anger, he realizes that his intemperate actions were partially responsible for the consequences he had to face. However, Father Giovanni reminds him that even Christ acted intemperately when he threw the moneylenders out of the temple premises in a display of righteous anger. Gandhi presents two ways of thought and two courses of action—both right and wrong in themselves. His mature vision of life recognizes that the right choice is not always clear and easy to make.

What of the people whose personal tragedies were shared with the man forced to facilitate their repatriation to India? Running in parallel is the story of Kandan, whose wife dies in childbirth due to the non-availability of a vehicle to transport her to the hospital in time. The overseer, insulted by the distraught Kandan for refusing to release a vehicle to take his wife to the hospital, exacts his revenge by ensuring that no one else is able to help either. Thus, tragic death, a common occurrence in the lives of deprived and powerless people, takes place in Kandan's home. His two motherless daughters are left in the care of their elderly grandparents when Kandan goes to work or out binge-drinking. The young and blooming Valli eventually forms a relationship with the Sinhalese fish vendor, Soma.

The poignant love story between two people from different backgrounds is described with delicacy and sensitivity. But everything weighs against such a relationship and the romance ends in tragedy. The overseer, who discovers the budding romance, rapes Kandan's daughter as revenge. Soma, who genuinely cares for the girl, defends her honour by killing the overseer and is locked away in prison for an indefinite period of time. Valli, on finding out that she is carrying Soma's child, is persuaded to accept a proposal of marriage from a much-older widower with several children, so that Soma's child would become legitimate. As her husband is one of those who was to be repatriated to India under the terms of the Indo–Ceylon pact, she eventually embarks on the first leg of her journey to India, having once again been raped by marauding thugs in a racially motivated attack on the plantation workers and leaving Soma's child in the care of her sister.

The picture that emerges from the novel is of a suffering, disenfranchised people at the mercy of chance, disease, ignorance, malnutrition, racist politics, and powerful God-like employers. The creative compassion that his grandfather spoke of is manifested in Gandhi's novel about these 'invisible' people. Yet, the novel affords no easy answers to the business of living.

It only offers a view of the choices made by each individual to understand what leads to Nimal's disastrous choices or why Dr Baptist, Soma, Valli, and others act the way they do. In the end, it stands as a testament to one man's nuanced view of the complexities of life and what it means to be fully human.

# 6

## GANDHI, MY FATHER
## A CREATION IN CONFLICT

#### FEROZ ABBAS KHAN

*Gandhi, My Father* is a result of a deep anguish. I have often questioned my motives for making this film. Am I to use the private pain of a very public family to feed the voyeuristic appetite of an entertainment hungry audience?

Was Mahatma Gandhi a father who failed or was it the relationship that failed? What moral credentials do I have to even attempt a judgement on an extraordinary man who could have been God, if he weren't a human being.

I abandoned the project several times. It was a burden that my conscience could not handle. But I felt deep within myself that I must find a way.

Harilal Gandhi was intelligent, handsome, romantic, strong-willed, fiery.

He was a beloved husband and a doting father.

The young Gandhi of South Africa was to be the natural heir to his revolutionary father. He challenged the cruel and racist regime in South Africa and courted arrest. At nineteen years of age, he was a seasoned freedom fighter.

Yet, five months after Mahatma Gandhi's death, he was picked up as a beggar on the street in Bombay and brought to a hospital where he died shortly thereafter. He passed on unknown—unsung.

Unscrupulous businessman used his surname as a dependable brand to defraud unsuspecting and gullible investors.

Muslim fanatics tried to use his conversion to Islam as a weapon to damage the Mahatma and confront Hindu fanatics in a dance of mutual annihilation.

In Harilal's pain as a young widower, he took to alcohol, debauchery, and public fury against his father. He lived with extreme poverty and a terminal illness.

Harilal Gandhi's life is a nightmare; a nightmare which Indian history would prefer to be in denial about. The combustible nature of his character conflicts with the aura of his surname.

I felt an obligation to tell the truth of this story, yet I want to make it clear that Harilal's tragedy cannot be a yardstick to measure the greatness of the Mahatma. Harilal's story is a reminder that all freedom struggles entail personal, social, and political sacrifices. He was caught at the wrong time in history with a difficult surname.

It is also a story of a desperate scream for love. He adored his father, he loved his father and the ultimate irony of love is that the one you love the most you hurt the most.

It is relatively simple to tell stories about heroes and villians. Harilal, the wronged son, and Mahatma Gandhi, the uncaring father. Period. Eulogies with platitudes or venomous denigration are some other models that can be used to understand Gandhi. Polarized politics use them to damage the truth.

Every film writer or pundit will advise you that we need a protagonist who is locked in conflict with the antagonist and eventually wins. But, can the complexity of a principled father's relationship with an aspiring son triggered by the socio-political turmoil of their time be reduced to a binary?

For me, between the shades of black and white is where the truth resides. These are real people documented with facts. Their struggle is life instructive. It would be too easy to reduce it to a petty domestic quarrel or empathize with their compulsions.

To the horror of many, the two main characters in the film oscillated between the protagonist and the antagonist. We were with the Mahatma several times yet it was Harilal who made us weep so often.

The final story, screenplay, and dialogues are a result of these big and small battles with perhaps millions of mutinies inside me.

The first day of shoot, 31 January 2005, early in the morning. I was driving to the location—the famous stepwells of Ahmedabad. We passed the Sabarmati Ashram. I asked the driver to turn around and reached the doors of Hriday Kunj. A part of the veranda was partitioned to create a small room where the Mahatma would sit, spinning, weaving, praying, and guiding the Indian freedom movement. The ashram was quiet and empty. A solitary janitor, braving the cold winter and cleaning the room, invited me to sit and pray in this most sanctified place. In those days, this room was not accessible to the visiting public.

This opportunity left me hardly able to hold back my tears. I sat there, weeping profusely, and I remember imploring Bapu for the strength to make a film that would not hurt the greatness of the Mahatma.

The experience shook me to my core.

There is a scene in the film which illustrates the impact of that experience on me well. In the scene, Harilal is sitting in a tiny room with a prostitute asking her to let him stay a bit longer, as he wants to talk to her. But she asks him to leave as she has to service other clients. Between the choices to shoot the scene with all its gory details and explicit vulgarity to sensationalize or to simply explore his loneliness, a man for whom the world had shut the doors, I chose the latter option. Every shot in the film bears the tension of this delicate balance of dignity, aesthetics, drama, facts, and cinematic grammar.

Marketing strategies are generally focused on getting the largest number of people to watch the film. These ideas are sometimes morally dubious and other times ideologically dangerous. Since a majority of the film-going audience is young, we were advised to project the film as a clash between the younger generation which represented the hopeful and the older generation which represented rigidity and dogma. Harilal was to be the young hero and Gandhi the vanquished villain.

A section of the media suggested we selectively highlight the provocative parts of the film and let the controversy rage and spread. This could prove to be a mutually beneficial arrangement. The argument between finance and ethics is fierce and delicate. All films are essentially driven by commerce.

After a lot of debate and soul-searching, we screened the film for the members of the Gandhi family. They had to be the ultimate arbiters of this legacy.

Deeply moved after watching the film, one of them told me that it felt like the movie had been made by a close family member; the film encapsulated for them the agony and anguish of Ba and Bapu as parents and the pain and helplessness of Harilal as a son, without judgement or prejudice.

The experience of making this film has left me grappling with the conflict between the freedom of expression and the responsibility to uphold the truth. Are we comfortable with imagined history serving commercial and ideological agendas camouflaged as free speech? Can art be burdened with conscience? And then in a post-truth world, do these questions even matter...?

# SECTION II

# HISTORY

7

'PA RISHI': GANDHI'S CONSTRUCTIVE
CRITIQUES OF PARSI CULTURE AND SOCIETY[1]

DINYAR PATEL

'Why,' Mohandas K. Gandhi asked in September 1921, 'does the world care for a community of eighty thousand men and women?' Gandhi, writing in the columns of Bombay's *Sanj Vartaman*, asked this question about the Parsis, a tiny ethno-religious community concentrated mostly in Bombay and southern Gujarat. For the Mahatma, the answer was simple. The Parsis' munificent charity, he noted, had made them 'renowned in the world'. Furthermore, the community had, throughout the nineteenth and early twentieth centuries, contributed many of the guiding spirits of India's political and economic development. These were reasons enough for Gandhi, normally generous with praise, to dollop an unusual amount of it on the Parsis. He quipped that a Parsi was really a 'pa rishi', or one-fourth of a sage. 'Every literate Parsi knows by now that I am simply in love with his community,' he concluded.

During the Non-Cooperation Movement, Gandhi initiated a sustained engagement with the Parsis of India. He praised their

---

[1] This article builds upon a paper that I wrote early in graduate school, based on a close reading of the *Collected Works of Mahatma Gandhi*. It includes material from subsequent archival research in the United States and India. I had shared my original paper with Gopalkrishna Gandhi in 2008. In spite of his responsibilities at the time as the governor of West Bengal, he was generous enough to meet with me. Since then, we have regularly conversed and shared insights on Mahatma Gandhi's various interactions with the Parsi community. I deeply appreciate the interest Gopal has taken in the Parsi community and its history. It is commonly assumed that Parsis remained aloof from Gandhian activism and politics, but Gopal has pushed against this perspective by pointing out Gandhi's numerous Parsi supporters and followers.

industry and generosity. However, he also sharply critiqued aspects of their culture and society. The Mahatma's critiques of his own Hindu society and religion are, of course, well known. But he felt familiar enough with members of another community to identify perceived social problems and sketch out a programme of internal reform. In spite of his quip about a Parsi being a 'pa rishi', Gandhi was an insightful and objective commentator on the community's internal affairs, poking holes in Parsis' self-assuredness and calling into question their self-congratulatory demeanour. This article delves into his specific critiques and investigates why Gandhi became so involved in the affairs of the Parsi community during the early 1920s.

Gandhi took issue with four particular aspects of Parsi culture: the spoken and written Parsi Gujarati dialect, their Anglicized ways, accumulation of material wealth, and their liberal attitudes towards alcohol (as well as the community's large stake in the Indian liquor industry). These were, in Gandhi's mind, interlinked phenomena. They overlapped with some social problems that the Mahatma identified in other communities. Notably, Gandhi's remedies neatly dovetailed with his constructive programme: his agenda for the social and moral regeneration of India. In other words, Gandhi realized the imperatives of keeping the Parsis in close orbit of his political campaigns.

What prompted Gandhi's particular interest in Parsi affairs? During his childhood, education, and early political career, the Mahatma developed a deep familiarity with Parsi society, borne out of a shared Gujarati culture and a plethora of Parsi friends and associates. In Porbandar and Rajkot, Parsis numbered amongst Gandhi's teachers, schoolmates, and family friends. In Durban and Johannesburg, he leaned heavily on two Parsi political colleagues, Rustomjee Gorkhodu (better known as 'Parsee Rustomjee') and Sorabji Shapurji Adajania, and attracted several other Parsi satyagrahis. Finally, Gandhi acknowledged his debts to Parsi politicians such as Mancherji Bhownaggree, Dadabhai Naoroji, Pherozeshah Mehta, and Dinshaw Wacha—these men championed the cause of Indian South Africans in the British Parliament, the Colonial and India offices in London, and the halls of power in Calcutta and Delhi. 'A strange relationship binds me to the Parsis,' Gandhi told a Colombo audience in 1927. 'The affection they have showered on me, a Hindu, wherever I have come in contact with them is something inexplicable and impregnable.'

Familiarity prompted commentary. Language, appropriately enough, formed the basis of some of Gandhi's earliest critiques of Parsi culture. Following in the footsteps of Gujarat's late nineteenth-century literary renaissance, Gandhi endorsed a rigid, Sanskrit-based shuddh Gujarati. In marked contrast to his later embrace of Hindustani, he disparaged the presence of Persian and Arabic loan words in the language. Parsi Gujarati, which liberally borrowed from the Perso-Arabic lexicon and featured idiosyncratic pronunciations and spellings, therefore piqued the Mahatma. 'The Parsis have disfigured Gujarati to such an extent that to enter into competition with them would be tantamount to murdering the language,' he complained in the columns of *Navajivan* in August 1921. He encouraged Parsis to 'improve their language' and pointed to a handful of Parsi authors who wrote in shuddh Gujarati, such as the social reformer Behramji Malabari and the poet Ardeshir Khabardar. 'A little pride in one's language is all that is required,' he lectured Parsi readers. Indeed, Gandhi believed that language reform was an intrinsic part of generating national pride and patriotism. He even suggested that 'our casual attitude to Gujarati'—the presence of different regional and community dialects—'bespeaks want of love on our part for our country and language.'

The Mahatma moderated his criticism of the Parsi dialect after discovering the extent to which spoken and written Gujarati, no matter how 'disfigured', was in retreat in certain quarters of the community. Gandhi despaired of the growing preponderance of English amongst Indian elites. The Parsis, who eagerly embraced English-medium education from the late nineteenth century onwards, therefore presented a particular conundrum. He bemoaned that some educated Parsis took pride in their wholesale adoption of English and consequent ignorance of Gujarati. 'This shows the unhappy condition of the community,' Gandhi declared. 'The English language is the craze of the day. I bear it no ill will. But it is one thing to learn that language and quite another to make it one's mother tongue.' In his correspondence with Parsi contacts, he lost few opportunities to encourage Gujarati writing and speaking. This was a long-term project. Thus, in 1944, he gently suggested to the industrialist J. R. D. Tata that he would 'love to write to you in Gujarati' rather than in English. Dadabhai Naoroji's granddaughters, the so-called 'Captain sisters', were regularly reminded to minimize their English usage with him. In spite of his veneration for Naoroji, Gandhi confessed to Nurgis Captain in 1925, 'I shall never forgive him for not insisting on you all becoming Gujarati scholars.'

The Parsis' steady adoption of English, Gandhi believed, was symptomatic of a deeper social malaise. He was profoundly dismayed by what he termed the 'Western drift' in the community: its supposedly 'thoughtless imitation' and adoption of Western culture. During the Non-Cooperation Movement, the Mahatma spent an unusual amount of time speaking on this topic in Gujarati towns with significant Parsi populations. Quite naturally, he reserved his strongest words for an event in Navsari, a large and ancient Parsi stronghold, held in April 1921. 'A whirlwind from the West has overwhelmed us,' he told audience members. 'It is not impossible that, fascinated by English education, your community will be swept off its feet by this Western wind.' Westernization, he suggested, was tantamount to a betrayal of Zoroastrian religious principles—no mild criticism in a town regarded as the headquarters of the Parsi priesthood. 'If you let yourselves be carried away by the wind from the West,' he continued, 'you will forget the divinity in you; and, if you forget the teachings of Zarathustra, you will lose that treasure for which you have become famous, [and] will exchange a pearl for a pebble.'

Zoroastrianism, the Mahatma believed, placed a particular emphasis on simplicity of lifestyle. He spoke approvingly of the simplicity and modesty of one of his father's Parsi friends in

Porbandar. Dadabhai Naoroji combined an ethos of simplicity with 'a strong religious, pious fervour' in his political work—Gandhi recalled seeing Naoroji toil away in a minuscule garret office in London, refusing to rely on a typewriter or secretary. Parsee Rustomjee, Gandhi held, was the very embodiment of austerity. 'Luxuries had no place in his life,' he noted. His old Parsi friend had arrived in South Africa with little education and a smattering of English, and yet had built himself into one of the most successful and respected merchants of Durban.

Gandhi held up these three men in contrast to what he now observed in Gujarat and Bombay: Parsis adopting unnecessarily cumbersome Western clothing, purchasing foreign cloth and luxury items, and hankering after Western technologies. These luxurious traits, the Mahatma believed, were not just an affront to Parsi religious tenets; they were also fundamentally against the interests of fellow Indians. Reliance on Western goods, after all, perpetuated the drain of wealth from the country. 'That we should trade with foreigners when millions in India are dying of hunger is a crime against ourselves,' he told Parsis.

In his speech in Navsari, the Mahatma spoke warmly of the Parsi tradition of charity, but he felt that this, too, was coming under assault. By 'hankering after pleasures and luxuries,' Parsis were now hoarding their wealth. 'There have been many multi-millionaires among the Parsis,' he acknowledged, noting the community's long mercantile history. 'Though they had earned such immense wealth, they did not give up simplicity, ever kept their hearts clean and never forgot God.' Previous generations of wealthy Parsis had liberally distributed charity across caste and religious boundaries. Gandhi once more had in mind Parsee Rustomjee, who had donated to mosques, madrassas, schools, and political work in South Africa and India. In contrast to Rustomjee's selflessness, the Mahatma held up recent charitable projects that were limited only to Parsis. By the early twentieth century, Parsis were increasingly funnelling their philanthropy towards intra-community projects like the baugs of Bombay, meant to house the community's poor, or Parsis-only medical facilities. 'Hospitals for Parsis, exclusive accommodation and other facilities for Parsis, separate funds for Parsis!' the Mahatma exclaimed in reaction. He felt that such projects meant that the community was now 'rolling in luxury'— and sternly warned that such philanthropy 'held the danger of the community's losing its present position' by promoting exclusivity. Parsis could hardly be accused of being alone in indulging in narrow community-based help, given the bulging coffers of certain Hindu, Muslim, and Christian institutions. Yet it was the sheer scale of intra-community charity, contrasted with the Parsis' miniscule population, that troubled the Mahatma. It smacked of excess. 'I have told Parsi friends that there was every danger of their spiritual growth being arrested because of excessive wealth,' he stated.

Gandhi was also increasingly disturbed by how Parsi wealth was being generated. He singled out one of the biggest sources of community philanthropy, the Tatas, for particular scorn. 'I dread the Rockefeller spirit that seems to be overtaking the great House of the Tatas,' he noted in *Young India* in March 1921. Gandhi had previously enjoyed good relations with the Tatas and remained on friendly terms with other Parsi business houses like the Godrejs. However, some of the Tatas' recent projects— such as the controversial Mulshi Dam, which triggered what was perhaps the world's first mass anti-dam movement—convinced him that capitalist prerogatives were diluting the nationalist ethos that animated much of Jamsetji Tata's work. In subsequent years, Gandhi's relations with the Tatas profoundly soured: Gandhi highlighted labour troubles, while the Tata Chairman, N. B. Saklatvala, bitterly opposed the Civil Disobedience Movement.

But no Parsi business venture attracted more of Gandhi's opprobrium than the community liquor trade. Parsis held a commanding position in India's liquor industry, owning large toddy plantations and pithas (taverns) in south Gujarat and distilleries and liquor stores across the country. The connection with alcohol production, retail, and consumption had an ancient pedigree stretching back to the community's origin in Iran. Yet the

Mahatma would have none of it. 'I shall never be convinced that the Prophet Zoroaster has sanctioned drinking,' he wrote in a Parsi-run newspaper in September 1921. He urged Parsis to give up drink and completely sever their relationship with the liquor industry. Here, even Gandhi realized the practical difficulties standing in the way of these goals. Amongst his Parsi audiences, after all, were men and women with surnames like Daruwalla, Toddywalla, and Rumwalla. Even Parsee Rustomjee, he ruefully noted, had gone back on his vow to become a teetotaller.

Nevertheless, as Gandhi wove prohibition ever closer into his constructive programme, he maintained a remarkably severe attitude towards the Parsis' involvement in the liquor trade. He told one liquor store owner to 'renounce trade in liquor even if he were to become a beggar in consequence'. When apprised of the fact that many Parsi widows supported themselves through family liquor stores, the Mahatma shot back that 'it was better for these women to break stones or even beg [for] their food than to sell liquor to the people'. Speaking to a gathering of Bombay liquor contractors in July 1921, he told the preponderant number of Parsis in attendance that they were destroying their community and hurting their country. This did not go down well.

Prohibition and the liquor trade provide us with a good opportunity to peg Parsi reactions to Gandhi's assorted critiques of the community. Many Parsis responded with alarm and incredulousness to the idea that they should renounce drink and cut their ties with the liquor industry. Alcohol consumption, they pointed out, was not proscribed in Zoroastrianism. They resented allegations that the Parsi liquor trade was injurious to themselves and to all of India. When prohibition finally came into force in Bombay in 1939 (ironically through a Parsi minister of public health and excise, Manchersha D. Gilder), Parsis flooded Gandhi's mailbox with angry letters, many containing language that caused the Mahatma to blush. 'Vulgarity is too mild a term for characterizing some of the writings,' he claimed. 'One writer uses language of violence which certainly brings him within penal laws.'

These outbursts clearly caught Gandhi off guard; he went so far as to call them the 'terrorism of minorities'.

From a much earlier date, Parsis rejected many of Gandhi's other critiques. His views on the Parsi–Gujarati dialect found few sympathizers.[2] Parsis dismissed the notion that they should give up the English language and their Westernized ways. 'Is it possible [...] to set back the hand of time?' a Parsi reporter quizzed Gandhi in June 1921. How could they, furthermore, put their families in jeopardy by resigning from government-affiliated schools, courts, and institutions, as the Mahatma called on them to do during the Non-Cooperation Movement? It was unreasonable for a community of rich merchants and professionals to take up some of Gandhi's more eccentric suggestions, such as abandoning cities for ancestral villages or curtailing their intake of meat and chicken (a particularly outrageous proposal for carnivorous Parsis).

Yet, amidst such pushback against Gandhi, something remarkable happened: a few of the Mahatma's critiques managed to resonate with a number of Parsis, drawing part of the community into the constructive programme. In particular, many Parsis were receptive to Gandhi's commentary about their materialism and overt Westernization. As a symbol of a commitment to simplicity, as well as solidarity with the poorest of Indians, the Mahatma urged Parsis to adopt and produce khadi cloth en masse—he wanted to see even the richest Parsis labouring over the charkha.

Numerous Parsis took up this suggestion with vigour. One of India's greatest proponents of khadi cloth in the 1920s was Burjorji F. Bharucha, who travelled from one end of India to the other to promote spinning and selling khadi. Gandhi himself marvelled at Bharucha's energy and dedication. The Captain sisters, meanwhile, popularized khadi products in Bombay: acknowledging Parsi fashion sensibilities, they produced finely embroidered items that catered to

---

[2]Aside from Ardeshir Khabardar, one important exception was Ratan Marshall (1911–2011), a prominent scholar of Parsi Gujarati literature. Marshall wrote and spoke in public in shuddh Gujarati, and he encouraged its use in the community.

the community's elite. Another granddaughter of Dadabhai Naoroji, Khurshedben Naoroji, introduced khadi cloth production in the impoverished villages of the North-West Frontier Province in the 1930s. She argued that khadi would provide economic uplift and social harmony in this restless region. And, in October 1921, an overjoyed Gandhi highlighted a unique Parsi wedding ceremony. This wedding, he told readers of *Navajivan*, was the first-ever all-khadi nuptial: the bride, bridegroom, priests, and attendees were all bedecked in khadi. Wedding gifts took the form of donations to the Tilak Swaraj Fund. 'Let us hope this regard for swadeshi and simplicity will be widely emulated,' the Mahatma declared.

Even Gandhi's lectures on prohibition caused some Parsis to set aside their nightly tipple. Although the Mahatma took care not to single out Parsi liquor stores for picketing during the Non-Cooperation Movement—especially after the Prince of Wales riots in November 1921 in Bombay, where rioters torched and vandalized many of these establishments—several Parsis came forward to take up this work. Two women led these efforts: Khurshedben Naoroji and Mithuben Petit.

Naoroji, whose grandfather had been an active proponent of temperance in both India and the United Kingdom, organized pickets during the Civil Disobedience Movement in the villages surrounding Ahmedabad. Petit, the daughter of one of Bombay's richest Parsi families, left her comfortable abode on Nepean Sea Road for the villages of south Gujarat. She originally took up khadi work. 'Belonging as she did to one of the most respectable Parsi families in Bombay, the effect of her going about in villages dressed in coarse Khadi and often barefooted with the message of Khadi on her lips and a bundle of Khadi on her shoulders was tremendous,' recalled Mahadev Desai. By the late 1920s, she endorsed prohibition with equal gusto. Petit was particularly drawn to the plight of the Kaliparaj, Adivasi peasants in Bardoli district who were ensnared in debt to liquor store owners, many of them Parsis. She popularized prohibition work amongst the Kaliparaj in spite of the threats of many of her co-religionists—who now faced dwindling revenues—

and general Parsi disapproval. Even her family disinherited Petit. Gandhi seized upon her inspiring example of self-sacrifice, using it to good effect in speeches while on his Salt March. 'Mithubehn is crazy about this cause,' he declared about her prohibition campaign. 'We should be ashamed of continuing to drink when a Parsi lady gives up her home because of it.'

The deeds of Mithuben Petit, Khurshedben Naoroji, Burjorji F. Bharucha, and countless other Parsi satyagrahis help us answer the question that Gandhi posed for *Sanj Vartaman* readers in 1921: why did the world care for this tiny community of 80,000? It is true that Gandhi hoped to tap Parsi wealth and resources for the Congress and its associated organizations. This explains why he courted some of the community's richest families, such as the Tatas, Petits, and Godrejs.

But that is only part of the story. The Mahatma, to put it simply, believed in the power of example. The Parsis' self-sacrifice, renunciation of privilege and wealth, and zealous dedication to the constructive programme could, he believed, stir the larger Indian body politic. Parsis could demonstrate that nationalist commitment pervaded even one of the richest and most Anglophile communities. This was precisely the reason why, during the Non-Cooperation Movement, Gandhi chose to spend an extraordinary amount of time courting and coaxing community members. And it was also why he persistently critiqued aspects of Parsi society. The Mahatma believed that such aspects hindered Parsi engagement with the constructive programme. Due to his familiarity and longstanding bonds with the community, he felt comfortable enough to speak his mind and suggest remedies. The Parsis might be 'pa rishi,' but this distinction was meaningless if they did not introspect and recognize their stake in the current political struggle.

Simplicity and sacrifice, Gandhi declared, were essential if the Parsis were to help India achieve swaraj. In the conclusion to his *Sanj Vartaman* article of September 1921, Gandhi once more invoked the community's reputation for liberal charity but added a twist. 'We are now in a position to understand the new meaning of philanthropy,' he stated. Parsi philanthropy, he continued, needed to take the form of single-minded dedication and nationalist commitment, rather than money. 'I beg the Parsi brothers and sisters that they dedicate to India all these powers,' the Mahatma wrote. 'I pray to God that it may be so.' It is to Gandhi's credit that he convinced so many Parsis to energetically take up this new philanthropic ideal.

8

# INTIMATE ENEMIES: RAJAJI AND KAMARAJ

## A. R. VENKATACHALAPATHY

The success of the Dravidian movement in the last half century often overshadows the long and robust history of nationalist politics in Tamil Nadu. It is worth recalling that the very first resolution at the inaugural session of the Indian National Congress in Bombay in 1885 was moved by G. Subramania Iyer, the founder of *The Hindu* and, that, in the 1950s, most people in Tamil Nadu believed K. Kamaraj would rule forever.

Since its inception, the Congress in Tamil Nadu had been dominated by Brahmins. A big challenge soon came in December 1916 in the form of the Non-Brahmin Manifesto issued in the name of P. Theagaraya Chetti, which declared, '[I]n what passes for the politics in Madras, [non-Brahmins] have not taken the part to which they are entitled.' This manifesto was followed by the launch of a non-Brahmin party, called the South Indian Liberal Federation or the Justice Party.

With non-Brahmins claiming political power, the ground rules of politics in South India changed. The political movement amalgamated with a cultural movement for Tamil identity and a radical social reform movement in the form of Periyar's Self-respect Movement. The Brahmin leaders of the Congress, who had little appeal among the public, were unable to mobilize the masses and the party was forced to cede ground to non-Brahmins.

By the mid-1930s it became clear that only a non-Brahmin could be the president of the Congress in Tamil Nadu. Three prominent non-Brahmin Congress leaders emerged following the birth of the Justice Party: E. V. Ramaswami (Periyar), Dr P. Varadarajulu

Naidu, and Thiru. Vi. Kalyanasundara Mudaliar (Thiru. Vi. Ka.). But even these three leaders remained uncomfortable in the Congress: Periyar left the party in 1925, Varadarajulu Naidu in 1934 (to rejoin it later in 1945), and an already marginalized Thiru. Vi. Ka. in the mid-1940s.

But what none of these stalwarts could achieve was later realized by Kamaraj: an unchallenged leadership of the Congress, a long stint in the chief minister's position, and a key role in national politics. The only counterweight to his rise was C. Rajagopalachari.

Through the parallel lives and careers of these two major political figures, Chakravarti Rajagopalachari or Rajaji (1878–1972) and Kumaraswami Kamaraj (1903–1975), the travails of nationalist politics in twentieth century Tamil Nadu can be narrated.

## Two Lives

Born in Thorapalli in present-day Krishnagiri district in Tamil Nadu, Rajaji studied in Bangalore before acquiring a law degree. Brought up in an orthodox Vaishnavite Brahmin family, as a young man, he had witnessed Swami Vivekananda's inspiring visit to Chennai in 1897. During the Swadeshi Movement, he had been drawn to Bal Gangadhar Tilak's politics, and had attended the stormy Surat session in which the Congress had split.

A successful lawyer in Salem, he plunged into local politics, eventually becoming the chairman of its municipal council in 1917. In the beginning of 1919, he moved to the city of Chennai as nationalist politics started gaining steam under Gandhi's leadership. The 1920s saw his steady rise in both provincial and national politics. This paralleled his close relationship with Gandhi. Though once described as Gandhi's conscience-keeper and heir apparent, eventually, Rajaji had to yield space to Jawaharlal Nehru.

In the interregnum between the Civil Disobedience Movement in 1930 and the first provincial elections in 1937, Kamaraj emerged as a major figure in Tamil Nadu politics, posing a tough challenge to Rajaji.

Born a quarter-century after Rajaji, in the trading town of Virudhupatti, present-day Virudhunagar, Kamaraj's ancestral community of Nadars had seen dramatic social mobility since the mid-nineteenth century. Indebted to British rule for their rise, they were staunch Raj loyalists and key supporters of the Justice Party and Periyar's Self-respect Movement well into the 1930s. But the rise of Kamaraj changed the tide.

A tall, lanky young man with little formal education, Kamaraj joined nationalist politics early on and volunteered in the Vaikom Satyagraha in 1924. By the time the Civil Disobedience Movement started, he was deeply involved in organizational work and was at the forefront of Congress agitations, even courting arrest on a number of occasions.

At this time there were two major factions in the Tamil Nadu Congress: one under Rajaji and the other led by S. Satyamurti. Kamaraj identified with the latter and so, when Satyamurti became the Tamil Nadu Congress Committee (TNCC) president in 1936, he took over as secretary.

From the time of the Non-Cooperation Movement, Rajaji had been a key man in the Tamil Nadu Congress's organizational politics. Though he was never made the Congress president, his stature in national politics was, however, never in question. In 1937, when the first elections were held under the Government of India Act of 1935 that gave provincial autonomy, the Congress won a sweeping victory under Rajaji's leadership, trouncing the Justice Party in the Madras Presidency. But the sidelining of his rival would have other repercussions when Satyamurti groomed Kamaraj to challenge Rajaji.

Rajaji's two-year-three-month term in office as premier was eventful. He enforced prohibition in a few districts, steered the Temple Entry Bill in the legislature, and introduced sales tax. But when he introduced compulsory Hindi in schools, a popular agitation rose against it under Periyar's leadership.

The war years further tested Rajaji. When the British government dragged India into the World War II without consulting the elected Congress provincial governments, they resigned in protest. Rajaji's support for the British war effort and opposition to the Quit India Movement further contributed to his distance from Gandhi.

In 1940, Kamaraj became the president of the Tamil Nadu Congress, defeating Rajaji's nominee. With no election being conducted due to the ongoing war and the Quit India Movement, he enjoyed a very long term. The election had been fought closely, and the margin was narrow: 103 to his opponent's 100. In 1955, the legendary journalist and early biographer of Kamaraj, T. S. Chockalingam remarked: 'Those three votes began the transformation of Tamil Nadu's history....'

One of Rajaji's critical proposals to solve the political deadlock between the All India Muslim League and the Indian National Congress, the Rajaji formula, which accommodated key elements of Jinnah's demands for Pakistan short of a partition so that India could swiftly progress towards Independence, was met with great opposition in the Congress. Kamaraj issued a show-cause notice forcing Rajaji to resign from the party. While he put up a brave face, emphasizing 'the value of discipline as well as the need for liberty of thought'—in the words of his biographer-grandson Rajmohan Gandhi—Rajaji had 'lost his Congress base'. His political weakness translated into Kamaraj's control over the party.

It was not until 1945 that Rajaji was rehabilitated, but not without controversy and bitterness. His attempt to re-enter the Congress was resented by the cadres who had experienced prison terms and police repression during the Quit India Movement. Although he was readmitted following his letter to the party president, Abul Kalam Azad, in August 1945, it came at great cost to the Congress party. News came suddenly of Rajaji's election to TNCC from Tiruchengode, where he had established and managed the Gandhi Ashram from the mid-1920s, in an election of which not even the party president, Kamaraj, was aware. This fuelled sentiments against Rajaji within the party.

The first TNCC meeting after the Quit India Movement and the Second World War was convened in Thiruparankundram near Madurai in October 1945. The Rajaji camp tried to mobilize support as the primary agenda of the meeting was to decide candidates for the ensuing provincial elections. Not only was the proposal to elect Rajaji as TNCC president defeated, but his election from Tiruchengode was also declared void.[1]

Once again, he tried to resolve the issue through his proximity to the central leadership. The matter was brought to the notice of Azad who appointed Asaf Ali to enquire. Asaf Ali spent a week in Chennai listening to views from both the camps. But even before he could submit his report, the parties worked out a compromise: the Tamil Nadu Parliamentary Board was constituted with three members from Rajaji's camp and five from Kamaraj's. Kamaraj was now the unrivalled leader of the Congress in Tamil Nadu while Rajaji had to stay content with his role in the all-India party. A remark by one of Rajaji's admirers that 'Kamaraj was a raging bull let loose' is not only reflective of the Rajaji camp's perspective but also captures the party's sentiments at the time.

Soon another controversy erupted: in January 1946, Gandhi was to visit Chennai by a special train. Fearing surging crowds, the railway station where he would alight was kept secret. Rajaji failed to inform Kamaraj of this. (How Kamaraj managed to be present to receive Gandhi in Ambattur Station is another story.) On his return, Gandhi, in a signed article in *Harijan*, said that a 'clique' was opposed to Rajaji while he had the full support of the party in Tamil Nadu. Deeply stung, Kamaraj resigned from the election committee. Such was his influence in the provincial organization that Kamaraj could even defy the Mahatma.

In the 1946 elections, the Congress won 165 out of the 205

---

[1]This controversy was captured by C. N. Annadurai in the phrase 'Kodu Uyarnthathu, Kundram Thazhnthathu'—the rise of (Tiruchen) code and the fall of (Thirupparan) kundram. In Tamil, both kodu and kundram mean a mountain. Annadurai was indicating that Brahmins had triumphed over non-Brahmins.

seats in the Madras province, which largely comprised legislators from the Tamil- and Telugu-speaking regions. Despite Gandhi's opposition to T. Prakasam's candidature as the premier, he won on the solid backing of the Andhra members. The divisions in the Tamil camp benefited Prakasam—the Rajaji faction abstained from voting when it became clear that he could not get a majority.

Kamaraj was largely responsible for the election of Prakasam instead of Rajaji. But Prakasam, who rubbed many members on the wrong side, besides Kamaraj, survived for less than a year in power. He was replaced by Omandur Ramaswami Reddiar—once again Kamaraj's choice—in March 1947. In two years' time he too was replaced—the result of Kamaraj's strained relationship with him. His next choice was P. S. Kumaraswami Raja. Due to the speed and effortlessness with which he anointed heads of the government, Kamaraj came to be known as kingmaker.

On the other hand, repeatedly defeated on his home ground, Rajaji now focused on national politics in the context of Independence. In 1947, he became the first governor of West Bengal. Soon, he became the first and last Indian governor-general. Though he narrowly missed becoming the first president of independent India, he was inducted into Nehru's cabinet as a minister without portfolio. Given his differences with Nehru, especially after Sardar Vallabhbhai Patel's death, this too did not last long. Right when his political career seemed to hit a dead end, the tide turned.

## 1952 and After

Held in early 1952, India's first general elections were historic: the world's largest democracy went to elections on a wave of universal adult franchise. In Tamil Nadu, too, it proved historic, for very different reasons. The party that had led India to Independence failed to win a majority. Even the chief minister lost. Though the bulk of the seats, 96 out of the 152 Congress legislators in a house of 375 seats, were from the Tamil region, it was nevertheless a huge blow to Kamaraj. It was in this situation that Rajaji made an unlikely return to Tamil Nadu politics.

Prakasam, who had left the Congress and lost his seat, cobbled up a united front and staked a claim to form the government. If Congress was to govern the state, this effort had to be defeated. When the first talks about Rajaji becoming the chief minister circulated, they were dismissed with disbelief. Commenting on the situation, Rajaji's alter ego, the accomplished writer and journalist Kalki R. Krishnamurthy, wrote with characteristic wit: 'It's like inviting Ramana Maharishi to become a municipal commissioner.'

However, Rajaji found the 'proposition...exciting—it had a scent of poetic justice'. To persuade him, Kamaraj himself went to Rajaji's home on Bazullah Road. His logic ran on these lines: 'If with his prestige [Rajaji] formed a ministry, it would survive, and most of the smaller parties and independents would support it.'

For someone who had expressed initial unwillingness to accept office due to ill-health, Rajaji was characteristically busy during his term in office. Quickly, he took on the Opposition with great gusto, especially the communists, to get legislation passed. In terms of administration, Rajaji did away with food control laws that enabled black-marketing and runaway prices. As an administrator, Rajaji had even won praise from his former British masters and bureaucrats. He was in full form, running an efficient administration, moving files, writing copious marginal notes, and keeping his officers busy. With a strong leader at the helm of the government, Kamaraj was forced to take a backseat. But trouble lurked in the corner.

The first signs appeared in the form of a Congressman, Potti Sriramulu, who was fasting unto death demanding a separate Telugu-speaking state of Andhra. Given his aversion to the linguistic reorganization of states—he called it 'a tribal idea'—Rajaji was seen as an inveterate opponent to the creation of an Andhra state. But, in fact, he objected purely to Andhra's claim to the city of Madras. After the formation of Andhra in October 1953, the Congress held a comfortable majority in the residuary Madras legislature. Rajaji was no more indispensable.

In early 1953, while the Andhra agitation was in progress,

Rajaji created trouble for himself with a new education scheme. Innocuously called the Modified Scheme of Elementary Education, it proved explosive. The scheme proposed half-day training in traditional crafts to school children in rural areas. Periyar's Dravidar Kazhagam (DK) and C. N. Annadurai's Dravida Munnetra Kazhagam (DMK), dubbed it as 'Kula Kalvi Thittam' ('casteist education scheme'), and led massive protests against it.

To add to this, Rajaji had also not taken his party into confidence—a matter that deeply agitated the Congress legislators who were already disgruntled for various reasons. Rajaji made it his personal project, making matters worse. Rajaji quipped to his critics: with whom did Ramanuja and Sankara consult before making their pronouncements? No doubt a good rejoinder, it was not appropriate in a democracy. There was mutiny in the ranks, leading to a curious situation where the ruling party was at war with the government. Fighting a rear-guard action, Rajaji's every effort to defend the scheme only fuelled further opposition.

Kamaraj, on the other hand, who also opposed the education scheme, was not at the forefront of the agitation. According to Chockalingam, the dissidents expressed their dissent through Kamaraj, but another sympathetic biographer noted that, 'Kamaraj had been critical of the scheme...and had advised Rajaji to withdraw it. Although he did not direct the agitation against the scheme, he did nothing to restrain the critics'. It became clear that Kamaraj was at the centre of all the manoeuvres to oust Rajaji. Ardent admirers of Rajaji pleaded with him to drop the scheme as it had put the government on the chopping block. Instead, he resigned in April 1954, citing ill-health rather than politics as the reason.

Rather than remain kingmaker, this time around, Kamaraj took the throne for himself. His rise to chief ministership was the culmination of the de-Brahminization of the Congress party in Tamil Nadu that had started in the 1930s. He contested the by-elections in the Gudiyattam constituency. In a surprise move, Periyar supported his candidature, calling him 'pachai Tamilan', the true-born Tamil. Periyar's support would continue through the decade: he made a distinction between Kamaraj and the Congress party, offering unconditional support to him as the defender of non-Brahmin interests.

After his resignation, Rajaji stayed out of politics for a while, producing an acclaimed retelling of the Ramayana in Tamil. But he remained the focus of the anti-Kamaraj faction, some of whom, unhappy with the candidate selection in the 1957 elections, formed the Congress Reform Party which received the blessings of Rajaji. The Congress won a resounding victory in an election where the DMK made its debut. In 1959, Rajaji formed the Swatantra Party, and became the primary challenger of Nehruvian socialism. If Periyar supported Kamaraj, his intimate enemy had now joined hands with the DMK and C. N. Annadurai. The two met occasionally from the latter part of the 1950s and evidently struck an excellent rapport. In the 1962 elections, the DMK and the Swatantra Party came rather close to clinching an alliance. In spite of the last-minute collapse of the talks, Rajaji campaigned for Anna in the Kanchipuram constituency. When Anna lost, he was elected to the Rajya Sabha with the help of Swatantra votes. Evidently, Rajaji saw in Anna's DMK the answer to Kamaraj.

Meanwhile, Kamaraj, as chief minister, led the party to victory in the 1957 and 1962 elections. Under his leadership, Tamil Nadu made solid progress in the fields of education and industry, laying the foundation for the state's development. The DMK's spirited performance in the 1962 elections gave him pause, and in 1963, he gave up office under a plan, called the K Plan or Kamaraj Plan, wherein senior leaders would resign from government office and work to strengthen the party. The next few years were halcyon days for Kamaraj. As the head of the 'syndicate' of regional Congress leaders, he was effectively the kingmaker even at the national level, playing a key role in the appointment of Lal Bahadur Shastri, after Nehru's death in May 1964, and of Indira Gandhi, after Shastri's death in January 1966, as prime ministers. However, the death knell for the party in Tamil Nadu came after Kamaraj relinquished his position, passing on the baton to M. Bhakatavatsalam who had no connect with the people.

In the 1967 assembly elections, the Congress faced a formidable challenge: the DMK had stitched an alliance with the Swatantra Party and the Communist Party of India (Marxist). A close fight was predicted but the DMK won a majority all on its own. Kamaraj was defeated in his pocket borough of Virudhunagar by a twenty-eight-year-old student leader. Injured in a road accident a few weeks before the election, he had vainly said that he would 'win lying down'. While Anna, humbled by the magnitude of the victory, expressed sadness, Rajaji, who had waited for two decades to defeat his bête noire, refused to comment on Kamaraj's defeat. Vengeance is a dessert best served cold.

### Rapprochement

But there was more drama to come. In an act of great magnanimity, Anna buried the hatchet with Periyar and dedicated the government to him, which rankled with Rajaji. Meanwhile, in a desperate move to demonstrate his popularity, Kamaraj contested the Nagercoil by-elections in January 1969. The region had seen fierce struggle in the 1950s to break-off from Travancore state and integrate with Tamil Nadu. Kamaraj, however, was unpopular due to his dismissal of the agitation. Now, fifteen years later, he had chosen to contest the seat that fell vacant with the death of A. Nesamony, the undisputed leader of the agitation. It was no coincidence that the district was dominated by Nadars, Kamaraj's own community. A leader who had near universal appeal had stooped to conquer. The result was a foregone conclusion: despite the ruling DMK's best efforts—M. Karunanidhi himself camped in Nagercoil to organize a concerted DMK campaign—Kamaraj won a thumping victory.

The year 1967 had delivered a double blow to Kamaraj. Across the country, the Congress lost in nine states and just about managed to retain power in the centre. Over the next two years, Indira Gandhi established herself as a leader in her own right, defeated the syndicate, and won undisputed command of the party, leading to the split in the Congress party.

In the meantime, the DMK was drifting away from the Swatantra Party. After Anna's tragic death in February 1969, he was succeeded by Karunanidhi, whose style of functioning was quite different. With the Congress divided, the DMK gave much-needed support to Indira Gandhi on which her government depended. This did not go down well with Rajaji who was already peeved by the DMK's support for the abolition of the privy purses. Towards the latter half of 1970, the drift hardened further.

When Indira Gandhi announced snap polls for January 1971, a politically astute Karunanidhi too decided to dissolve the assembly and face the electorate. There were already signs of a rapprochement between Rajaji and Kamaraj, and Karunanidhi, fearing Kamaraj's mastery of the mechanics of electioneering, decided to give little time for their partnership to work. The desperation of Indira Gandhi led her Congress (R) to a peculiar alliance with the DMK: her party did not contest any assembly seats and stood in only nine parliamentary seats. Karunanidhi, out to prove that he had inherited Anna's legacy, led the fight from the front.

In the 1971 elections, a DMK conference in Salem organized by Periyar vitiated an already bitter fight, alleging that the Hindu gods had been insulted and blasphemed. Rajaji launched a strident attack. 'Cho' Ramaswamy's fortnightly, *Thuglaq*, fed the fire and the Brahmin-dominated media joined the chorus. Karunanidhi dug in his heels and defended the government. Reminding Rajaji of how he had soft-pedalled Periyar's Pillaiyar idol-breaking agitation in 1953, Karunanidhi charged him with spewing 'caste venom'. A few days before the polling, on 25 February, both Rajaji and Kamaraj addressed a mammoth election meeting on the Marina Beach. It appeared as though the DMK would be routed.

But the election results turned out to be a washout for the Rajaji–Kamaraj combine. Barring Kamaraj, all other seats were won by the DMK alliance and the party won 184 out of the 234 assembly seats on its own.

In retrospect, Rajaji and Kamaraj had gone for overkill.

Photographs of the nonagenarian Rajaji applying tilak on the forehead of Kamaraj, whom he had once dismissed as 'a raven crow', did not go down well—it invoked fears of a return of Brahmin Raj.

Rajaji died the following year. A broken man, Kamaraj too passed away on Gandhi Jayanti in 1975, a few months after the Emergency was announced. With the death of these colossal personalities, the legacy of nationalist politics in Tamil Nadu ended as well.

# 9

# JHINU KANTVU: TO SPIN A FINE YARN

## TRIDIP SUHRUD

Gopalkrishna Gandhi has a deep fascination for and a nuanced understanding of the subtle shades of meanings and expression of Gandhi's Gujarati. He is among those rare readers of Gandhi's prose who can discern the play between pitrubhakta (devoted to father) and vishaybhakta (devoted to passions). Not just the play of words but also Gandhi's belief that his pitru was an asakta—attracted to passions—just as he was at one stage of his life.

In 1919, a curious thing happened: Gandhi decided to offer his candidature for the presidentship of the Gujarati Sahitya Parishad, a body of Gujarati writers that had elected Govardhanram Tripathi, author of *Sarasvatichandra*, a four-part novel that Gandhi had read and admired and whose impact on the intellectual and social life of Gujarat he was well aware of, as its first president in 1905. But the literary class of Gujarat preferred an officer of the Baroda state, Hargovinddas Kantawala to Gandhi. Somewhat—just somewhat—embarrassed by this, the Gujarati Sahitya Parishad has, like Milan Kundera's *The Joke*, decided to airbrush this event from our literary history. Unfortunately, in this wilful amnesia, there is no laughter. But the unease that the writers felt then about Gandhi's literary sensibility and the merit of his writing has not disappeared today, just that we are able to mask it better (not for nothing that we invented the mask) and his Mahatmaship helps us to outweigh the 'crudity' of his prose.

It is safe to assume that in 1919 (as in 2019) most Gujarati writers would not have read *Hind Swaraj*, even as a banned book (and even less likely in Gandhi's own English translation of it). If they had they would have been wonderstruck by his Gujarati prose and his ability to be a bilingual thinker—by not only thinking and writing in two languages but also theorizing about civilizational conditions in two languages simultaneously. The bilingualism I wish to suggest indicates simultaneity; it suggests a process where an idea is conceived and thought in one language and expressed in another; where it becomes possible to speak of a concept, a notion alien to one linguistic/semantic universe through another tongue. Let us first consider the curious case of the title itself. Gandhi's handwritten manuscript as well as the first *Indian Opinion* edition consistently used the term rajya; it is *Hind Swarajya* and not *Hind Swaraj*. The term rajya is used in the text as well; for example, chapter 4 is 'swarajya te shu?' And not 'swaraj te shu?' But when the English translation was completed and published on 20 March 1910, the term rajya was substituted by raj. This usage was standardized in subsequent editions in the Gujarati, beginning with the 1914 edition.

The reason for this change becomes clear if we examine the English rendering. Published under the title *Indian Home Rule*,[1] the term swarajya/swaraj was rendered as home rule in the English edition in the initial chapters. For example, in chapter 1, the term swarajya/swaraj occurs twenty times. In every instance, save one, the term has been translated as home rule. Once it has been rendered as self-government while in one instance, it has been rendered as 'home or self-rule'.

By chapter 4, a semantic shift is introduced, where all seven usages of the term swarajya/swaraj have been rendered as swaraj in the English edition. This shift became necessary, as Gandhi wanted to introduce a basic semantic difference between the terms home rule and swaraj as conceived by him. The term home rule had both

---

[1] The title of the English edition was changed to *Hind Swaraj or Indian Home Rule* in 1921; all subsequent editions of the English text appear under this combined title, except the 1924 American edition edited by Haridas T. Muzumdar which was titled *Sermon on the Sea*.

a pre-history and an identifiable political organization and persons who aspired for home rule. Swaraj, as Gandhi thought of it, was constituted by a different philosophical ground. This difference was clearly articulated in chapter 14. He says that hitherto the reader and the editor had been considering the conditions of freeing India 'indirectly', but would now do so 'directly.' The term 'directly' is an inadequate rendering of the Gujarati, term swa-rupe, in its 'intrinsic form'. The difference between home rule and swaraj for Gandhi is of this intrinsic form. This is the reason he needed the two terms to speak of the basic differences between both the visions and the two methods of obtaining them.

◆

This distance between home rule and swaraj is latent in the Gujarati version. Gandhi did not distinguish between home rule and swaraj in such a shared sense; he continued to use swaraj to mean both home rule and swaraj in its 'intrinsic form'. But the difference was before his eyes even while he wrote the Gujarati *Hind Swaraj*. The change from rajya to raj is indicative of that. The term rajya, both in the Sanskrit and in the Gujarati has a sense of territoriality. Rajya is rendered as kingdom, country, or realm. Raj, on the other hand, suggests 'to reign' or 'to rule over'. The idea of reigning in the sense to 'rule ourselves' is basic to Gandhi's idea of swaraj.

'It is swaraj when we learn to rule ourselves.' The change from rajya to raj was necessary. In the Gujarati, he needed to distinguish between two notions of rule, one that denoted territoriality and the other which suggested rule over oneself. The term rajya did not allow the second and more primary sense to be foregrounded. The nature of this imperative becomes clear when we read the two texts together where the idea of self-rule, self-control, and the possibility of knowing oneself are clearly marked. It is for this reason that he rendered swaraj as 'rule himself'.

Far more instructive is the notion that forms the core of *Hind Swaraj*, the idea of sudhar. The word in Gujarati has a lineage. Before Gandhi, the term was used largely to indicate the idea and process of social and religious reform. The term sudhar in the sense of reform did include the idea that su-dhar was the good path, the righteous path. And it is in the sense of su-dhar being the good path that sudharo could be equated with 'good conduct'. But in the history of the term, sudharo was not indicative of 'that mode of conduct that points out to man the path of duty', where 'performance of duty and observance of morality' become 'convertible terms' which allow us to 'attain mastery over our mind and passion' and 'so doing, we know ourselves'.

Sudharo that makes possible self-knowledge and self-rule are unique to Gandhi's vision. Even a century after the publication of *Hind Swaraj*, the term sudhar/sudharo is used in Gujarati primarily in the nineteenth century sense of reform.

Let us examine this usage more closely. The term sudhar/sudharo occurs ninety-six times in the Gujarati text, more than either the term vachak (reader) or adhipati (editor). Only when we read the text bilingually do we begin to understand the multiple meanings with which Gandhi imbued the term. In the English rendering sudhar/sudharo has been conceived as civilization, modern civilization, European civilization, ancient civilization, Indian civilization, reform, progress, and even ephemeral civilization. The term thus has been conceived and rendered in eight distinct senses. It is clear that Gandhi thought through these distinct terms in English and rendered them into Gujarati through the generic usage sudharo. The choice of the term sudharo is somewhat perplexing. At the time of writing *Hind Swaraj*, Gandhi was aware of the nineteenth-century reform movement in Gujarat and Gujarati. He had read the works of Narmad, Manibhai Nabhubhai, and Govardhanram Tripathi[2] as also Mahipatram Rupram Mehta and Karsandas Mulji's accounts of English life. He was aware of the contributions of Parsi reformers like Behramji Malabari.

---

[2]The identification of reformers with the act of writing is very strong in Gandhi. In fact he rendered Paschim Na Sudharako (Western Reformers) as Western Writers.

Gandhi had a choice of two other and more prevalent usages to indicate civilization. These are sabhyata and sanskriti. In fact, when Gandhi writes in the English that 'the Gujarati equivalent for civilization means 'good conduct', he is referring to sabhyata rather than sudharo. According to the Gujarati lexicon *Bhagvad Go Mandal* the equivalent of sanskriti means civilization. Gandhi may not have preferred a notion of civilization that is intrinsically tied to Sanskrit and all the modes of thought and practices that were articulated through that language. But this still does not explain the choice of the term sudhar.

Gandhi was clearly invoking sudhar in two senses which have been latent in Gujarati. Su-dhar not just as good path, but one that holds, bears; from the Sanskrit root dhri, dharayati. One, which holds and bears human society, is sudhar and only such sudhar could point out to man the path of duty and open the possibility of self-knowledge. Sudhar is civilization in this sense. Secondly, sudhar, unlike the other two terms, has a sense of movement. Sudhar, according to *Bhagvad Go Mandal,* suggests a movement towards virtue. It entails a choice in favour of the good and active shunning of all that is undesirable. It is this active, choice-enabling, virtue-enhancing possibility of sudhar that Gandhi desired from civilization.

Moreover, sudhar in the more prevalent usage could also suggest reform, progress, contemporariness, change, and influence of the modern West, all the other senses which are present in the English rendering.

There are instances in the Gujarati text where Gandhi has qualified the term sudharo. The term modern civilization of the English text occurs in three distinct ways in the Gujarati text; as sudharo, as aaj-kal no sudharo, and as adhunik sudharo. The term aaj-kal in Gujarati literally means today and tomorrow. It is used to indicate the contemporary and therefore transient nature of things; the term modern lacks this pronounced sense of transience. Interestingly, the term adhunik which occurs only twice in the Gujarati text also has a sense of transience, of lack of permanence in Gujarati. Narmad in his *Narma-Kosha* explained adhunika, that which is of the present moment, as Na take tevu (that which will not last—ephemeral).[3] By describing civilization as adhunik sudharo, Gandhi wished to emphasize not so much its modernity but the transient nature of what passes under the name of civilization.

He declared that 'this civilization is such that one has only to be patient and it will be self-destroyed'. In the Gujarati text he emphasized the self-destructive nature of modern civilization by stating that 'te sudharo nashkarak ane nashvant che' (this civilization is destructive and certain to be destroyed.) This added emphasis is absent in the English text. In contemporary Gujarati, both sudharo as civilization and adhunik as ephemeral have become recessive; we speak of adhunik in the sense of navin and, hence, modern.

In the Gujarati text, the term kudhar/kudharo (the wrong path) creates a play between sudhar and kudhar. The term occurs nine times in the Gujarati text, which has been rendered in English as 'civilization only in name', 'civilization as a disease', and 'reverse of civilization'. In fact, six out of nine times Gandhi did not render the term kudhar in the English text. This is true of many of the idiomatic Gujarati phrases. Gandhi either does not render them in English, or chooses to provide a literal translation. He does not resort to equivalent idiomatic usages in English. For example, the Gujarati idiom 'Miya ne Mahadev ne na bane' (Miya and Mahadev will always quarrel) is used to frame the argument about Hindu–Muslim relations and the 'had ver' (inborn enmity) between the two communities. This idiom is used twice in the Gujarati text. Gandhi chose not to render it in English at all. Once he rendered it as 'our very proverbs prove it', and in the second instance as 'the proverbs you have quoted'. While in case of 'jenu man changa che tene gher bethe ganga che', he provided a literal translation: 'those

---

[3]The first part of *Narma-Kosha* was published in November 1861, the second in December 1862, the third in September 1864, and the fourth part in August 1866. The complete *Narma-Kosha* was published in 1873. The term adhunik is described on p. 58.

whose hearts were aglow with righteousness have the Ganges in their own home.'

Of the fifteen proverbs in *Hind Swaraj*, one of the most evocative is 'sangha Dwaraka e na jashe' (we will not reach Dwarka. With the passage of time Mahadev Desai and Gandhi together would have probably rendered it as 'we will not find our Jerusalem'), which he translated as 'we are not likely to agree at all'. This creativity of Gandhi's Gujarati stayed with him. He would repeatedly employ metaphors from craft practices that he came to know, appreciate, and practise to restore almost single-handedly (in many instances, it was a two-handed affair, savayasaachi that he was) the semantic universe of craft and hand-work to the Gujarati language. His letters to Devadas Gandhi—hitherto unpublished[4]—often bring the stylist in Gujarati to the fore. Devadas himself was a wordsmith and often corrected his father's quirky Hindustani. In a letter written in 1934, Gandhi invoked the craft-based words gunthan (knitting) and parvo-vun (threading or stringing) to describe his mind's preoccupation with work and also thoughts about loved ones. In another letter of 1935, he employed a very unusual but apposite term to describe a letter that had gone missing: 'rakhdi gayo' is a harmless loiter, amble, very fitting for a letter that had gone a-missing, innocently. Gandhi was a very attractive and effective communicator in Hindustani. His Hindi carried till the very end marks of imperfection, which in no way took away the beauty of his expression. He frequently used Gujarati words—like chanchupat (to dip one's beak) in Hindustani. To Lakshmi Gandhi, he wrote in Hindi in the fond hope that she, a native speaker of Tamil, would become less hesitant in Hindustani. In time she became a fine exponent of Hindi, surpassing any expectation that he might have cherished for her, rendering in Hindi Rajaji's retelling of the Mahabharata and the Ramayana. Her ease with Hindi probably had something to do with delightfully imperfect expressions like 'merey

---

[4]These letters are to be published in the original Gujarati and in English translation (*Scorching Love*), edited and translated by Gopalkrishna Gandhi and Tridip Suhrud.

najdik' meaning 'near me' to convey the intended meaning 'merey nazar me', 'in my eyes' that Gandhi used in his letters to her.

Gandhi's Gujarati writings are suffused with poetry—the one form of literature he was drawn to and knew intimately. A discerning reader of poetry, he helped create through his practice of recitation the *Ashram Bhajanavali*—the anthology of Bhakti poetry that remains one of the finest collections of its kind. He was also an accomplished translator of verse, albeit in prose form. Tulsidas and Surdas, Mira and Narsinh Mehta, Shamal Bhatt, Akho, Dhiro Bhagat were, like the Bhagavad Gita and Isa Upanishad, 'by-hearted' by him. Their verses, quite often just a fleeting image from a poem, found their way into his writing. His autobiography in Gujarati and in a very different way in English is immersed in poetry. At least four titles of his chapters are in poetic verse. In fact, the only title to appear untranslated in English is Surdas's 'Nirbal Ke Bal Ram'. The poetic sensibility also informs the English translation. For instance, in the chapter 'Nirbal Ke Bal Ram' the combined sensibility of Gandhi and Mahadev Desai is on display. A set of prosaic sentences in Gujarati soar in the English translation with the help of verses. The Gujarati states: 'Banne haath hetha pade' (when all actions become futile) is translated through Henry Francis Lyte's hymn 'Abide with Me' with the lines 'when helpers fail and comforts flee'. A few lines later the phrase 'hriday ni nirmalta' (purity of heart) is translated as 'emptied of all but love' from Charles Wesley's hymn. Soon thereafter, he writes of 'gagan gami sur' (music reaching to the heavens) which is rendered through a line from Alfred Tennyson's 'Locksley Hall' as 'trembling pass in music out of sight'.

He also used the term 'apurva avasar' from the title of Raychand Mehta's poem of the same title to describe the sublime moment of death, a moment when one comes face to face with one's God.

But of all the terms that Gandhi coined and gave meaning to through his practise and usage, my favourite is from the act of spinning: 'jhinu kantvu', to spin a fine yarn. This captures his striving not only in turning the coarse yarn of khadi spun on the spinning wheel into a fine yarn such that a saree woven from it would not sit heavy on the frail body of Kastur Ba but also in other semantic senses that it came to be used by him. 'Jhinu kantvu' also means to pay attention to detail, to make a complex argument with elegant subtlety and not allow the thread of thought, relationship, and care to be broken. It is also something that joins him to Kabirdas.

For me the best way to describe Gopalkrishna Gandhi is by using one of Gandhi's favourite expressions, 'object lesson', in the art and craft of 'jhinu kantvu'. There is nothing coarse around him. That his language (in all the tongues that he speaks in) and demeanour have exquisite courtesy is known to even those who have had even a fleeting acquaintance with him. His scholarship that sits easy on him is a source of delight. He is among the few with whom I share the fondness for the increasingly recessive practice of writing footnotes. But what would have endeared him to Bapu the most is his capacity for care, when needed as an embrace and other times like a beacon—ever-present, watchful, showing the path. May he continue to spin a 'jhini chadariya'.

# 10

## HAROLD LASKI AND INDIAN INDEPENDENCE

ISAAC KRAMNICK

In 1993 Gopalkrishna Gandhi was the Minister (Culture) at the High Commission of India in London and the Director of the Nehru Centre. On the evening of 17 May 1993, he presided over the Centre's 'Commemoration of Harold Laski and his association with V. K. Krishna Menon and India'. The guest of honour was Shri K. R. Narayanan, then Vice President of the Republic of India, who had been a student of Laski's at the London School of Economics (LSE) at the end of World War II, now on a state visit to Britain. In Narayanan's moving tribute to his beloved teacher, he spoke of the day he informed Laski that he was an 'untouchable'. The Jewish professor responded by saying, the Vice President remembered, 'my people have been history's untouchables Mr. Narayanan.'

Gopal Gandhi had also asked others to speak that evening: Dr L. M. Singhvi, the High Commissioner for India; Barry Sheerman, Labour M. P. for Huddersfield in the British House of Commons, and me, co-authors of the recently published biography of *Laski: A Life on the Left*; the book's publisher, Andrew Franklin of Hamish Hamilton; and Gopal Gandhi himself, the Director of the Nehru Centre. To capture Laski's historic connection to the founding of the Indian republic and its early leadership, Gopal spoke of there always being an empty seat set aside for Laski's ghost at post-Independence cabinet meetings. For my part, I, that night, traced Laski's career-long involvement with Indian affairs. To honour Gopalkrishna Gandhi now, a quarter of a century later, on his 75th birthday, I will revisit those comments on the profound role Laski played in bringing about free India.

Harold Joseph Laski (1893–1950) was an academic luminary in politics and history at the LSE for thirty-six years, a man whose scores of books and articles on social theory made him the leading English-speaking socialist intellectual in the first half of the twentieth century. Laski's socialism was a reflection of both conventional Marxism and European democratic socialism in general, and the English Fabian tradition, in particular. It was a statist ideal focused on central government nationalization and management of the means of production, as well as of essential natural resources and modes of transportation. Central planning for the national interest, not laissez-faire free market profit-seeking, was to dictate economic decision-making. The political system in his socialist vision was democratic and grounded in free parliamentary party electoral decision making, which was not determined by violence and revolutionary class struggle.

He was also a committed civil-libertarian, embracing statist interference in economic life, but fearful and suspicious of any state control of individual human rights to speak, think, and believe freely. He was also a political activist at the center of British politics. Indeed, he was the Leader of the Labour Party in its surprise defeat of Churchill in 1945.

Despite having been a champion of its independence, Laski never set a foot in India. Not so his father, Nathan, whose company, based in Manchester and co-owned with his brother Noah, was one of Lancashire's largest and best-known cotton-goods export houses. In his lifetime Nathan is said to have made some forty trips to India, purchasing cotton or selling finished cotton goods.

Harold Laski's interest in India, while stoked perhaps by his family's business interests, took political shape in a most unpredictable of ways: he was called to jury service. For five weeks from 1 May to 6 June 1924, and for five hours a day, Laski was one of twelve special jurors in the notorious libel case '*O'Dwyer vs Nair*'. Sir Michael O'Dwyer had been the civilian Lieutenant-

Governor of the Punjab in 1919 when General Reginald E. H. Dyer ordered British troops to fire on non-violent civilians assembled at the Jallianwala Bagh in Amritsar. Although, the official number of people killed is 379, the real figure is believed to have been much more. In a book published in 1922, *Gandhi and Anarchy*, Sir C. Sankaran Nair, an eminent Indian jurist and critic of Gandhi's methods, accused O'Dwyer of terrorism in the events leading up to the massacre and of being responsible for atrocities committed by the civil government. O'Dwyer sued Nair for libel and the trial in London reopened the whole Amritsar affair with the 'diehards' of the Tory right wing seeking vindication for O'Dwyer.

From the jury box in an almost unprecedented spectacle Laski interjected himself with questions and comments to witnesses, counsel and the judge. He had done his homework, reading up on the duties of an administrator under martial law. He interrupted eight times during the trial. Once he asked for greater details about rules for flogging and another time he noted that in England no one could be whipped and made to crawl down streets on their hands and knees.

The tone of the trial, despite Laski's intervention, was embarrassingly supportive of British repression in India as well as utterly insensitive to Indian institutions and values. Counsel and witnesses for O'Dwyer and the judge joked about Indian life and behavior. In his summing-up for the jury, Judge Henry McCardie opined that General Dyer had been 'wrongly punished by the Secretary of State for India since grave evils may sometimes demand grave remedies'. He repeated his personal view that 'General Dyer, in the grave and exceptional circumstances, acted rightly'.

With such a charge, the jury, after deliberating for two hours and twenty-five minutes, returned to say that they were unable to decide on a verdict. The parties then agreed to accept the verdict of the majority, and the foreman announced that eleven jurors were in favor of the plaintiff and that one juryman, Laski, dissented.

The legacy of *O'Dwyer vs Nair* endured. Indians would not forget the outcome, and sixteen years later, in March 1940, Sir

Michael O'Dwyer was assassinated by an Indian revolutionary, Udham Singh. The trial also had a profound effect on Laski, introducing him, he wrote, 'to the depth of color prejudice.' For him there was only one final verdict on British rule in India: 'I hate it and I personally favour our withdrawal from there.'

The case marked the real beginning of Laski's commitment to the cause of Indian independence. Many of the legions of Indian students who came to study with Laski at the LSE did so partly because of it. Amritsar had turned Gandhi and Nehru into revolutionaries and no Indian nationalist failed to forget the one person out of 12 who stood for justice and decency. Thirty years later, on 15 August 1954, at the inauguration of the Harold Laski Institute of Political Science in Ahmedabad, the foreign minister of India, Krishna Menon, noted that 'since the days that he sat on the jury in the Michael O'Dwyer case, Professor Laski became one of us'.

Menon knew what he spoke of, for in 1925 he had become a student of Laski's at the LSE, graduating with a first-class degree in 1927, and for two decades while he worked as a lawyer, in publishing, (as a founding editor of Penguin Books) and running the fiercely pro-independence India League, he and Laski collaborated closely. Menon's socialism was inspired by Laski. He had once suggested that 'Laski was a very great man' and 'that it would take one hundred years to realize the profundity of his thought'. Menon had more than the gratitude of the pupil; he 'learned to love and respect him in a way that I treasure very preciously. He had been a profound influence on my own life.'

Their relationship was much closer than just a teacher–student. Laski took a domestic interest in the frail, handsome, depression-prone ascetic, who seemed to survive on tea and buns. In turn, Menon was constantly a presence in the Laski home after 1925. 'The telephone in the house', Laski's wife, Frida, wrote, 'belonged to him. At nine every morning there would be a ring and I used to say 'that must be Krishna 'and sure enough it was.' The Laskis sometimes helped Menon with money and he was a frequent attendee at their Sunday open house. At a particularly suicidal moment during his years in London, it was the visit of Laski and Frida to his garret room in St. Pancras that, according to Menon's biographer, T. J. S. George, 'put him on the road to recovery.' Through Menon, secretary to the India League, Laski met Gandhi and Nehru on their visits to Britain, and he, in turn, became an advocate for India's cause that Menon could always call upon; whether it was to lecture Indian students, speak to India League rallies or lobby with the Labour party.

Menon and Laski were close political allies and friends for decades. Speaking at the Indian Independence Day celebration in London in 1949, Laski commented:

> I do not know how many times I have gone to meetings that I did not want to attend, have made speeches that I did not want to make, have written articles that I had no time to write, because I was under the grim control of this irrepressible embodiment of the will of India to be free, and I look back and what I owe Krishna Menon for having made me attend as a member of his army is a debt that I can never repay.

In MacDonald's 1929 Labour government Professor Laski, by then an influential figure in the Party, served diligently as a foot soldier in Menon's army. As an adviser to Lord Sankey, Labour's Lord Chancellor, Laski was, as Beatrice Webb noted 'always running between various groups of Indians, Mohammedan and Hindu.' There was, of course, a long tradition in British politics of academics assisting government ministers with research and writing, but seldom with the intensity and regularity of Professor Laski, who one day a week worked on Sankey's correspondence, read Cabinet papers for him, wrote memoranda, and suggested sources of study. In the spring of 1930, Sankey asked him to help plan the forthcoming Indian Round Table Conference, which would deal with the principles of a federal constitution, a subject on which Laski was an expert. Sankey also knew Laski's standing with Indian activists in Britain like Krishna Menon and his London-based India League.

India preoccupied MacDonald's Labour government. Lord

Irwin (later Lord Halifax), Viceroy of India, made it clear in October 1929 that India would some day have dominion status. Gandhi responded by demanding it immediately and began 1930 with a dramatic new campaign of civil disobedience, marching to Dandi and defying the British salt monopoly by extracting and using crystals of untaxed salt. During the Civil Disobedience campaign that followed, along with Gandhi more than 90,000 of his fellow Indians were imprisoned. MacDonald then decided to speed up the process and called the First Indian Round Table Conference for November 1930. Neither Gandhi nor the Indian National Congress attended.

Laski prepared memoranda on constitutional history for Sankey, and when the delegates arrived he briefed them on the history of federalism as well as its practice in Europe and America. He was struck by the enormity of the problem, the goodwill of people like Irwin and MacDonald confronting bitter religious strife between Hindu and Moslem. 'We can't govern it and it is not fit to govern itself,' he wrote, wondering whether Britain 'was not about to face the biggest crisis in our colonial affairs since 1776.' Laski's greatest fear was that 'India will become the Ireland of the next generation—a prospect to me of unmitigated horror'. He was worried by the analogous role of religion, for his meetings with the Indians convinced him that 'the depths of their religious fervor makes any plan for effective justice between them a matter of extreme difficulty'.

The First Round Table Conference ended on an optimistic note, with the Indian princes in attendance agreeing in principle to a future Indian federation. Laski had been a good teacher and Sankey thanked him on Christmas Day for his 'wise counsel and advice'. Some of the hopes for an easy settlement were dimmed during the great parliamentary debate on India held on 22 January 1931 in which, Stanley Baldwin and the Tory leadership supported the government's existing India policy; Churchill announced his implacable opposition to dominion status and to any conciliation of Indian nationalism. He spoke of 'warrior races' and 'the grandeur of the British Empire' as he resigned from the Conservative Shadow Cabinet, beginning the long years of isolation from Tory leadership circles that would end only with the outbreak of World War II.

When the Second Round Table Conference met later that year, Gandhi attended as the sole representative of the Indian National Congress. Gandhi lived in Kingsley Hall, a settlement house in the East End, where he had his goat's milk and spun on his spinning-wheel daily. Krishna Menon brought Gandhi, the man Churchill labelled a 'naked fakir' to meet Laski. Involved closely in the second negotiations, especially on the constitutional questions related to the political control of a contemplated federal Indian army, Laski also worked on a criminal code and its implementation through the various levels of the projected structure.

Sankey asked Laski to confer with both Aga Khan and Gandhi on the future constitutional status of religion in India and the likelihood of Moslem acceptance of secular institutions. Laski had little luck with the Moslem spiritual leader: 'It was like talking to a wall. His religion was the ultimate truth,' Laski wrote. The general talks did not go well either and, after the first few weeks, Gandhi resented having come. The different tone of this conference was attributed by Laski to the late-summer change in government after MacDonald's 'betrayal' in which the new National government had a Tory Secretary of State for India, Sir Samuel Hoare, who was sympathetic to Churchill's position. Laski even suspected that some Tories were backing the Moslems behind the scenes to wreck the talks.

When the Second Round Table Conference broke up in utter failure, Laski wrote to his close American friend Felix Frankfurter, the future Supreme Court Justice, that Gandhi had told him that he was returning to India ' helpless, homeless, and empty-handed.' For Laski the debacle was the inevitable result of Sir Samuel Hoare's belief 'that the white man ought not be asked to give way to the black' and Gandhi's 'haunting fear that the white man in India will always take a yard for each inch of compromise'. Laski predicted 'an India in flames for the next few years and out of that tragedies too vast even to think of'. Gandhi left London, travelled through Europe, arrived in India, and immediately renewed his campaign of satyagraha.

The evening before he left London, Gandhi met with a group of Labour Party sympathizers that included Kingsley Martin, Leonard Woolf, H.W. Nevinson, H.N. Brailsford, and Laski. Gandhi asked the group what course he should follow on his return to India. He asked each person in the room to tell him how he read the break up of negotiations and what he should do. Leonard Woolf's account of what then happened provides a fascinating contemporary portrait of Gandhi's 'friend Harold Laski':

> When we had all had our say, there followed one of the most brilliant intellectual pyrotechnic displays which I have ever listened to. Gandhi thanked us and said it would greatly help him if his friend Harold Laski, who was one of us, would try to sum up the various lines of judgement and advice which had emerged. Harold then stood up in front of the fireplace and gave the most lucid, faultless summary of the complicated, diverse exposition of ten or fifteen people to which he had been listening in the previous hour and a half. He spoke for twenty minutes; he gave a perfect sketch of the pattern into which the various statements and opinions logically composed themselves; he never hesitated for a word or thought, and as far as I could see, he never missed a point. There was a kind of beauty in his exposition, a flawless certainty and simplicity which one feels in some works of art.

◆

Churchill had fundamentally different views on India than Laski did. While Churchill regarded the Indian Raj as 'the crown jewel' in the glorious British empire, for Laski it was 'the slum of empire'. After the collapse of the Round Table Conferences on India, Laski remained an outspoken advocate of Indian independence. He protested the cycle of arrests and repression in India and became increasingly dismayed by the complications in the quest for Indian independence due to the hardening positions of Jinnah and the Muslim League. In lectures for Menon's India League in London, Laski always constantly lamented the absurdity of the British teaching Indian students the ideas of Milton, Locke, and Mill and then sending them to be second-class citizens in their own country.

Laski ridiculed what he saw as Churchill's nostalgic fantasy of Victoria's empire. 'We hold India,' Laski wrote, 'not by the quality of our rule, not by a reciprocal interest born of mutual good-will; we hold India by the sword...no country is held by good-will when fifty thousand people have to be sent to jail.' The British were unwilling to recognize that 'Indian nationalism is part of a basic revolt of the East against Western tutelage, to which there is no answer save that of freedom.' It was a lesson that should have been learned from America and Ireland. But it was also 'a lesson that an imperial race can understand only when it is too late. That is the price of empire.'

As was so often the case with Laski, his politics got wrapped up with friendships and during the 1930s his commitment to Indian independence was intensified by his relationship with Jawaharlal Nehru. Three years older than Laski, educated at Harrow and Cambridge, Nehru, who saw Laski on his visits to England in 1935 and 1938, was much more compatible with Laski than Gandhi was. A secular intellectual, Nehru had a vision of free India that was socialist, where national planning and economic modernization would end centuries of poverty and traditional institutions like child marriage. Nehru adopted Menon's worshipful respect for Laski, who had stood so bravely in the Amritsar trial, who took such interest in Indian students, who spoke out so forcefully for independence, and whose writings outlined the political and economic pattern of India's future. When Nehru's daughter, Indira Gandhi, came to England for school and then Oxford in 1936, Nehru urged her to seek out Laski for advice on books to read.

Nehru's admiration for Laski was matched by Laski's for him. What he particularly admired was that Nehru was fighting not only for India's right to govern itself, but also for a fundamental transformation in who would rule. He wrote in his weekly *Daily Herald* column that Nehru 'wants not merely a political revolution, which would free India from foreign domination; he wants also a social revolution, which would effect a complete change in India's economic system'. Even more revealing was Laski's private assessment. In a letter of 1938, Laski told his American friend Felix Frankfurter that 'Nehru I regard as one of the few really great people I have ever met—worlds above Gandhi in strength of character and insight'.

Despite his admiration for Nehru and his commitment to the independence ideals of Menon's India League, Laski failed to convince his fellow members of the Labour Party's National Executive Committee to include Indian independence as part of Labour's demands in 1940 for agreeing to join the wartime coalition government. He was more successful in 1944 when as Vice-Chairman of its Executive Committee he presided over Labour's Annual Party Conference.

Since 1942, many of the leaders of the Indian independence movement had been imprisoned for their refusal to back the British in the war against Japan. Nehru was willing to support the war if self-government were granted, but when the British insisted on postponing action until the war was over and only if it were demanded by a Constituent Assembly, he and Gandhi, and the Indian National Congress turned to civil disobedience and were jailed.

Krishna Menon worked throughout the autumn of 1944 with Laski on a strategy to bring the India question before the Labour Conference. On the last day of the conference, they persuaded the powerful National Union of Railwaymen (NUR) to move a resolution affirming the Party's conviction that 'the granting of freedom to the people of India to establish an independent Indian National government will be a decisive factor in the fight against fascism'. The resolution called for the release of all Indian political leaders from prison and the beginnings of negotiations 'with a view to the formation of a responsible National government'.

The NUR resolution was carried by a large majority and the

Labour Party stood strongly committed to an independent India. It was a sweet victory for Laski, who throughout the war had objected to the party's refusal to push Indian independence as part of its price for sharing power with the adamant foe of independence, Churchill.

In the autumn of 1945, a month after taking office, the Labour government announced a general election for India to decide its future, but the Congress Party, afraid that this was merely a way to postpone real action, decided to put pressure on the government. Krishna Menon organized a massive celebration of Nehru's fifty-sixth birthday on 14 November at St Pancras Town Hall and invited Laski as the principal speaker. Laski's speech, in the opinion of Menon's biographer 'must be considered a landmark in the history of India's struggle for freedom'. Every paper in London carried his words.

> Indian freedom is inevitable and inescapable, and what we have to decide is whether that freedom shall come gracefully by British cooperation or, instead, by British hostility. We have to make up our minds. A Labour Party which is unwilling to play its full part in the emancipation of India will, sooner or later, be unwilling to play its full part in the emancipation of the British working class. As a movement that is part of the international movement for human emancipation, a Labour Party which fails this test will pass from the historic scene, for the Indian problem is part of a much wider and more vital issue. The end of imperialism everywhere.... Freedom and democracy know no bar of colour, religion, class, or birth.

The strategy worked and Labour quickly set in motion the process by which independence was granted to India. Laski, fittingly enough, was the speaker at the London celebration of Indian Independence Day. That same year, 1947, he was invited by Nehru to visit India and lecture at various universities in the winter term of 1947–48. Laski anticipated that his request for leave would be denied because of the pressures on the LSE with returning servicemen and colonial students flocking to Houghton Street, and told Nehru that his visit must wait. It would never come to pass, but Laski did see his student Menon become the first ambassador from a free India to the Court of St James nearly a quarter-century after the Amritsar trial when Laski became according to Menon, 'one of us'.

Laski, a constant smoker, died from a burst lung abscess on 24 March 1950, one month after the Labour party defeated Churchill for a second time, albeit with a drastically reduced majority from its spectacular 1945 victory. His simple funeral took place four days later at the Golders Green Crematorium. Krishna Menon made available the Indian High Commission's Rolls-Royce for the use of Laski's family during the funeral of 'one of us', as he put it.

Richard Crossman claimed that Laski's ideology 'influenced half the leaders of the colonial revolution...making them not passionately anti-British and pro-communist but liberalistic and pro-British.' John Kenneth Galbraith, former American Ambassador to India, contended that 'the center of Nehru's thinking was Laski' and that 'India was the country most influenced by Laski's ideas.' Nehru, who used to joke that he was 'the last Englishman to rule India' saw Laski as the voice of Fabian socialism with its vision of a central role for the state in a managed and planned economy.

With his work for independence and his influence on the political elite through Nehru, Menon, and the legions of his LSE students, like Narayanan, in the government and civil service, Laski's reputation in India was widespread. No surprise then that Gopalkrishna Gandhi could, indeed, claim on the evening of 17 May 1993, that 'in its early years there was always a vacant chair at every cabinet meeting in India, reserved for the ghost of Professor Harold Laski.'

# 11

## ASHOKA AND GANDHI

### UPINDER SINGH

The worldwide phenomenon of spiralling violence, its spawning of novel forms and manifestations, and the nurturing and celebration of cultures of anger and hate have led to a yearning for a mitigation, if not elimination, of the madness. This sensitivity lends an especially urgent edge to an exploration of violence in history. But should the ancient Indian past be used as a resource to deal with our troubled present? What are the lessons, if any, to be drawn from it? While exploring violence in history what if we, consciously or unconsciously, manipulate the entire exercise in order to find the results we want to find?

The idea of a peaceful, non-violent ancient India is pure fantasy, created through a clever sleight of hand. By selecting a few iconic figures (Mahavira, the Buddha, Ashoka), a remote, non-violent ancient India is magically connected with the more recent past, with Gandhi and the Indian freedom struggle. This involves skimming over the medieval period, which has in any case never been associated with non-violence in historical writing or popular perception. This makes us feel special—members of a primordial Indian civilization which embodies deep wisdom and offers an important message for humanity, giving us the right, in fact, the duty, to teach civilizational values to the world.

The problem is that there is overwhelming evidence against the construct of a non-violent ancient India. The tedious, seemingly endless lists of bloody wars that are part of political history include intra-elite contests, conflicts with other states, and violent interactions with forest people. Like states at all times and places, those of ancient India used coercive force or the threat thereof in order to tax subjects. Like them, they asserted the right to punish and take life in the name of maintaining social order. There was a connection between the growth and systemization of state violence and the increasingly sophisticated attempts to mask, invisibilize, justify, and aestheticize this violence in various ways. Violence and the threat of violence are also inherent in all hierarchical and exploitative social institutions and structures based on inequality. In the context of ancient India, these included varna, caste, slavery, untouchability, and the patriarchal family. So, the narrative of a non-violent ancient India, which hops, skips, and jumps from the Buddha to Ashoka to Gandhi and edits out all the other bits is bad history.

◆

Confronting the ugly parts of the past and recognizing that ancient India was mired in inequity, oppression, and violence of various kinds is an important reality check that pulls us out of our self-congratulatory stupor of civilizational superiority. But it leaves little to feel good or cheerful about, let alone celebrate. The way out of the conundrum is to steer clear of the extremes of glorification and denigration. It involves investigating the various ways in which violence was built into the lives of people who lived long ago, into their social and political structures, religious practice, ways of thinking and doing things. It involves recognizing violence in its blatantly apparent forms and uncovering its surreptitious, hidden workings. It also involves confronting the vexed issue of what exactly violence *is*, perhaps realizing that there can be no fixed or adequate definitions.

Political practice and political thought are interrelated, but if they are disentangled, it becomes apparent that although ancient Indians were by no means non-violent people, ancient Indian thought displays a unique, intense, and prolonged engagement with the tension between violence and non-violence. That a certain amount of violence was necessary for kings was not only the view of the Mahabharata and *Arthashastra*. It was also the view of the religions of non-violence, Jainism and Buddhism. At the same time, political discourse consistently distinguished legitimate force from illegitimate force and kept open a window for interrogating the state's violence. So the meaningful question is: how did ancient Indian thinkers deal with the problem of violence while living in the midst of their violent worlds? The important resources for the present have to be located in the realm of ideas.

Exploring an issue which resonates so strongly in our own time forces a historian to move beyond the comfortable cocoon of long ago to confront the age-old questions about the relationship between history and the present. Such a confrontation can lead to strange and unexpected places, in my case, to a juxtaposing of two historical figures—Ashoka and Gandhi. I know that both these men have a special place in Gopalkrishna Gandhi's heart, so I offer this comparison as a token of my respect for his ideas, his writings, and all that he represents as an exceptionally fine human being.

♦

I can hear the protests about the exercise. On their own, Ashoka and Gandhi would make it to any list of famous proponents of non-violence. But an attempt to connect them, even through comparison, could be summarily dismissed as anachronistic and pointless. Why compare two men who were separated from each other by over two millennia? Why compare an ancient emperor with a person who, many centuries later, devoted himself to dismantling an empire? Is it meaningful to compare an individual whose ideas are compressed into a few sets of monologues inscribed on pillars and rocks with one who has left to posterity a copious record of his thoughts and actions, his collected works running into almost a hundred published volumes?

We do not know what Ashoka looked like. Gandhi's face and figure are well known within India, indeed, all over the world. Ashoka is the only ancient Indian king who speaks in the first person in his inscriptions; yet his biographical details are few. He lived in the third century BCE. Inscriptions and Sri Lankan texts call him Devanampiya ('beloved of the gods') and Piyadasi ('of gracious mien'). Four of his inscriptions give the name Asoka (Ashoka is the Sanskritized form), 'free from sorrow'. This may have been a name he chose after seeking refuge in the Buddha's teaching, whose core deals with suffering and its elimination. Ashoka tells us—and there is no reason to disbelieve him—that the Kalinga war was a life-transforming experience. But, apart from this, we know little about his inner demons and much more about the resolve that emerged from his struggles with them. Ashoka lives on through his inscriptions, but he lives on even more strongly in legend, as a paradigmatic king in the Asian Buddhist world. In sharp contrast, the factual details of Mohandas Karamchand Gandhi's life are minutely documented. Apart from the year, month, and date of his birth and death, a great deal is known about what happened in between. Gandhi's experiments with truth are revealed in his autobiography, diaries, articles, letters, and speeches, as well as through the records maintained by his close associates, admirers, and others with whom he interacted. He too had his transformative moment, not on the battlefield but when he was thrown out of a train in South Africa. It was one of many personal and political crises that he described meticulously in his own words.

Despite the immense chronological distance and the asymmetry in information, a case can be made for comparing Ashoka and Gandhi, and it does not rest on the desire to say something new and startling. Their writings (let us consider Ashoka's inscriptions as his writings, even though he may have dictated them orally), marked by a unique kind of reflection, introspection, honesty, and frankness, allow an exploration of the ways in which two very different men, living in very different times, struggled with the problem of violence. A comparison reveals many surprising similarities, as well as many striking differences. I will explore both, with a tilt towards Ashoka, because I know him better.

Ashoka and Gandhi were political beings who sought to connect the political, social, and moral spheres, asserting the supremacy of the moral. Both were political and moral activists who at a certain point in their lives, began to consciously, consistently, persistently, and passionately practice and propagate non-violence as an essential basis for a good life. In Ashoka's case, this commitment to non-violence emerged primarily, but not exclusively, from a creative, idiosyncratic engagement with Buddhism, and in Gandhi's case, from a creative, idiosyncratic engagement with a variety of philosophical and religious traditions, including Hinduism, Jainism, Christianity, and Islam.

Both men believed in persuasion and saw their persuasive skills as having a profound social impact. Both adopted a dialogic approach based on communication and direct mass contact. Ashoka set up massive machinery to spread dhamma (goodness, virtue), including a special cadre of dhamma officials whose responsibility was to go around spreading goodness. The emperor himself was involved in a marathon 265-day mass contact dhamma campaign. Since Gandhi lived in the locomotive era, the extent of his travels and public outreach far exceeded those of Ashoka. And yet he wrote to Kasturba, 'One cannot propagate dharma by travelling in trains or cars, nor in bullock carts. That can be done only on foot.' Ashoka would have agreed.

Ashoka and Gandhi believed in the connection between the inner and outer worlds and between the personal and the social. They led through example, energy, and commitment. Both believed in human imperfection and perfectibility, and the need to live in accordance with a transcendent, higher dharma. They believed in grounding action in ethics and were obsessed with non-violence, truth, and controlling the passions. Although Ashoka talks about controlling the passions, we do not know about his personal attitude towards sexuality; Gandhi's obsession with brahmacharya is well known, as are his unorthodox experiments to test his commitment to complete and true celibacy. Ashoka's dhamma included individual virtues such as self-control, truthfulness, purity of thought, liberality, and gratitude. The idea of duty is central to how he thought of his role as a king and in the code of ethics he propounded to his subjects. Proper social conduct comprised obedience to mother and father; respect for elders; courtesy and liberality towards Brahmins and renunciants; courtesy to slaves and servants; liberality towards friends, acquaintances, and relatives; moderation in expenditure and possessions; and guarding one's speech. The appropriate behaviour towards all living beings—humans and animals—included gentleness, compassion, and abstention from injuring and from killing. Gandhi would have agreed with all of this, especially the emphasis on non-violence, self-control, and frugality as part of the definition of the good. He would have agreed with Ashoka's view that a life lived according to the dictates of goodness, virtue, and duty was the foundation for happiness in this life and the next. Ashoka and Gandhi practised non-violence personally and sought to create non-violent societies. Both had a strong sense of self and mission; they saw themselves as important, innovative figures within the longer-term politico-intellectual tradition. Both engaged with the world in order to change it.

Ashoka and Gandhi's obsession with ethics was combined with shrewd political pragmatism. Gandhi's calling off of the Non-cooperation Movement due to the violence at Chauri Chaura displayed a stubborn unwillingness to compromise on the issue of non-violence, but in many other situations, his strong political instincts led him towards pragmatic compromise. In his thirteenth rock edict, where Ashoka gave a strong, reasoned critique of war, he also struck a pragmatic note when he warned the forest tribes that he would not hesitate to use force against them, if required.

There is a similarity in Ashoka and Gandhi's attitude towards religion. Both were deeply religious but rejected institutional religious authority. Ashoka's personal religion included a faith in Buddhism combined with a belief in the gods, heaven and hell, karma, ethics, punya (merit), and papa (demerit). Although Gandhi did not believe in the outer trappings of religion, he was a devout Hindu; at the same time, he had an intense curiosity about other religions. Ashoka and Gandhi recognized the existence of religious conflict and struggled to foster interaction and harmony between religious communities. Ashoka's plea for concord (samavaya, similar in meaning to the Hindi word samvad) between the various pasandas (religious sects) was a plea for mutual respect and dialogue, much more than what is conveyed in the bland and rather negative phrase 'religious tolerance'. Religious concord was close to Gandhi's heart too. Of course the magnitude of religious conflict and violence that he dealt with, especially during the prelude to and aftermath of the Partition, were much more frightening in scale and intensity than anything that Ashoka might have faced or even imagined.

Apart from all these similarities, there are, of course, several important differences between Ashoka and Gandhi in their ideas and practice. In his advocacy of non-violence, Ashoka's main focus was on personal behaviour and social ethics and livelihoods. Gandhi was, in addition, concerned with using non-violence as a political instrument in the form of innovative strategies such as non-cooperation, satyagraha, and fasting. In many important respects, Gandhian non-violence marks a break with older Indian traditions, not only in terms of its time frame and colonial context, but also in the nature of the political movement it was part of, one that involved the use of non-violence as a strategy against the colonial state.

Another difference lies in their attitude towards social inequality. Ashoka asserted that dhamma and its rewards (heaven, happiness in this life and the next) were open to all, high and low. By third-century BCE standards, this was quite radical, but other than this, Ashoka did not directly question or challenge the prevailing forms of social inequality. Gandhi's views on varna and caste changed over time. Although there are diametrically different assessments of his stand on these issues, there is no doubt that he was acutely conscious of social inequality, especially the scourge of untouchability, which he considered immoral and unjust, and a great deal of his social activism focused on this problem.

Ashoka and Gandhi's personalities are marked by extraordinary confidence and conviction. In the case of Ashoka, there was a change over time—the frank admission of his inability to impose vegetarianism in the royal household in an early inscription made way in later years for more arrogant assertions of the resounding success of his dhamma propagation, and claims that he had succeeded in transforming the minds, hearts, and behaviour of people. Gandhi was much more aware of his shortcomings and failures and in fact revelled in laying them bare to the world. His inability to find common ground with Ambedkar, to preserve Hindu–Muslim concord, and to prevent the Partition of India were issues of great sorrow to him. Over time, Ashoka seems to have become more and more convinced of the success of his mission, while Gandhi became increasingly disillusioned and pained by his failure to arrest or reverse the relentless unfolding of events.

The differences between the two men can be seen not only in their life but also in their death. Gandhi met a violent, public death at the hands of a religious fanatic who did not relish his ideas of Hindu–Muslim amity. We do not know for sure how Ashoka died. Buddhist legend suggests a peaceful, pious solitary end; some legends suggest he became a monk, others say he died a king, after giving everything away to the sangha.

There is one more important thing that Gandhi and Ashoka have in common. Both have become symbols, icons of non-violence, but empty, hollow ones. Their convictions about the moral basis of politics have little real traction in today's Kautilyan political world. Ashoka has been reduced to an emblem, his Sarnath lions stamped routinely on state letterheads and coins. He is mentioned in school textbooks but has been robbed of complexity or profundity, his radical ideas turned into tepid, tedious platitudes. Gandhi is the father of the nation, invoked routinely on the anniversaries of his birth and assassination. His disembodied spectacles have become a symbol for a clean Bharat. But the ideals he stood for, lived and died for, have been whittled away, and his vision of an India where non-violence, inter-religious dialogue and harmony reigned has been replaced by a narrow idea of a muscular nation that thrives on exclusion and conflict.

The aim of this comparative exercise is not to draw a straight line from Ashoka to Gandhi, nor to suggest that Gandhi was inspired by Ashoka's ideas or example. We do not know whether Ashoka could read or write, and if he did, what he read. The extent to which his understanding of Buddhism and the world was based on texts or on information given to him by monks and others is unclear. Gandhi, on the other hand, was a voracious reader and we have a very good idea of what he read at different points in his life. There is no indication that he ever read Ashoka's inscriptions. So Ashoka and Gandhi are not directly connected. The aim in comparing them is to see how two men, living centuries apart, responded to the problem of the violence around them.

Further, a long history of the interface between violence and non-violence in political theory and practice cannot begin in the nineteenth century; it has to begin in ancient India. This does not mean a simplistic harking back to the past in order to show that we knew it all, had it all. It involves identifying interesting points of continuity and convergence, but also the many striking points of change and divergence in political ideas and practice. Such a history can illuminate the many different perspectives through which political thinkers and practitioners in our part of the world grappled with the perennial problem of violence.

There is also exciting material here for a larger, global comparative history. Without essentializing cultures or falling into the traps of cultural bias or chauvinism, there is the possibility of a comparative history of violence and non-violence which identifies the common threads, but also qualitative differences in forms, structures, intensity, ideologies, and attitudes. The factors that define violence and the normalizing processes that make some kinds of harming or killing by the state or against the state seem justified are deeply embedded in social and political structures, institutions, and ideologies, as well as in moral and religious values. A global comparative history of violence would examine the ways in which these factors coalesced across cultures and times.

The structure and ideologies of ancient Indian monarchies and the modern democratic nation state are drastically different. The modern democratic state is based—at least in theory—on ideas such as equality, freedom, and liberty of the individual. These ideas were never in the picture in ancient India, where social inequality and hierarchy were taken for granted, with a few religious traditions accepting equality in the context of devotion to a deity or the potential to achieve liberation from samsara—the cycle of birth, death, and rebirth. Modern states have far greater potential for violence than their ancient counterparts, much more sophisticated means to justify this violence, and enormous powers to manipulate public opinion. But there are some similarities between ancient and contemporary states, for instance, in the acceptance of the idea of the fundamental duties of the state—the protection of subjects, ensuring their well-being and prosperity, the dispensing of justice, and the maintenance of social order. Further, all states at all times and places in history have sought to mask, justify, and legitimize their use of violence through an ideology that presents the state's violence as necessary force. In ancient times, this violence was presented as necessary to uphold the kingdom, today it is presented as necessary to uphold the nation.

An exploration of violence and non-violence in Indian history will have to take into account the current phase where behind the occasional rhetoric, the state has, in fact, rejected the Ashokan and Gandhian values of truth, non-violence, and religious concord. But in a long history of political ideas and practice, like all things, this too will pass.

## 12

## TRACKING A PRIME MINISTER'S TRAVELS TO AJANTA AND ELLORA

### NAYANJOT LAHIRI

Past events are recorded in diverse ways depending on the medium and intent of the recorders. While the question is then one of deciding which of these is more authentic, the researcher often realizes that there is no one definitive account and thus, by implication, no singular history with a capital 'H'. As I will show, the prime ministerial visit, which is the subject of this essay, is recorded differently in various sources. Even though each tells a discrete story, it is all of them combined that makes it possible to capture the flavours and the context—the political and the personal, the mundane and the historic—that make up that visit. Gopalkrishna Gandhi himself is fond of using various evidentiary threads, from personal letters to material relics, in writing wonderful prose. This has been written in the hope that he would approve of an attempt to pick out letters and newspaper reporting, photographs, and file notings to highlight a little researched episode that reveals Jawaharlal Nehru as both a man and a prime minister steeped in history and sensitive to India's ancient heritage.

♦

On 2 and 3 February 1957, some professional archaeologists, a few politicians, and an Englishwoman with Indian connections congregated to visit the ancient cave shrines of Ajanta and Ellora. Madhusudan Narhar Deshpande, the Aurangabad-based superintendent of the Archaeological Survey of India, was there to make sure that the pre-eminent politician of India, Jawaharlal

Nehru, and his companion, Lady Edwina Mountbatten, were fittingly shepherded through the caves with their stunningly painted ceilings and walls, and sculptures.

Other attendees included heavyweight politicians like Yashwantrao Balwantrao Chavan, the Congress chief minister of Bombay state, while among the archaeologists was the Ajanta officer-in-charge, Abdul Wahid Khan, and the chief archaeological chemist of the Survey. This visit can well be treated as routine, since Nehru used to visit places that interested him as he went about the country in the course of his prime ministerial duties or while electioneering for his party. But this was no ordinary visit. While it had indeed been arranged for Nehru, the request had been made by him personally, so that he could see the caves with Edwina.

The visit had been long in the making. As the relevant volume of the *Selected Works of Jawaharlal Nehru* reveals, Nehru wrote to Edwina in December 1948 about a tentative programme for her impending visit to India where the Bombay leg was slated to include Ajanta and Ellora. He added that he would like to accompany her there but was not sure if he would be able to manage it. 'A Prime Minister must not go sightseeing too much', he said, seemingly in jest. Keen to visit places with her, in the same letter, he also made plans to go to Konarak. This was some months after the Mountbattens had left India. Edwina had come as vicereine, accompanying her husband, Louis Mountbatten, the last viceroy of India, on 24 March 1947.

Soon after her arrival, she developed a close rapport with Nehru which quickly turned into an intimate romantic friendship that continued well after the last British viceroyalty ended. She came to India practically every year while he spent time with her during his visits to England. Their relationship endured until Edwina's untimely death in 1960, with Nehru's letters by her side.

But tracing back our footsteps to 1948, the visit to the caves did not materialize. Nehru and Edwina, along with many others, did go to Konarak. She developed a high fever during the course of that trip, which was possibly the reason they did not visit Ajanta and Ellora. Some years later, this visit was planned again but could not take place due to Edwina's collapse in Malta. She, however, extracted a promise from Nehru that they would go there in the near future. Nearly ten years after the initial plan, he, as promised, had organized a visit. And Deshpande was present as the primary sutradhara.

◆

Deshpande had first seen the splendorous caves of Ajanta and Ellora when he was a teenager in the 1930s. This was around the same time, as we shall see, that Nehru first visited the caves. At the time, Deshpande's father had been trying to dissuade him from following the family medical profession. The father had told his son that he was meant for something else. What that was exactly he didn't say. He did, however, take the son around historic places, ranging from Ajanta and Ellora near Aurangabad to the Gol Gumbaz of Bijapur. These were sites where, later, Deshpande would do some of his most important work. Simultaneously, his father exposed him to the growing Indian national movement, towing him along for various Congress meetings, including the Faizpur session of the Indian National Congress. This was held in December 1936, and the excursion to the monuments of the father-son duo would have been organized before or after it.

Now, in 1957, as a professional archaeologist, Deshpande was looking after the South-Western Circle of the Survey, having arrived in Aurangabad the previous year. This was five years after the Indian parliament in 1951 had declared a large number of monuments in the former princely states to be of national importance. Two years later, the Archaeological Survey had taken direct charge of the Ajanta and Ellora caves.

Before the parliamentary intervention, the Hyderabad state had been tasked as the institutional guardian of the caves; even in 1949, the state had appointed a committee to study their proper preservation and maintenance. The committee was headed by

Ghulam Yazdani, the author of the excellent volumes on Ajanta. I have sometimes wondered why Yazdani's services were not sought by the Archaeological Survey when Nehru and Edwina visited. He was, after all, not only the author of the Ajanta volumes but had been intimately involved in the preservation of those caves. And several others. The reason was probably age. Yazdani was, by then, seventy-seven years old, compared with the thirty-six-year-old Deshpande.

There was something in the air that year, 1956, when Deshpande moved to Aurangabad. The Archaeological Survey was apparently expecting a high-profile visitor. This can be sniffed out from the unusually large number of letters and notings relating to the cave sites in the Aurangabad Circle files of that year. In April, Amalananda Ghosh, director general of the Survey, visited Ajanta and Ellora with Deshpande and the archaeological engineer, Shankar Das. He followed this up with a long letter in which he described the programme of conservation required at both the sites. Even before Ghosh's visit, Shankar Das and Deshpande had gone over the Ellora caves with a fine-toothed comb. Das was particularly alarmed with some of the repairs which, he declared, were either poor work or very modern-looking. He put down his caustic observations of the caves. In Cave 1, for instance, he highlighted how the cement concrete on the floor showed longitudinal joints all over, which he claimed looked 'like snakes stretching from one end to the other. The entire look is modern and it was this modern look which has always been avoided in the past.' Many sculptures, he noted, also showed 'revolting pointing' carried out in cement. This, he stated, should be taken out and the cracks filled suitably with the help of a modeller. He probably knew that there was an excellent modeller who worked at the Ellora caves at this time. This was none other than Ram Sutar who went on to become an iconic and famous sculptor. Not many know that he began his career at the Archaeological Survey.

On 9 August, the lighting at Ajanta was taken in hand. B. R. R. Iyengar, the officiating superintending engineer of what was called

'Hydro & Districts' (Hyderabad Division), visited the caves. He was there on the orders of the Secretary, Public Works Department, to examine the arrangement for the lighting of the caves and suggest modifications to make it better. Incidentally, visitors used to pay five rupees for an entry ticket that included getting light for one-and-a-half hours to see the caves. Attendants who held the lights in their hands were not averse to threatening visitors with a penalty if they exceeded their time limit. This is not something that Iyengar would have faced but he was unhappy about three separate diesel sets servicing the area and, instead, suggested it was better to have one diesel station which would supply power to all the points. It would still be some years before the power backup and lighting of Ajanta would be adequately resolved.

As it so happened, the existing generators were not in great shape even on the eve of Nehru's visit. We know this because as newspapers began reporting the forthcoming visit in the third week of January, the officer-in-charge at Ajanta, Abdul Wahid Khan, was in a flap since the Aurangabad office had still not supplied parts for the generator sets that would ensure they were ready for providing a regular supply of electricity to light up the caves. Khan also urgently asked for other stuff—phenyl, Dettol, joss sticks, and incense to ensure clean and, it seems, fragrant bathrooms and public areas.

If there was a prime minister who was waiting to finally bring his female friend to see a historic site beloved to him, and there was a superintendent who wanted to make this a memorable visit for them, there was an officer at Ajanta who wanted to get the basics right. The visitors are unlikely to have even been aware of these last-minute arrangements. But one can entirely empathize with Khan, because whatever planning may have gone into the trip, without attention to illumination and hygiene, the pleasure of the visit for Edwina and Nehru would definitely have been diminished. Many years later, Nehru's daughter, also as prime minister, visited the Elephanta caves near Bombay. Indira Gandhi would pointedly complain about the lack of cleanliness in the bathrooms there and felt that the site should be shut down for tourists if basic amenities could not be provided.

◆

Nehru's visit in February coincided with a particularly hectic domestic phase for him. The general elections were to be held in March that year. Since much of the appeal of the Congress stemmed from his personal popularity, he was in the midst of electioneering tours which went on side by side with his work as a prime minister. What struck me, though, is how often the past figured in Nehru's speeches and in his tours. I draw attention to just three such occasions in the weeks before he went with Edwina to the cave shrines.

Less than a month before he went there, the prime minister was in Indore for the meeting of the Congress Working Committee and an open session of the Congress. He also made a speech at a public meeting on 7 January after having visited medieval Mandu. He went, as he mentioned in the meeting, because he had 'a holiday' on that day, in a manner of speaking, presumably squeezing in a morning admiring its ruins. Mandu is some 90-odd kilometres from Indore and Nehru was quite happy spending the day in the vicinity of those monuments. He began his speech, in fact, by explaining why the past mattered to him even as he remained absorbed in the day-to-day problems of the present: 'I went to Mandu to refresh myself mentally and physically, and to cast a backward glance at our past, away from the problems of the present. I do not like to look back too often because we have to live in the present, understand the problems of this age and find a solution for them. But if we are tied to the present, with no sense of the past or the future, there will be no continuity. We have to build on the foundations of the past for the future that is to come. In this way, the link between the past, present, and the future remains unbroken.' This curiously resonates with E. H. Carr's words about 'an unending dialogue between the past and the present' who he used in this phraseology to describe the nature of history in Carr's now famous 1961 George Macaulay

Trevelyan lectures at Cambridge published as *What is History?*

Some days later, on 13 January, Nehru was in Cuttack for the inauguration of the Hirakud dam. Here, he drew attention to the extraordinary beauty of the Konarak and Bhubaneshwar temples and the people who came there to either worship or admire their architecture. He then spoke about how productive labour should be worshipped, underlining that while there had been a tradition of building temples and worshipping them, now 'that tradition needs to be linked to the modern temples and a new form of worship. Places like Hirakud are the modern centres of pilgrimage for us', he declared. The very next day, 14 January, when Nehru inaugurated the forty-fourth session of the Indian Science Congress in Calcutta, he returned to the connection between the past and the present and reminisced about how in the last two days, as he had been at Nalanda and at Hirakud. The Nalanda visit on 12 January had been in the company of the Dalai Lama, Panchen Lama, and the Chinese ambassador on the occasion of handing over the relics of the ancient Chinese pilgrim, Xuanzang. His words at the Science Congress are wonderfully evocative as he drew links across time — from ancient Nalanda to modern Hirakud:

> And so, I wondered at the close association of this ceremony at Nalanda and the memories of the Buddha coming to me and of subsequent events of that University, and the next day at a product of modern science — this Hirakud dam — and today, I am here before you at this Science Congress. And the centuries seem to come together before me, and again I thought, how India is a bundle of centuries, where you can find almost every century represented here from the remote past to the modern age. Somehow we jog along with the past and the present, and even work for the future together, and the cow and the tractor march together in this country. I do know what the future will hold. It does not seem terribly incongruous that the cow and the tractor are side by side.

If Nehru was alive, while he would approve of the fact that the cow and tractor continue to coexist in India, he would also not fail to notice how much more the lives of cows matter today than those of the people whose livelihoods depend on them. But, going back to January 1957, these visits and speeches give us a sense of how the tours of the prime minister were organized where he wandered from the past to the present, physically and mentally, as he put it. The fact is that in making space for Ajanta and Ellora during the time he spent between 1 and 3 February in Poona and Aurangabad, it could well be said that he was doing what he usually tried to do elsewhere, whenever he could.

But there was more to the Ajanta visit than this; even if Nehru went around ancient places, there was something about the cave shrines that made the visit different for him from every other historic site in India. One is struck by the number of times he visited the caves, on some four occasions or so. Ajanta also figured prominently in his letters and other writings. As a letter to his daughter reveals, much like Edwina's visit, his maiden pilgrimage to it eventually took place much later than he had planned. He wrote to Indira from prison in 1932, that some seven or eight years ago, after going to Ellora, he had got down at a station to travel to Ajanta but couldn't find a car to go there. He seems to have finally gone there in late 1936. He would write about his visit and his reaction to what he saw soon after this, on 2 January 1937, to Padmaja Naidu. She was the Congress leader Sarojini Naidu's daughter. Nehru had a long romantic relationship with her, one which continued till his death. Apart from anything else, it was marked by an affinity with all things Buddhist, as is obvious from the letters they exchanged. Naturally, Nehru wrote to her about how he saw Ajanta:

> What shall I write to you about Ajanta? It seems almost vulgar and profane to use foolish words of praise which have been so cheapened in the market place. The joy of seeing these pictures of long ago almost becomes a pain, to see beauty of form and beautify of life that are unattainable, unrealizable. What manner of people were they who created this dream

world out of a few colours and lines? What was the texture of their lives—how rich it must have been! How can one forget the Bodhisattva even after seeing a picture—and the lovely women of Ajanta. I wish one did forget for they disturb.

Nehru's letters to Padmaja ooze with an attractive chemistry, and bring alive an uncommonly attractive man, one who could be simultaneously emotional and intellectual. Especially when he linked an ancient apsara at Ajanta with his modern one. 'How terribly near you are all the time to me since the Ajanta Princess has come and taken possession of my room,' he wrote to her after she presented him with a reproduction of that famous apsara and asked, apparently rhetorically, why he thought of her whenever he looked at it.

But coming back to Nehru's first visit there towards the end of December 1936, when the Faizpur session of the Congress was held. Faizpur is some 80 kilometres from Ajanta, even closer than Aurangabad to the caves. It was also during this session that the young Deshpande came to Faizpur with his father who took him around Ajanta and Ellora. So, the first visits of Nehru and Deshpande to the cave shrines where they would meet in 1957 as an archaeologist and a prime minister, took place around the same time.

Beyond Ajanta's presence in intimate letters exchanged, Nehru's admiration for the caves and the women depicted there shine through in his publications. In *The Discovery of India*, he waxed lyrical about how Ajanta took 'one back into a distant dream-like and yet very real world'. But his most perceptive and eloquent comments were for the women there whose beauty he juxtaposed with the prescriptive preaching of the clergy:

> These frescoes were painted by the Buddhist monks. Keep away from women, do not even look at them, for they are dangerous, has said their Master long ago. And yet we have here women in plenty, beautiful women, princesses, singers, dancers, seated and standing, beautifying themselves, or in

procession. The women of Ajanta had become famous. How well those painter-monks must have known the world and the moving drama of life, how lovingly they have painted it....

Later, too, in 1954, as the prime minister, in his preface to Madanjeet Singh's book on the paintings of Ajanta, *India: Paintings from Ajanta Caves*, he confides that 'if I were asked to name three or four places of paramount interest in India, which would give some glimpse into India's mind in successive ages, I would mention Ajanta as one of them.' As before, he drew the attention of the readers to the female figures there by noting that the 'women of Ajanta are famous. History becomes human and living and not merely a record of some distant age which we can hardly understand.'

We have no way of knowing if Edwina was aware of these connections, both artistic and real, that Nehru felt with Ajanta which made representations of a remote age pulsate with a contemporary human resonance. But, to us, looking back, they are hard to miss. It is women who endow interconnectedness to Nehru's writings and musings, wanderings, and visions about and around Ajanta.

◆

To now turn to the sojourns at the Ajanta and Ellora caves, there is a qualitative difference in how the media covered the events and what is revealed by the photographs. The newspaper reports of the monument visits kept their focus, unsurprisingly, on Nehru. Having arrived the previous day on an Indian Air Force Meghdoot at Poona, he left the next morning by the same plane for Aurangabad, from where the party drove down to Ajanta. The Press Trust of India report mentions that on reaching there, he spent two hours exploring the caves, accompanied by Lady Mountbatten. The report captures his eagerness to explain the paintings and their significance to her: 'The Prime Minister ran up 200 feet of the flight of steps to the caves without showing the slightest signs of fatigue and immediately on arrival inside the caves started explaining the history of the caves to Lady Mountbatten.' Even when Abdul Wahid Khan gave details of the art, he intervened a number of times to explain their special significance and historical background, we are told. Also, Nehru asked questions about how ancient artists prepared pigments for which the chief chemical analyst of the Survey gave explanations. Did he also see the several hollows in the cave floors which were used for grinding the pigments? Who knows. Certainly, they spent a lot of time seeing a new discovery— presumably at Cave 12—which had been unearthed some nine months ago. This had cells for monks and it was reported that 'Mr Nehru went through three cells meant for monks, with stone cots and stone pillows. Mr Nehru said they were similar to stone cots found in Rome.'

But with no photographs accompanying the Press Trust report, it seems somewhat dead in its description. Interestingly, in the Deshpande family papers, there are several photographed moments at Ajanta and at Ellora, and all kinds of people figure there, especially the archaeologist-sutradhara and the prime minister with his companion. If in the Nehru archives, as also in those of the Archaeological Survey of India, the focus is on the planning that went into the visit and, in newspaper reports, the figure of the prime minister looms large, the intimate elements of those visits are captured in these pictures. It is to those that I now turn since they form a collage of visual memories which simply do not figure anywhere else.

The first thing which stands out is that these are not compositions for the camera. The photographs were taken as the visitors and the escorts went about the caves. The second feature is the crowd accompanying the prime minister as can be clearly seen in this Ajanta photograph.

*Nehru coming down the steps at Ajanta*

There seem to have been two dozen or so, from politicos and archaeologists, to security and protocol officers. Their clothes too stand out. The politicians looked casual while the protocol entourage was formal and stuffy. Deshpande, too, wore a buttoned-up short bandgala coat like many others. In contrast, it is striking how informally Nehru himself was dressed. Abandoning his usual sherwani, he wore a kurta over his churidar, with his characteristic cap, carrying in his hand, as he often did, a short stick.

*Y. B. Chavan, Nehru, Edwina, and Deshpande at Ajanta.*

His laced shoes, in photographs of Caves 1 and 2, are well polished, but by the time he was coming down the staircase that led to Caves 10 to 12, they look dusty and in desperate need of cleaning. While Nehru looks youthful for his seventy years, Edwina, on the other hand, appears tired. Possibly, her attire was too buttoned up for all the climbing up and down that is part of exploring Ajanta's cave shrines. But it is also possible that she wasn't well. In any case, her coiffured hair, pearl string, and fancy sandals fail to draw attention away from her drawn face.

By next morning Edwina looks somewhat revived as revealed in the photographs from Ellora. Nehru was back to his usual formal, achkaned self and the buttonhole, as always, had a fresh rose. He was flying back to Delhi and straight into a flurry of meetings. Deshpande, like him, is also wearing an achkan and churidar. The photographs reveal that they visited Caves 10, 12, 16, and 29, which would mean they saw the Buddhist caves as well as the Hindu ones. Cave 16, the most famous Kailasa (or Kailasanatha) Temple, was where they spent considerable time, taking in the carvings around Shiva and stories relating to him, his devotees, and other figures, with Deshpande evidently explaining the mythologies recorded in the panels. In one of the photographs, the archaeologist is standing with Nehru and Edwina at the top of a staircase looking down at a panel. In a most unselfconscious way, he has his leg up on the rock, describing in an amazingly animated way what they are looking at on the opposite wall.

*Deshpande explaining Ravana shaking Mount Kailasa at Ellora to Nehru and Edwina*

The staircase happens to face the relief-carving of Ravana shaking Mount Kailasa. Ravana, he might well have been telling them, even though he is standing below an array that includes Shiva and Parvati, appears to be far larger and more arresting than those celestial figures. At least, that is how he appears to modern visitors.

Certainly, Deshpande's telling has everyone looking at the carving and responding to the sheer majesty of the demon with his multiple arms and heads carved in the round. In another photograph, he is looking at what Edwina and Nehru, with their heads together, appear to be discussing about the beautiful panel of Shiva and Parvati in Cave 29.

*Deshpande, Edwina, Nehru, and Chavan in Cave 29 at Ellora*

The expression, though, on Yashwantrao Chavan's face, is priceless. He too appears to be looking at the couple—Nehru and Edwina—also wondering about them and their sense of camaraderie in the midst of a cave with representations of another, more ancient, celestial couple. None in the crowd, though, seems to have in any way disturbed this couple's concentration, an ability, presumably, people who lead public lives develop as part of their persona.

◆

Historians are hardly ever witnesses to the events that they write about. We can only produce representations of them by retrieving recordings and imprints. As we recover those, we realize there is never one way of remembering an event. The prime ministerial visit I have described here was no different. It appears in various forms depending on who is recording, and yet, it is those multiple lenses that flesh out its ambience and its significance. This also means that being an eyewitness is never enough. Rather, it is the historian's 'act of representation that lifts us', as John Lewis Gaddis put it so well in *The Landscape of History* (2002), 'above the familiar to let us experience vicariously what we can't experience directly: a wider view' of events and processes.

---

Photos courtesy Ashok Deshpande

## 13

## PACIFIST, ANARCHIST, SATIRIST, AND HISTORIAN OF THE WATER CLOSET[1]

VENU MADHAV GOVINDU

In early March 1930, India was in a mood of anticipation. Gandhi was about to inaugurate a major civil disobedience campaign and there were rumours of a letter being sent to Viceroy Irwin. The press zeroed in on Motilal Nehru as a potential courier of this important missive. His laughing denials further fuelled their suspicion. Instead, on 4 March, a most unlikely representative of the Mahatma arrived at the Viceregal House in Delhi. It was galling enough that he strode past the ceremonial mounted guards and entered the Raj's imperial chambers dressed in khadi shorts and sporting a Gandhi cap. What made it worse was that he was not a cocky Indian nationalist but a flaxen-haired, twenty-five-year-old Englishman. Soon a name was flashed across the wire earning its bearer instant fame in India and notoriety back home. Thus was launched the unusual public career of Reginald Reynolds.

Reginald Arthur Reynolds was born on 17 October 1905 in Glastonbury, England. He was the third of five children in a Quaker family. Also known as the Religious Society of Friends, the Quakers are a Christian sect with origins in the political turmoil of seventeenth-century England. Their faith is characterized by a commitment to a plain lifestyle, pacifism, social reform, and teetotalism. Their beliefs also found a home in America where the emphasis on social change included an opposition to the slave trade.

---

[1]The title of this essay is taken from a photo caption in Robert Huxter's *Reg and Ethel: Reginald Reynolds, His Life and Work and His Marriage to Ethel Mannin*, York: Sessions Book Trust, 1992.

In the 1930s and 40s, a significant number of Gandhi's supporters in Britain were drawn from this community.

While Reynolds did well enough in school, his plans of enrolling for a university degree floundered when he failed his 'Inter' exams owing to a poor grasp of Latin. Subsequently, he proved equally inadept at his family trade in sheepskin rugs. Lacking professional success and suffering from heartbreak in matters of love, by 1929, Reynolds found himself in a mood of despondency. His tutor, Horace Alexander, had travelled in India and met Gandhi the previous year. Alexander suggested the remedy of packing Reynolds off to India to spend time at Gandhi's ashram in Ahmedabad. The problem of finances was fortuitously solved by prematurely encashing his share in the family business. Richer by £200, Reynolds sailed for India, and in October 1929 arrived at Sabarmati Ashram in Ahmedabad.

Reynolds settled into ashram life as best as an Englishman could, in other words, not very well. He also travelled around India and attended the momentous 1929 Lahore Session where the Congress declared purna swaraj or complete independence as its goal. When Alexander had proposed a stint at Sabarmati, Reynolds was surprised that he could just walk into Gandhi's ashram. Indeed, it is a measure of Gandhi's generosity that while he was working towards perhaps the most important political campaign of his life, he would take under his care a young Englishman who had little to offer in return. While Alexander's good offices would have helped in the acceptance of Reynolds, it was rather rare for Englishmen to be so interested in the Indian cause. Inevitably, Reynolds found himself catapulted into the heart of the Indian campaign for freedom.

Located as he was, Reynolds had a ringside view of Indian history in the making. He regularly sent letters back home that were also privately circulated. Decades later, in 1952, he used these letters and his journals to write a most incisive and delightful memoir of his time at Sabarmati, his travels in India, and his relationship with the Mahatma, *A Quest for Gandhi: To Live in Mankind*. In his letters from 1929–30, the young Reynolds displayed some of the hallmarks of his later oeuvre—an eye for detail, shrewd observation of people, and a sardonic and rapier wit. At the same time, he also demonstrated many Western prejudices against Indian habits, lifestyle, and culture. This included using a most hackneyed colonial trope for his series of letters. They were called 'Tropical Budgets'.

Gandhi had refused to allow Reynolds to join the Dandi March. Instead, Gandhi stipulated that once Mahadev Desai and he were arrested, Reynolds should take charge of the weekly *Young India*. In the event, Reynolds did not take charge of Gandhi's journal. The ashram at Sabarmati was largely deserted as most of its residents were either conducting Civil Disobedience campaigns or in prison. With little to do and suffering from poor health owing to his high blood pressure, by June 1930, Reynolds decided to return home by boarding a ship in Ceylon (now Sri Lanka). Reynolds had become a controversial figure by now and the mere act of entertaining him created problems for his hosts, such as the English priest and later anthropologist Verrier Elwin. His host in Madurai, the American missionary R. R. 'Dick' Keithahn, was summarily sent back home by his church for the sin of being present when local Congressmen met with Reynolds.

In India, over a period of nine months, Reynolds was witness to the struggle between might and right. In the early days of his visit he had evinced unease about the militancy of the Civil Disobedience campaign. But having witnessed the brutal violence unleashed by the Raj, he was transformed. Horace Alexander had wisely advised Reynolds to leave the problem of what to do with him in Gandhi's hands. Now, the die was cast. Touched by Gandhi's personal solicitude of his welfare and motivated by the justness of the Indian cause, Reynolds decided to make Indian freedom the primary concern of his life.

During his travels in India, Reynolds had met a number of his countrymen and women. He was dismayed by their ignorance of India and their smug display of prejudice and bigotry. Back home, he was incensed by the indifference of his people to the lives in India that Britain ruled over. He found that his fellow Quakers adhered to a false pacifism that he deemed cowardly and, most devastatingly, shifty. Instead of owning up to their moral duty, they criticized the idea of Indian civil disobedience for its 'un-Christian' and 'unpacifist' character. Here, it must be remembered that the Quaker-led India Conciliation Group was formed in later times. Reynolds also found that the Labour Party was as much an upholder of the empire as the Conservatives. In later years, he marvelled at his own stupidity in supporting the Labour Party till 1929 ('more at home in dinner jackets than they are in overalls') and at his patience with the communists in the early 1930s. However, the biggest impediment to making the Indian case was the British press which produced 'an endless cataract of misquotation, misrepresentation, and crude falsehood' with regard to the events in India and the role played by Gandhi and his fellow nationalists in it.

Reynolds keenly wished to make personal amends—to the extent that any one individual could—'for all the degradation that Indians had suffered from the British'. Now, under extremely unfavourable circumstances, he set about campaigning for Indian freedom through letters and articles to counter pro-Empire propaganda, publishing explanatory pamphlets, and speaking in public. Soon, despite his young age, he became an important contact for Indian nationalists such as Jawaharlal Nehru, who filled Reynolds in on the rapidly evolving political events in India. Undoubtedly, the significance accorded to Reynolds had as much to do with his precocious intelligence and fierce commitment as the sheer scarcity of campaigners for India's swaraj in Britain.

Reynolds had felt that Gandhi's 'scorching passion for truth was almost terrifying'. But he was also struck by Gandhi's open engagement with people and ideas. Speaking from personal experience, Reynolds argued that Gandhi's greatness lay in the fact that he 'never saw people merely as they were, but as what they could become'. Indeed, Gandhi had affectionately given Reynolds the nickname of Angad, Rama's vanara emissary to Ravana's court in the Ramayana. He addressed Reynolds by this moniker in his letters over the years. But Reynolds was no unquestioning follower. When he heard of the Gandhi–Irwin Pact, an incensed Reynolds wrote a strongly worded letter to Gandhi as he was unable to see what India had gained in the process. He was equally upset when he heard the news that Gandhi would be arriving in London to attend the Second Round Table Conference. 'I don't think,' he argued, 'Bapu's coming over will bring so much as the shadow of independence to India.' While Reynolds saw Gandhi's new position as capitulation, he was nevertheless delighted with the opportunity to meet the Mahatma again.

Upon returning home, Reynolds had helped set up a small organization called Friends of India and had even sold three of Gandhi's letters to raise funds for it. He canvassed extensively for the Indian cause. Now, he noted with alarm that others had taken charge of Gandhi's visit and Reynolds and his colleagues were in danger of being completely edged out. Unwilling to be so outmanoeuvred, Reynolds devised an ingenious solution.

His open association with Gandhi had marked out Reynolds as a dangerous figure by the establishment. Within an hour of his arrival at Sabarmati Ashram, he had been interrogated by a policeman. As one can see from archival records, much before he arrived in Delhi with Gandhi's letter to Irwin, Reynolds was closely monitored, his room searched on occasion, and his mail intercepted. While he did not pick up many Gandhian traits, Reynolds had observed in Ahmedabad that the residents of the ashram always treated policemen with courtesy and openness. Soon after he returned to England, when he figured out that he was being followed by plain-clothes policemen, Reynolds startled them by introducing himself. The manner in which he did this is a delightful story unto itself and the interested reader can profit from reading about this and other impish adventures in his 1956 autobiography, *My Life and Crimes*. To return to our narrative, soon Reynolds was on terms of mutual familiarity with the various policemen on a roster ordered to follow him as he went about his life in London.

When Gandhi's ship anchored at Folkestone, Reynolds was refused his request to be the first to meet him as there was already a ponderous list of 'representatives of the India Office and possibly other government departments, Members of Parliament, representatives of leading newspapers' and other worthies who wished to do the same. Using his 'good offices' with Scotland Yard, Reynolds did the next best thing. He managed to have his name added to the list which was presented to Gandhi. Reynolds was confident that this would do the trick as he 'knew the old man would put loyal comrades and old friendships before any official obligations'. Sure enough, Reynolds was the first person called up the gangway to meet his friend from Sabarmati.

During the 1930s, Reynolds was increasingly caught up in the endless and ineffective debates on ideology, strategy, and method between pacifists, communists, socialists, and liberals of varied stripes in Britain. The details of these tortuous wrangles and the many internecine battles need not detain us here. By now Reynolds had rejected both Christian pacifism and communism. Despite his abiding affection, he had also drifted away from 'Gandhi's philosophy of life and conduct'. He found himself 'moving fairly steadily to the left until I could see the Trotskyists at some distance to my right, looking very conservative'. Reynolds continued to collaborate with individuals such as C. F. Andrews as well as Friends of India, but was politically drawn to Jawaharlal Nehru and other Indian socialists.

As part of the internal battle amongst leftists in England, the publisher Secker and Warburg wished to publish a series of books with a leftist tilt but against the 'popular line of Left orthodoxy' of the more famous Victor Gollancz. To his surprise and delight, Reynolds was asked to write a volume on India as he had been studying Indian social and economic history for some years and had been writing regularly on these matters. The result was the first of a dozen books that Reynolds would go on to produce, *White Sahibs in India*, published in 1937. Strikingly, the foreword was not by Gandhi but Reynolds' newfound hero, Jawaharlal Nehru. Nehru commended the book for it was neither imperialist nor sentimental in its outlook towards the problems of India. In an indication of his own ideological preoccupation, Nehru welcomed the publication of a book that 'helps us to understand *scientifically* the background of the Indian struggle' (emphasis added).

Reynolds dedicated his book to the Indians in prison for 'the crime of patriotism' and argued that '[i]mpartiality is a virtue of a knave or a fool's wisdom'. Desiring neither, he presented an unrelenting catalogue of British crimes in India from the time of the John Company. Reynolds, of course, was not the first Englishman to write such a polemic. In 1925, the novelist and historian Edward J. Thompson had written *The Other Side of the Medal*, an exposé of British atrocities during the events of 1857. But if Thompson was tempered in his criticism of fellow Englishmen, Reynolds saw no reason to soften the blow. Chapter titles such as 'The Bloody Sceptre', 'Applying the Lancet', and 'They Made a Wilderness' were indicative of his harsh denunciation of what Britain had inflicted on India. While Thompson's volume presented the darkness of British imperialism in India, it did not accord much significance to the growing Indian nationalist aspirations against colonial rule. In contrast, Reynolds devoted a significant portion of his book delineating the events of the 1920s and 1930s and the role of the Congress in it. In keeping with his political bearings at the time, in *White Sahibs,* Reynolds also placed much unwarranted faith in the ability of the newly formed Congress Socialist Party to move India towards a social revolution. Reynolds had already achieved fame and notoriety for being Gandhi's messenger. But he saw *White Sahibs* as his most significant contribution towards Indian freedom. While the Raj banned it in India as 'a poisonous book', Reynolds was justly satisfied to note that *White Sahibs* had made many in Britain examine their assumptions and think seriously about India for the first time.

While he was focused on India, Reynolds was also involved in a number of other causes. A prolific pamphleteer and writer on political matters, he was also a much sought-after speaker for his grasp of details and easy rapport with his audience. Reynolds presented a commitment to socialism as well as a fierce opposition to war. In various overlapping phases of his political evolution, he supported the Independent Labour Party and became the secretary of the No More War Movement. He also had a long-term association with the War Resisters International. He criticized pacifism for its inordinate emphasis on a simplistic notion of peace without adequate attention to social, political, and economic injustice. Reynolds viewed himself as a radical pacifist who abhorred all forms of government.

Reynolds knew a number of political and literary figures in 1930s London. Soon, his political sensibilities would find echo in his personal life. Earlier, Reynolds had been engaged and jilted, but now he was in a romantic relationship with Ethel Mannin (1900–1984). A prolific writer of poetry, novels, and political essays, Mannin was well-travelled and involved with anarchists such as Emma Goldman. Mannin viewed the Soviet Union with 'admiration and mistrust'. She was also well known for her liberated sexuality. As the biographer of the Reynolds–Mannin duo, Robert Huxter, recounts in *Reg and Ethel*, Mannin had a number of liaisons and affairs with men, both famous and unknown. Her 1930 volume *Confessions and Impressions* was a bestseller but as it was 'considered daringly outspoken and morally shocking', it also resulted in a number of libel cases. Reynolds and Mannin married in 1938, although in keeping with Mannin's disdain for social mores theirs was a 'semi-detached' relationship with the two living fairly independent lives. Curiously enough, in one of his letters, Gandhi evinced tender affection while sternly disapproving of the sexual liaison that Reynolds had entered into with Mannin. While Gandhi's views on these matters are along expected lines, what is striking is that despite their political distance, Reynolds had felt it necessary to write to the Mahatma detailing the nature of his sexual relationship with Mannin before their marriage. In any event, one may safely assume that Gandhi was saved from being even more scandalized than he was, since it is extremely unlikely that he was aware of Ethel Mannin's views on these matters.

Their companionable relationship apart, Reynolds and Mannin were now jointly involved in the political causes that each espoused. As the war clouds loomed over Europe, like many of their friends, the two were gripped by a need for urgent action which was backed by a quiet, steely resolve. They found themselves deeply involved in political activities aimed against General Franco in the Spanish Civil War. When plans were made to charter a ship to carry foodstuff in an attempt to break Franco's blockade of Bilbao, Mannin offered her entire savings for the purpose.

World War II brought additional challenges. With the severe crackdown against the Congress in India, and the imprisonment of its leadership, Reynolds spent much time explaining the Indian position to a hostile wartime Britain. He wrote a number of newspaper articles and pamphlets delineating the role of Britain in the 1943 famine in Bengal and the devastating consequences of British exploitation of India's resources for the war. Particularly noteworthy is his pamphlet, *The New Indian Rope Trick*, which was a critical expose of Britain's treachery on the question of the Sterling Balances it owed India. During the war, Britain had extracted enormous food and other material from India to aid its global war effort. But when it came to paying India what it owed as a result of its extraction of materiel, Britain demurred and drastically reduced its debt. Reynolds argued that this was akin to the Indian rope trick of yore, for the debt that Britain owed India kept rising up till it suddenly disappeared into thin air!

Over the years, Reynolds had contributed much to a literary form central to political activism, the pamphlet. It was therefore natural that he would take a particular interest in genres specific to his inclinations. He edited a two-volume collection of writings titled *British Pamphleteers*, the first volume being co-edited by George Orwell. Prior to these volumes, in 1938, he had co-edited *Prison Anthology* drawing from a number of sources diverse in style but all converging on the experience of gaol.

Reynolds spent a lifetime dealing with serious matters and fighting for many a lost cause. But while this usually entailed a grim demeanour, what probably saved him was his wry sense of humour which was often laced with gleeful sarcasm. In *A Quest for Gandhi*, Reynolds details his observations on some of the humourless and insincere people who kept Gandhi company at Sabarmati. He also recounted a biting and most apposite observation made by an Indian on many of the Gandhians after the Mahatma's demise—'when Fate could not destroy a great man it sent him disciples in revenge'. It was only natural that he would find a kindred spirit in that enemy of cant and humbug, Gandhi's long-standing compatriot J. B. Kripalani. 'A gaunt figure with an almost Mephistophelian expression', Kripalani was the most amusing person that Reynolds had met in India in 1930.

With his radical views and disdain for convention, it was natural that Reynolds would deploy his mordant wit towards a most noble end—political satire. Between 1940 and his death in 1958, Reynolds wrote a large number of verses for the *New Statesman*. Some of these were republished in a 1946 volume titled *Og and Other Ogres*. In the words of his biographer, Robert Huxter, in them one could see 'mutations of his comic spirit, for here can be found bitter satire, irony, gallows-humour, ribaldry, whimsy, drollery and fantasy'. The poet John Betjeman argued that Reynolds's satire was deadly but it had humanism at its heart. However, one is not sure that those at the receiving end saw Reynolds in such kindly light. As a sample, we will make do with the first stanza of 'Afterthoughts on the Election' that reflects an enduring, universal sentiment:

> A tattered poster on the wall,
> A paper man, stuck to the bricks
> (Whose bloated face serves to recall
> All that I loathe in politics)
> Is not so dead as those who sent
> Such cretins back to Parliament.

Earnest in his effort and certain of his convictions, Reynolds was quite critical of those he knew. But he had that rare virtue of not taking himself too seriously. Indeed, while his memoir is filled with all manner of humorous episodes, it would barely let you know of the significance of his work and the depths of his wisdom. When he applied to become the secretary of the No More War Movement, he was asked to state his qualifications. Reynolds had no formal degree in hand, so on the form he scrawled 'Mens sana in corpore sano' which translates as 'A healthy mind in a healthy body'. For a movement wracked with dissensions and desertion by many of its members, this was qualification enough. Reynolds got the job.

While satirical verse had its uses, Reynolds needed a larger canvas to indulge his appetite for drollery and the absurd. Thus was born in 1943 *Cleanliness and Godliness*, a book-length historical and literary disquisition on toilets. A Rabelaisian romp through the scatological habits of different cultures and ages, the book also had a serious ecological message that was impressed upon him in 1930 by a forest officer in India. Much more important than mere hygiene, Reynolds argued, 'dung is a link in the chain of life, the source of vegetable fertility, the means whereby we make payment to nature for that which we have from her'. *Cleanliness and Godliness* was a big success in America and the publisher urged Reynolds to write 'another preposterous book on an improbable subject, with the same light-hearted treatment of scholars and scholarship'. *Beards: Their Social Standing, Religious Involvements, Decorative Possibilities, and Value, Offence and Defence through the Ages* appeared in 1949, written, it must be noted, by Reynolds who was clean shaven all his life. This was followed up in 1952 by *Beds: With Many Noteworthy Instances of Lying on, under or about Them*.

By the war period, Reynolds had cemented a reputation of being an 'enfant terrible' who was beyond the pale. His finances were always strained and he suffered from poor health. But he could look back with pride and satisfaction for having lived by his convictions. Yet, for all his reputation as a political activist battling it out with the establishment, Reynolds had a niggling problem. He had never been arrested. It is true that in 1930 when he left Ahmedabad en route to Ceylon, while travelling on a train with satyagrahis, he was detained. However, much to his disappointment, he was immediately released. A decade later, while living in rural England, Reynolds was hauled up in court for riding a bicycle at night without a light. Having worked on so many political causes, and edited an anthology of jail experiences, he was not about to forgo such a singular opportunity. When he was asked to pay a tiny fine to be let off, Reynolds queried the perplexed jury as to what the alternative was. Thus, he went to prison for a week. He told the jailer that while it was probably easy for him to arrange for the fine, 'I don't want to. I want to spend a week here.'

During World War II, Reynolds registered as a conscientious objector and worked with an ambulance service. The experiences of the war and the suffering in the world—especially the bombing of Hiroshima—led to a reassessment of his convictions and a renewal of faith. As a result, 'having spent fifteen years in the wilderness of secular politics' Reynolds returned to his spiritual roots as a Quaker. Along with the ethical lessons of Gandhi's life, Reynolds found sustenance closer home in the writings of the eighteenth-century American Quaker and early abolitionist, John Woolman. In 1948, Reynolds signalled his return to the Quaker fold by producing an anthology titled *The Wisdom of John Woolman*.

Gandhi had told Reynolds that Sabarmati was his second home, but Reynolds could not return owing to a lack of financial means for the trip. In 1949, a year after the Mahatma was assassinated, he finally got the opportunity when he was invited to attend the World Pacifist Meeting that was originally intended to enable pacifists to engage with Gandhi in the aftermath of a catastrophic global war. Revisiting Sabarmati was a pilgrimage for Reynolds and he must have felt some satisfaction in having contributed his bit towards India's swaraj.

India was free but there were other injustices to fight. Both Mannin and Reynolds had been critical of Zionism and supported the Palestinian cause. Reynolds also took a special interest in the struggles in Africa. In 1953, he travelled for six months across that continent. This resulted in the book *Cairo to Cape Town: A Pilgrimage in Search of Hope*. In 1958, shortly after he finished the manuscript for a children's book, *The True Book about Mahatma Gandhi*, Reynolds travelled to Australia for a Quaker event. There, in Adelaide, he suffered a brain haemorrhage. On 16 December 1958,

Reginald Arthur Reynolds, friend of India, champion of peace and justice, passed away. He was fifty-three.

When he died, Reynolds had £200 and the goodwill and respect of countless people around the world as his assets. Despite stark differences, Reynolds was loyal to Gandhi in that he lived up to the truth of his convictions. He could have looked back on his life with a claim that few can make—he had all along tried to 'Live in Mankind'.

# SECTION III

# THE ENVIRONMENT

# 14

## GRASSLANDS LOST IN THE WOODS

### JANAKI LENIN

The battle for territory between grasses and trees waged for tens of thousands of years on the hills of the Western Ghats. As dry and cold climate swept in, grasslands flourished. When conditions swung towards damp and warmth, woodlands gained ground. Hiking up above 1,400 metres, the first humans saw an undulating sward from horizon to horizon with patches of stunted trees, called sholas, darkening the valleys. The same circumstances created two distinct habitats, groves and grasslands, the yin and yang of this landscape up in the sky. But foresters misunderstood this duality and gave the trees undue importance for more than a century, irreversibly transforming the ecology of these southern hills. This entrenched bias has infected even non-government organizations and civil society movements, threatening savannas, deserts, and grasslands across the country.

The open country and cool weather charmed British colonial explorers of the early nineteenth century. In this 'Scotland of the tropics', they could enjoy a respite from the blistering plains. Even as officials and businessmen made plans for settlements, the Forest Department puzzled over the treeless panoramas. Why were evergreen forests limited to sheltered valleys? Oddly, the grasslands didn't gradually transition to trees. Where the green turf ended, sholas rose as abruptly as if someone had trimmed the untidy edges. In the lowlands, logging and planting trees were the foresters' full-time occupation, and they viewed the dichotomy between sholas and grasslands with prejudice. They arrived at a conclusion that couldn't be more wrong: the indigenous inhabitants had clear-cut entire massifs, and using fire, had maintained the meadows for their livestock. This 'wasteland', as they denigrated it, had to be restored. They appropriated the lands and began to tree the high mountains. Although it wasn't apparent then, the shola forests had won a powerful ally in their aeons-old battle.

The planting enterprise took on urgency as the first settlements, Kodaikanal in the Palanis, and Ootacamund, or Ooty, in the Nilgiris, were established in the mid-nineteenth century. Settlers needed wood for cooking and heating. The gnarled trees in the valleys were the only source, and their damp timber didn't burn well. The administration passed legislation to protect these forests and penalized anyone who cut them without permission, set fire, or grazed livestock. These protection measures, it believed, safeguarded the water security not only of the outposts but also the plains below.

The colonial Forest Department planted acres of fast-growing Mexican pine and Australian acacias and eucalyptus. Although it tried to grow native trees, they didn't survive. Timber made the 'wastelands' productive, and the thirsty roots of these imports drained marshes and prevented pesky insects from breeding. In the wetter Nilgiris, commercial plantations of tea, coffee, and cinchona monopolized entire hillsides.

The colonial British administration embarked on a disastrous endeavour, but the forest department of independent India took it to ruinous heights. In 1948, imports of wattle bark extract from South Africa were banned, opening the market for a homegrown product. The leather factories used the substance to tan hides. The department went on a planting spree, setting down saplings of a dozen wattle species. Black wattle's (*Acacia mearnsii*) frost-resistance made it an ideal candidate for surviving in the open country.

Industries needed viscose to make rayon and wood pulp for paper and plywood. Although plantings of eucalyptus and pine continued apace, wattle was the favourite. As demand for timber increased, plantations replaced the greensward. The department didn't spare watersheds either. With every year, it raised more and more non-native trees on land that had grown nothing so tall for millennia.

Alongside these massive planting operations, in the 1970s, the agency auctioned vast tracts of grasslands in the Palanis under a scheme called kumari cultivation. Farmers who made winning bids planted potatoes. 'This was the biggest source of employment in Kodaikanal at that time,' says C. Jayakaran, who undertook such leases but later championed environmental causes. The department co-opted the potato-growers to further its goal. It distributed wattle, eucalyptus, and pine seedlings to the tenants who planted them with their tuber crop. When the lease ran out, timber trees had been established in many more acres. Such conversion to woodlots affected the Palani grasslands more than the Nilgiris or Anamalais.

Wattle found favour with residents who preferred its logs for the strong, even fire it produced. But the trees weren't free for the taking. If forestry guards caught anyone with a headload of harvested wood, they levied fines and confiscated the lot. Inhabitants surreptitiously turned to sholas instead.

Conservation awareness arrived with the 1980s. Self-taught botanists Robert Stewart and Tanya Balcar from Britain set up the Vattakanal Conservation Trust (VCT) in the Palani hills. At first they raised wattle saplings for distribution to farmers so they didn't cut logs from the Vattakanal shola, less than 10 kilometres from Kodaikanal. Later, they grew native species in a nursery and planted them inside plantations and along roadsides.

Another NGO, the Palni Hills Conservation Council (PHCC), petitioned the government to stop planting commercial timber trees on the grasslands of the Palanis, and to declare the Palani Hills National Park. Although Father K. M. Matthew, a renowned botanist at the Anglade Institute of Natural History, Shembaganur, and author of *The Flora of the Palni Hills, South India*, was the vice president of the organization since its founding year until his death in 2004, its focus remained on sholas.

The theory that indigenous people axed the forests and denuded the landscape held strong until scientists settled the controversy in the 1990s. Radiocarbon dating studies concluded grasslands existed 40,000 years ago, long before humans arrived on the scene. But the evidence had been stacking up since 1967 when pollen analysis of soil samples from the Nilgiris showed the antiquity of a treeless landscape. A combination of frost and topography kept the two distinct habitats from encroaching into each other's turf at these high altitudes. Ice-tolerant grasses couldn't thrive in shaded woodlands, and sheltered shola saplings didn't survive in the open expanse of grasslands.

Across India, trees have been romanticized since colonial times as the saviours of ecosystems, increasing rainfall, reducing soil erosion, and recharging streams. Public service messages exhorted everyone to grow them. Tree planters received awards and conservation organizations distributed saplings. Woods no doubt have their value but only as long as they don't replace other habitats. Those who viewed the world through the prism of trees described savannas and grasslands as wastelands. These landscapes may be devoid of forests, but they support wildlife such as wolves and bustards and the livelihoods of pastoral communities. Without considering the uniqueness of these habitats, the forest department planted trees, dug trenches for soil and water conservation, and the department of energy installed solar and wind farms.

This tree-centric view prevailed in the hilltops as most were not aware of the scientific evidence. The plight of the Nilgiri tahr, a wild mountain goat, the flagship species of the highlands, didn't change minds. A creature of the open grasslands, it had suffered from decades of hunting and a shrinking habitat. The idea of a recent and dramatic transformation of these hilltops remains entrenched even today. Except, the humans in question were not indigenous people but forestry officials.

Conservationists demanded the removal of plantations out of concern for sholas. The seeds of foreign-origin trees were rooted inside native forests, they said. The imported species had become naturalized. Institutions such as the Kerala Forest Research Institute agreed with these observations. This infiltration could eventually be fatal for the sholas, feared the activists.

Despite these protests, the cycle of planting and harvesting continued until 1996, when the Supreme Court ordered all tree felling to stop in the country unless mandated by the department's working plans. By then the viscose company had shuttered on charges of pollution, and imports of tannin extracts from South Africa had resumed. The leather industry preferred the superior and cheaper imported product to the locally produced one. Although the demand for wattle bark vanished, paper and plywood industries pressed for timber until the court order put an end to that. Since exploitation of the plantations was out of the question, planting operations stopped.

The department clear-felled non-native trees along roads for traffic visibility in the Nilgiris and Palanis. This removal was small in scale, but that didn't prevent the PHCC declaring in its annual report for 2004–05, 'This is a welcome move for biodiversity conservation in the wet temperate sholas of Kodaikanal.' It spoke too soon. Within months, the stumps sprouted and saplings clogged the gaps between the rows. Their thirsty roots drilled underground searching and draining water.

As tourists poured into the highlands, seeking a break from the plains during the hot summers, concern over water scarcity grew. Everyone accused the plantations of depleting the groundwater.

In 2006, the VCT, in collaboration with the department, began to restore the grasslands around Vattaparai Marsh on the edge of Kodaikanal. It's hard to pinpoint what caused the turnaround that focused the trust's energies on the neglected little plants of the open country. By then, Stewart and Balcar had befriended a group of pioneering restorers at the Gurukula Botanical Sanctuary in Wayanad, Kerala. For over two decades, the sanctuary's team rescued and propagated endangered plants such as ferns, orchids, and grasses from high altitudes. Perhaps this work influenced the couple from Vattakanal. Or maybe their careful observations of the plant world had led them independently to conclude that the open country needed more help. Whatever the cause, the grasslands of the Palanis had finally won champions.

The department cut wattle and VCT planted nursery-raised grassland plants. Weeding the successive waves of foreign species seedlings from this small patch was a back-breaking endeavour even for a dedicated group. The collaboration proved short-lived, and wattle saplings recolonized the area.

By then the water problem became a full-blown crisis. Perennial streams parched, and the water table receded in depth. In 2007, two reservoirs that supplied water to Kodaikanal dried up, despite receiving normal rains. The Berijam Marsh, about 20 kilometres southwest of Kodaikanal, was so dry, you could walk across without getting your feet wet, wrote Stewart and Balcar. These developments galvanized the clamour to remove the plantations.

But the couple advised caution. The towering timber trees dwarfing the diminutive native species gave the wrong impression. Despite the claims of conservationists, the alien species couldn't overwhelm the sholas since their sun-loving seeds cannot germinate under a canopy, whether it was forest or plantation. On the contrary, Stewart and Balcar said, native tree species were taking over plantations because they preferred the dull light and frost-free conditions. Their observations baffled the rest of the conservation community who had concentrated on the sholas for much of this time.

Although indigenous species flourishing under foreign trees seemed novel, it's a principle used in forest restoration elsewhere. Barren, degraded land can be hostile to fragile, shade-loving native saplings. Hardy pioneers, often from other countries, create humidity, improve fertility, and shield the soil, encouraging local trees to take root. Tree planters would have recognized the shola succession underway in plantations. The forest department had inadvertently created the conditions for the afforestation of the montane savanna.

Even rare and endangered plants made a bold appearance. A fern *Dryopteris wallichiana var madrasensis*, known to science only in 1989, popped up among wattles behind Pillar Rocks, a popular picnic spot in Kodaikanal. Stewart and Balcar also found six ground orchids growing in another plantation.

If the timber trees were axed as the conservationists demanded, seeds lying dormant in the soil would be only too eager to germinate. The evidence lay along the roadsides that had been logged by the foresters. Neither shola nor grassland species could gain a toehold with such tough competition. Denser stands of the same species would replace plantations.

It was better to leave the timber trees alone, Stewart and Tanya warned, and let nature take its course. The grasslands may not return, but at least a forest of native species would one day inherit the land from plantations.

Others who had argued against vast stands of timber trees were reluctant to accept this. Ian Lockwood, a photographer whose family had long roots in Kodaikanal, was one of them. He had grown up listening to his father's descriptions of extensive grasslands and was convinced the trees had to go until he saw the hybrid ecosystem for himself. The closer a plantation was to a shola, the better the infiltration by local species. The forests were expanding outward from their edges. He also recognized that every attempt at removing the woodlots had only made matters worse. Lockwood photographed a Malabar trogon, an unusual bird for these altitudes, in one such plantation-forest, showing how wildlife took advantage of this rich ecosystem.

Gaur, the world's largest wild cattle, browsed their way through the stands of timber trees. After suffering from a virulent epidemic of rinderpest in the 1950s and widespread hunting, the species rebounded. The animals sauntered through Kodaikanal town and market as if they owned the place. According to common perception, the plantations were squeezing the bovines out of their habitat. In reality, shola saplings emerging in the extensive woodlots provided rich fodder.

One pioneering indigenous species was *Actinodaphne malabarica*, found only in Blackburne shola, to the northeast of Kodaikanal, along the Palani range. Thousands of its saplings carpeted the plantation adjoining the forest. In 2014, Stewart and Balcar would count nearly a hundred native species growing here. This local invasion wasn't restricted to the Palanis alone. It was underway in the Nilgiris and Anamalais.

Their observations were backed by students from TERI University who catalogued the adventurous shola species and analysed the factors that encouraged their growth. Still, a hands-off policy for mature stands of alien species was a hard sell. Even this problem may resolve, Stewart and Balcar said. Mature wattle trees were dying en masse.

The species reached a maximum height of 4 to 5 metres in their native Australia, but the abundant monsoons and underground water in the Western Ghats made them shoot up to 15 metres. After emptying groundwater reserves, trunks of the distressed wattle cracked, allowing a native fungus to infect them. Most trees developed enormous blister-like swellings called cankers and death followed. In several plantations, wattle did not flower and seed. The stage was set for the shola conquest of lands that had at one time been grasslands. However, wattle trees weren't dying everywhere across the highlands. Felling them all the same would only encourage a virulent resurgence of their saplings.

In 2013, a long-standing proposal by PHCC to create a protected area in the Palanis, which had been moving its way through bureaucracy, received approval as Kodaikanal Wildlife Sanctuary. Logging any tree within the 600-square-kilometre reserve, even one ruinous to the well-being of the place, became illegal.

The following year, a lawyer filed a Public Interest Litigation before the Madurai bench of the Madras High Court, seeking the removal of the plantations in the Western Ghats. The arguments against the timber species played on nationalist sentiments: the foreign usurpers flourished at the expense of poor natives. In statements to the press, forestry officials, the architects of this mismanagement, decried the terrible impacts of the plantations on local ecology. The rumour mill whispered the court case had been instigated by the timber lobby.

In an interim order, the judges instructed the forest department to restore the sholas. Even the court went to the aid of forests and not the original grasslands. But the order put the department in an untenable situation. Not only was it to undertake a stupendous exercise for which it wasn't equipped, but it was being forced to act against the Supreme Court order banning the felling of trees. To obey the judges, the department would need to seek approvals from several agencies.

In the Palanis, the forest department felled timber trees along the roads leading out of Kodaikanal to the neighbouring areas of Berijam, Poombarai, Mannavanur, and Kukkal. It carted off the logs and set fire to the debris, singeing, and burning native species growing nearby. Machinery used to bring the trees down ploughed up the topsoil. In the carnage left behind, foresters planted shola saplings, sometimes in the dry season. The exercise was a disaster because the department made two basic mistakes: first, young forest plants cannot endure the sun; second, they need moisture to survive. Deprived of these essential conditions, the plants shrivelled from exposure and thirst.

Stewart and Balcar had spotted *Exacum anamallayanum*, a herb with pretty purple flowers, at a wattle plantation at Mathikettan on Berijam Road in 2012. Botanists had thought it had gone extinct. But their excitement died with the plant, a casualty of the department's clear-felling operation.

Worse, fire unleashed the dormant seeds of timber trees which burst forth under the open sky. Weeds such as eupatorium, lantana, and bramble grew in an impenetrable tangle that even a rat couldn't squeeze its way through, Stewart and Balcar commented caustically.

Kurinji (*Strobilanthes kunthiana*), the iconic plant of the grasslands, painted the landscape lavender once every twelve years. In 2018, tourists had to travel 40 kilometres from Kodaikanal to Akkaraikadu, near Poondi, to see the spectacular sight, says Baladhandayutham of the PHCC. Forty years ago, they saw the communal flowering around Berijam.

Despite continued concern by conservationists, judges, and the department, sholas were in better shape than they had feared. But, unnoticed native and foreign trees were wresting territory from grasslands.

The Forest Survey of India assesses the state of woodlands every two years. As its name reveals, it categorizes the country based on how wooded they are, even counting plantations as 'tree cover'. This emphasis on trees and forests meant no institution tracked the status of natural treeless landscapes.

A 2019 study investigated the status of grasslands across the Western Ghats for the first time. Over a forty-five-year period (1973–2017), the hills had lost 38 per cent of open country. This doesn't capture the full extent of the transformation that the plateau suffered for more than a century. Scientists could only look back as far as 1973, the first year satellite maps were available. The most degraded grasslands were the extensive high elevation massifs of the Nilgiris, Palanis, and Anamalais. In that time, hardly any shola disappeared.

While the future of the next generation of timber trees was dim within plantations, it was bright outside. The species marched outwards into the grasslands, expanding from the woodlot edges as forest vegetation ventured into plantations. Undeterred by frost and sunlight, the saplings thrived. Plantations weren't invading sholas; they were encroaching on grasslands. Since 2003, long after the department stopped planting, timber trees extended their territory, unaided by humans, into 60 square kilometres of grasslands in the Palanis and 44 square kilometres in the Nilgiris.

At one time, green turf covered 75 per cent of the upper reaches of the Palani massif. Now 66 per cent has disappeared, leaving only slivers of grasslands. Besides plantations, researchers tagged agriculture as a growing threat. The Palanis suffered most from these changes.

Under severe pressure, grasslands needed restoration, but that was easier said than done. If VCT's experience at Vattaparai was anything to go by, tending recovering grassland required years of sustained gardening. To replicate this over several thousand acres, some in remote areas, would be a Herculean endeavour. The history of the department's actions so far doesn't give confidence in its ability. A one-time felling operation followed by a half-hearted planting effort will make a bad situation worse. If it were to try restoring the plantations, it would have to jump in with both feet as VCT had done on a smaller scale at Vattaparai.

If the department cannot commit to decades of pulling weeds and saplings, it's better to cut the losses and instead focus on the remaining grasslands. The natural process of sholas replacing plantations is the least poor option. But the invading front of timber trees could be kept in check with their judicious felling along the periphery. At best some land can be reclaimed for the grasslands, but they lost the battle for territory a long time ago.

However, climate change has thrown a monkeywrench into the bargain and no winners may emerge. Godwin Bosco, who restores grasslands in the Nilgiris, reports that sholas are dying in the wetter parts of the high ghats, such as the Nilgiris and Anamalais. Even eucalyptus trees are distressed. Common grasses aren't flowering. This hasn't been confirmed by scientists, but many factors, including climate change, could be the culprits. These effects aren't apparent in the Palanis as it's on the rain shadow side of the Ghats.

If climate change is a danger, mitigating it is another. Since the 1980s, the country promoted one of the largest afforestation schemes in the world. In the past decade, government programmes such as Green India Mission and the draft National Forest Policy call for planting millions of trees to trap carbon. Many of them may be set in savannas, leading to the decimation of already ravaged habitats. Non-government organizations promote the greening of treeless ecosystems such as the deserts of Thar and Ladakh, and the terai grasslands.

The colonial misunderstanding of grasslands and savannas continues to transform entire landscapes and inform policies. When trees burn in wildfires, they release carbon back into the atmosphere. Grasses lock it underground. For this ability, they ought to be part of the climate mitigation package. But in the myopic view of policy makers and civil society leaders, trees seem to hold the key to carbon sequestration at the expense of other natural vegetation.

The one silver lining in this saga is that more people have begun to recognize grasslands as unique and as important as forests. The little plants need all the allies they can get to make the last stand for their survival.

---

Thanks (in alphabetical order) to G. Baladhandayutham (Bala), Godwin Vasanth Bosco, C. Jayakaran, Ian Lockwood, Jayashree Ratnam, Suprabha Seshan, Robert Stewart, Robin Vijayan, and Romulus Whitaker.

# 15

# ON BIRDSONG AND HUMAN WELL-BEING

## VIVEK MENON

## The Purpose of Birdsong

Birds sing not to charm the human ear, but to stay alive and to pass on their genes to their progeny. In order to do so, they use song to defend territories, to establish dominance hierarchies or to woo and court their mates. But we don't call all bird sounds as songs. A crow caws, a goose hisses, a parakeet screeches, and owls hoot—they don't sing. All birds produce sounds or calls using short, crisp notes and some of them sonate by ruffling feathers, booming vocal sacs and rattling bills. Bird language is complex and in some birds such as ravens and a bird familiar to the Western Ghats, the shama, they seem to communicate with each other by specific calls as if by 'name'. This challenges the Aristotelian assertion that only humans use language, which was refuted by Immanuel Kant saying that birdsong traditions appear to be the truest (language) in the world. Song, a more complex and lengthy series of notes that the human ear labels as melodious, is well developed in the smaller bird forms, especially the passerines. In India, most birdwatchers would accord the title of supreme songster to the shama, a long-tailed magpie-robin, that in the words of naturalist-writer M. Krishnan's words 'would begin to sing before sunrise, a welling, liquid flow of cascading delight and sudden, deep pools of sadness'. In the West, Shelley's skylark is a classic example of a passerine 'singing still dost soar, and soaring ever singest'. The fact that many birds sing by soaring into the air or sitting on top of high branches is postulated to be to achieve an elevation where their songs can carry to the maximum limits of the avian voice box or syrinx.

In most bird species, especially those that live in temperate zones, only the males sing, but in Australia and southern Africa, females of many birds sing as well. Even more interestingly, birds sing most during the dawn chorus, a period that lasts till forty minutes after daybreak. This is, of course, the quietest period of the day with regard to anthropogenic sounds and perhaps the stillness of the morning carries the birdsong further.

*A green-tailed sunbird celebrates dawn on the mountaintops of Arunachal Pradesh*

Another hypothesis states that the bird that is able to sing when its energy levels (after a whole night of fasting) is at its lowest can signal to a potential mate or rival that they are a truly healthy specimen who should be well noted!

One of the first modern studies on birdsong was by the British ethologist William Thorpe, who kept young chaffinches in isolation, away from adult males. All of them grew up singing odd notes. But the moment they heard older cocks sing, they began to sing like true blue chaffinches. It became clear that the birds learned how to sing in their first year by listening to other birds, overlaying the notes that they heard on a template embedded in their brains: nurture layering nature. And then they learnt more variation by practice and innovation.

There have been many other studies on the geographical variations of song. The cultural and genetic drift and sexual and natural selection were found to cause many of these variations. Vocal chords and beak sizes also played a part in the dialect that the bird used. Therefore, the chaffinches singing in St James Park in London sing almost entirely differently from the Himalayan chaffinches which use a Central Asian dialect! Which makes one wonder—does the migrant chaffinch miss its local mates when it sings in gardens across the seas, or do enough birds move alongside to let it speak its language unabashed and unbridled?

Yet another long-standing conundrum has been to understand how birds hear other birds when they sing. Field guides and ornithological literature try to anthropomorphize complex birdsongs either by translating them into English with unmelodious phrases like 'tzee-whitt, tzee-whitt, tzee, tzee' or by describing it using pitch, tempo, syllables, and notes. But there are more modern studies that analyse inter-note intervals, frequency sweeps, and glides of species-typical song that suggest that birds may be listening to other birds in much more precise detail than we do. The English naturalist and columnist Simon Barnes, while listening to the wren in his backyard for 8.5 seconds, slowed it down to 66 seconds through playback and found the transformation startling 'from the chrysalis of a dry and rather mechanical trill you find emerging, like a butterfly, a gloriously sweet melodic line. Analysis revealed that the wren sang 103 separate notes in the course of that eight-second song'. Now, do the birds that listen to other birdsongs have similar reactions to humans who listen to song?

A recent neurobiological study on song sparrows shows that females in a breeding state that were played a male sparrow's song responded like humans listening to their favourite music; this measured through changes registered in the mesolimbic reward pathway of the brain. However, males listening to other males sing showed an amygdala response—the way humans respond when listening to horror movie music! The researchers concluded that 'the neural response[1] to birdsong appears to depend on social context, which can be the case with humans as well'.... Both birdsong[2] and music elicit responses not only in brain regions associated directly with reward, but also in interconnected regions that are thought to regulate emotion. That suggests they both may activate evolutionarily ancient mechanisms that are necessary for reproduction and survival.

*A russet sparrow chirrups in the terai in Corbett National Park*

## Birdsong and the Human Ear

Even if not sung primarily for the human ear, birdsong has fascinated the early human across civilizations. In Japanese haiku poetry, the Japanese bush warbler is celebrated as uguisu whose call

---

[1] 'Neural response', *Medical Xpress*, available at <https://medicalxpress.com/tags/neural+ response/>.
[2] 'Birdsong', *Medical Xpress*, available at <https://medicalxpress.com/tags/birdsong/>.

heralds spring. The chataka in Sanskrit and Tamil refers perhaps to the Jacobin cuckoo whose call coincides with the onset of monsoon. The call of the hoopoe as he assembles the birds in the quest to find the mythical simurgh, resonates through Farid ud din Attar's twelfth-century epic poem, 'The Conference of the Birds'. The Polynesian demi-god Maui listening to the enchanting song of the 'I'iwi and concealing the bird and its song from humans is a Hawaiian fable that portrays birdsong as what makes their islands special. It is not only ancient man but also relatively modern human beings, especially those with a creative mind, who have profited from birdsong. Keats writing his 'Ode to the Skylark' or Emily Dickinson's 'Hope is a Thing with Feathers' are both testaments to a bird's impact on the poet. Vivaldi's 'Goldfinch' concert, Girolamo Frescobaldi's 'Capriccio sopra Cucho', Beethoven's second movement of the 'Pastoral Symphony No. 6' and Wagner's 'The Bird in the Woods' in his opera *Siegfried* celebrate the songs of the goldfinch, the cuckoo, the nightingale, and the quail respectively. Famously, the musician Olivier Messiaen attributed the inspiration for the founding of several musical instruments to birdsong. He celebrated the most complex of all songsters, the Australian lyrebird, which he said 'represented a source of "pure" music, undefiled by the modern world.' The celebration of birdsong is thus both ancient and universal in the human world.

## Human Ill-being in the Anthropocene

The modern world we live in, however, is not exactly what our ancestors inhabited. The Anthropocene is as yet an unrecognized era that we live in, but has been postulated sufficiently different geologically from the Holocene in physical, chemical, and biological process terms. A key, unique factor about the Anthropocene is the unimaginable planetary impact that one species has had over a million others in only the last few centuries of our existence. But the other difference is the huge effect our actions are having on our own species—one that is causing a sense of ill-being individually and in our society. Intolerance, pessimism, helplessness, hopelessness, sickness, and stress are at an all-time high. In 2007, it was estimated that depression cost the British economy £7.5 billion and anxiety cost £8.9 billion in health costs and lost workdays. The phenomenon of deaths due to overworking has engendered modern-day terms, such as Karoshi in Japan, Guolaosi in China, and Gwarosa in Korea, showing that ill-being is not just a Western occurrence.

In 2017, Kate Raworth published in the medical journal *Lancet*, a concept of a doughnut in the Anthropocene as humanity's compass in the twenty-first century.[3] In this work, she drew a doughnut with the outer boundaries as ecological ceilings and the inner circle as social ceilings. Whenever humanity exceeds the ecological ceiling the doughnut overshoots with dire red alerts related to climate change, freshwater withdrawals, land conversions, air and water pollutions, or biodiversity loss. Similarly, she postulated that when social parameters such as education, health, food, water, energy, networks, housing, social and gender equity, peace, and justice are not met, we end up in the red as a shortfall to our social well-being. According to her theory, 'Between these two sets of boundaries lies an ecologically safe and socially just space in which all of humanity has the chance to thrive' or 'in other words' would constitute human well-being. The doughnut seeks to 'highlight the dependence of human well-being on planetary health'. However, where it falls short is that her social parameters actually do not have nature or biodiversity as a measurable parameter that could 'help to focus attention on addressing such inequalities when both theorizing and pursuing human well-being'. This brings us to an essential question. Other than the fact that human existence is dependent on the well-being of the natural world around us, does the natural world influence human well-being?

---

[3]Kate Raworth, 'A Doughnut for the Anthropocene: humanity's compass in the 21st century', *Lancet*, May 2017.

## Birdsong and its Effect on Human Well-being

The science of birdsong has been well studied for at least half a century. The art of birdsong, on the other hand, has been far less studied. What does birdsong do to human minds?

A popular view is that evolution over millennia has hardwired the human mind to know the environment around us is safe when birds are singing. This is easy to understand for a layman but difficult to test or prove in science. What is it about birdsong that makes you feel a sense of well-being? Or what about the lack of birdsong makes you feel uneasy, with a deep, dark foreboding of doom? Walking through the silent forests of Southeast Asia, amidst towering rainforest trees, but with no sounds of mammals and birds, has been more traumatizing to many people than walking through a landscape devoid of all vegetation. Where there is nothing you do not expect anything, it seems; but where there are semblances of the natural world, we expect birdsong. Not having our hearing soothed by the lullabies of birds can bring about a sense of calamity.

In contrast, a recent study on the restorative effect of birdsong reported that 'in particular, listening to a single bird sound enabled many participants to imagine detailed and varied environments and to revisit familiar places in their mind's eye'. And most such feelings were found to be restorative in nature. Another rigorously tested theory of human ill-being and neighbourhood nature found that the 'metrics of nature that were most visible during the day and so most likely to be experienced by people, namely vegetation-cover and afternoon bird abundances, were positively associated with a lower population prevalence of depression, anxiety, and stress' among people with mild mental illnesses. This could, of course, be directly connected to our evolutionary past. As Julian Treasure put it, 'Our developed appreciation of birdsong may be there because listening to it is a significant physical manifestation of our connection with nature—a connection that modern living has severed for many millions of people.'

All birdsong does not, however, have restorative qualities. A key piece of research in the UK concluded that 'individuals generally perceive bird sounds to be restorative, but that these perceptions vary between different types of sounds in accordance with certain acoustic and aesthetic properties. Furthermore...bird sounds are associated with different types of meanings that may also relate to perceptions of their restorative potential.' For example, the hooting of owls had a negative valence for many of those included in the study. Another piece of research found that this could be associated with low fundamental frequencies and pitches of the owl, the raven, the gull, or the magpie unlike the high frequency and rising notes of a warbler, skylark, or nightingale. The negative feeling associated with certain kinds of birdsong is not restricted to empirical studies such as this one, as even in ancient Indian texts certain bird sounds, especially of the ulluka (owl), were considered to be the harbinger of nairrta or ill-fortune.

A final thought is that birdsong is not only a comforting pillow to rest an uneasy mind on but also one that brings you close to home. The effect of birdsong on alienation among migrant humans has sparked a recent study. What a fantastic thought. An Englishwoman born and bred on robin notes mourns when sent to geriatric isolation in Australia with her children, that 'the very devil now speaks to me every morning from the bush outside my window'. The reference to the devil had to do with the magpie whose sharp metallic submachine chatter is no doubt a call of great comfort for the Aussies, but a call of an alien for an Englishwoman. Our brains, it seems, store away the aural backgrounds of our lives and when we hear strange, unfamiliar sounds, we feel alienated. Clearly, in this personal aural mindscape of ours, birds play a major part. So an Indian immigrant to Birmingham misses the bulbul carousing in the mornings and Africans in America miss the noisy chorus of the superb starling that wakes up the great continent in cacophony. A participant in the study on the restorative effects of birdsong said that listening to a certain bird reminded her of home. She said, 'I think it's the wood pigeon. That kind of reminds me of summer and sort of long, hot summers and so when I hear that sometimes it takes you back and you feel, like, you know, so your childhood, nice, yeah.' For frequent travellers, birdsong works even better than melatonin to set the body clock right after a night on the red-eye.

*A familiar wake-up call is a male red jungle fowl announcing the break of day*

Economists and policymakers don't like connecting birdsong to human well-being. 'The problem is that focusing on lollipops and birdsong feeds the perception of well-being as a fluffy agenda that lies outside the economic sphere—or, even worse, an indulgence for the better-off, out of touch with people's lives in tough economic times', writes Christine Berry. And, indeed, human well-being cannot all be attributed to nature and birdsong. But, surely, like the lovelorn Shelley writing his 'Ode to a Skylark', we too can look up to the skies and sing:

*Teach me half the gladness*
*That thy brain must know,*
*Such harmonious madness*
*From my lips would flow*
*The world should listen then, as I am listening now.*

In that 'half-gladness' we might find a measure of well-being that we seek in the Anthropocene.

---

Photos courtesy Vivek Menon

16

# THE ENVIRONMENT
## A RENEGOTIATION WITH OURSELVES

SOPAN JOSHI

The first time I met Gopalkrishna Gandhi was in 1998. The President's Estate in New Delhi was hosting people and organizations working on environmental matters. K. R. Narayanan, the president at the time and a man of diverse learning, had a keen interest in the environment, having held the science and technology portfolio earlier in his political life. Such was his commitment to environmental efforts that he flew to a village in Rajasthan to honour its water management work, which it had accomplished with time-tested wisdom and in the face of great difficulty. Back in Delhi, a team of experts was handpicked to create rainwater harvesting systems on the sprawling President's Estate. Such social and environmental interventions had as much to do with President Narayanan as with his secretary, Gopalkrishna Gandhi, who always had time—and ideas—for environmental activists.

The 1990s was a decade of rude awakening in India. Environmental matters were coming to a head but there wasn't even the language to talk about them in public. For the most part, the terms of environmental discussions were too technical for ordinary people; it remains so today. In popular culture, environmental topics are discussed with two contrary sensibilities. One is burdened with the frightening imagery of environmental destruction; it tries to jolt people into comprehending imminent dangers. The other attempts to simplify and inspire people with feel-good slogans like 'save/regreen the planet', 'plant more trees' or 'reduce reuse recycle'. Call it carrot-and-stick-environmentalism, if you will. None of the three idioms does the job of explaining a complex matter to ordinary people. Why is that so? It's a difficult question with several possible answers. What can be said without any doubt is that the environment is a new subject requiring expertise; it lacks an ordinary vocabulary. Yet the roots of environmentalism in India do not lie in academic expertise.

The seeds of India's environmental movement lay in the 1970s in folk movements such as Chipko Andolan, which was about forest conservation in the Himalaya, and Mitti Bachao Andolan, a soil conservation campaign in the Narmada river valley, as also in the union government bringing in legislation to protect wildlife (1972) and forests (1980). The new environmental consciousness unleashed a wide range of researchers and activists; they began collaborating in the 1980s to put together the bigger environmental picture. The 1987 drought provided added urgency to the research; international research funding gave additional impetus, especially because India was viewed as the ideal laboratory for finding solutions to drought and famine in several African countries. The anti-dam movements of the 1980s had already shown that water management was, actually, land management. Large dams created large reservoirs that submerged forests and farms and villages, displacing large populations. In southern Bihar (now Jharkhand), the Scheduled Tribes—particularly the Munda villages in and around Khunti, south of Ranchi—agitated to create a popular movement against a dam project on the Koel and Karo rivers.

This new consciousness of the 1980s bore fruit in the 1990s. Its initial thrust was water. That something was drastically wrong with India's water management had become obvious. The value of traditional methods of rainwater harvesting appeared in high relief. A great variety of water systems were researched and written about; it became clear that they shared certain basic ideas but their varied designs were specific to local and regional conditions. It had become obvious that India had forgotten its traditional water management systems under the influence of modern hydrological engineering, introduced in the colonial era.

The reappraisal of traditional rainwater harvesting systems revealed that the planning of villages and cities had allocated land for water management; there was evidence of this even from some sites of the Indus Valley civilization. There were fundamental differences between the traditional and modern approaches to hydrology. For one, the old approach saw the monsoon as a great gift, its variability notwithstanding; it eagerly awaited the rainy season, celebrated the monsoon in its festivals and calendars, worked tirelessly to harvest the seasonal water bounty—in socially diffused and decentralized ways. The Sanskrit and Hindi word for the year, varsh, is a cognate of the word for rain, varsha. There was no doubt we are, whatever else, a people of the monsoon.

In contrast, the British colonial state adopted more centralized systems of water management. With the society lacking the means of managing these, the government took over the knowledge and ownership of modern water systems. Large capital investments came from the state, not to mention the recurring costs of maintenance. This new approach had a different view of the monsoon: it considered the monsoon a problem. Planning documents and newspaper articles began to speak of freeing ourselves of the 'vagaries of the monsoon', a mimetic phrase loaded with the acquisition of all agency by the state to unfetter us from the caprices of nature. Highly publicized government-sponsored programmes promised the creation of engineered hardware—dams and canals and pipes—to liberate us not merely from our environmental limitations but also the burden of decentralized folksy water management. Knowledge derived from the 'natural sciences' was now going to help subdue nature, all for the cause of human progress. Hard data and planning expertise was all set to free us from the tyranny of the customary. A new, enlightened dawn was looming.

The 1990s revealed this was a pipe dream. While the centralized approach did secure water supply for powerful people in big cities and for industry through the large-scale transfer of water over long distances, there was no way it was going to deliver for a great majority. Irrigation canals began to fail in the last mile of supply;

inefficiencies crept up like the sediment that silted up reservoirs; there were competing—and numerous—demands for limited water. All schemes to rehabilitate people displaced by the dam projects were falling woefully short. The development projects demanded large-scale human sacrifice, the horror of which was veiled with red tape. If the 1970s and 1980s were filled with the optimism of the Green Revolution in agriculture, the 1990s had revealed that its bounty came from the overexploitation of groundwater.

The monsoon had revealed itself indomitable. Chaturanan Mishra, cabinet minister in the late 1990s, used to say that the monsoon—and not he—was the real agriculture minister of India. But the people of the monsoon had lost respect for the greatest hydrological transfer from the southern hemisphere. A people who had planned to conserve every drop of rainwater without any formal hydrological training had now become consumers who demanded water supply as if it was their entitlement. When the supply did not arrive, they protested and even rioted. State governments became increasingly embroiled in bitter battles for water from rivers and canals, their disputes reaching the judiciary and requiring the creation of special tribunals.

Modern hydrology was preventing water from flowing according to gravity; it now flowed in the direction of political and financial power. Cities began to plunder their rivers and nearby water sources; when they proved inadequate, they drew—actually stole—water from ever increasing distances. Since cheap water was available from great distances, cities began to turn their own rivers and water bodies into the receptacles of water *after* it had been used. Sewage, in other words. Cities that earlier looked after their water bodies now began to pollute them. By 1986, the Ganga was polluted enough for the creation of the Ganga Action Plan. In about a decade, the ineffectiveness of this centralized programme had become apparent. As water bodies got polluted, domestic water purifying systems have become common in rich households; rich people have a low interest in cleaning up public water supply systems because they do not depend on them.

A scary image was emerging grain by grain on other environmental fronts also. By the 1990s, India became aware of the carcinogenic aftermath of synthetic pesticides. Toxic insecticides used to control pests in agriculture were now becoming ineffective as insects acquired resistance to them; friendly insects, however, were succumbing to the synthetic chemicals. Reports of suicides by distressed farmers had become common by the late 1990s. It wasn't just the consumer who was in danger from residues of poisons used on crops; farmers had begun ingesting the new-fangled pesticides that were failing to protect their crops. In order to profit from new technologies, farmers had begun to take risks with cash crops grown with large loans. Pest attacks were contributing to an increasing cost of cultivation, the biggest reason being the lack of irrigation; groundwater was getting milked, the plunder leading to plummeting water tables across the country. This race to the bottom demanded an ever-increasing investment in deeper and deeper bore wells. Recurring crop failure was multiplying farm indebtedness. Agriculture was turning into an unremunerative occupation for a large number of farmers. The farming sector was crying out for a great renewal. The government, however, was preoccupied with the structural readjustment of the economy beginning in the early 1990s.

Forest exploitation was approaching a tipping point. After witnessing the denuding of pristine forests in the Nilgiris in Kerala, a man called T. N. Godavarman wrote a postcard in protest against deforestation and sent it to the Supreme Court in 1995. The court took cognizance and passed an order that applied to all forests across the country. This snowballed into unprecedented forest litigation, dramatically questioning even the definition of a forest. In some cases, the case has prevented the felling of forests; it also flared up the colonial legacy of unsettled claims of forest-dwelling Scheduled Tribes. In several places, the forest department took the Supreme Court's interest to mean it could simply do away with the unsettled claims that emerged from grave injustices of the past, both during colonial rule and after the country's Independence.

The Supreme Court became the cynosure of a new kind of environmental activism in this period. A case filed in 1985 snowballed into dramatic legal drama as Delhi's air quality worsened in the 1990s. Disappointed by the government's lack of seriousness in tackling the national capital's air quality, the court created a statutory authority in 1998 to monitor all air-pollution-related matters on its behalf. This led to an unprecedented shift of the city's public transport from diesel to compressed natural gas, paving the way for the installation of an elaborate natural gas supply network. Yet the gains from these efforts are ebbing away in the absence of follow-up measures. The rich in our cities have begun to install air purifiers for indoor spaces to go with the water purifiers in their kitchens. It's as if the elite has abdicated from the common resources of air and water; behind gated communities, their land is also their own. It is hardly surprising that the environmental campaign is in the hands of popular protest movements or the courts.

The spurt in judicial activism has to do with the government's apathy towards environmental matters. It is not unusual for judges to pull up government agencies that are supposed to uphold the 'Right to Life' guaranteed in Article 21 of the Constitution of India. Several decisions of the courts were grounded in this, including the orders in the Delhi air pollution case; this unveiled a great potential in legal recourse on environmental matters. The government had been caught napping. Repeatedly—and on various fronts—the government was looking for a way to avoid enforcing environmental laws. It was a legacy issue. After Independence, the government had to manage a country ravaged and impoverished by two centuries of colonialism. The government chose to centralize its operations to deal with contingencies on several fronts. It took upon itself the task of industrializing the country. It incubated and established research facilities for modern science and technology, but they required time to deliver. For quick results, technological assistance had to come from the industrialized West.

Europe had been the cradle of the industrial revolution. Its industrial development had created unprecedented technological power that was deployed in epic proportions in the two world wars. Through human history, war has remained a powerful vehicle of technological transformation. The world wars had created an entirely new technological order. One example of this was the establishment of factories that could make—'fix'—nitrogen from the air through the Haber-Bosch process. Vaclav Smil, a scientist with an acclaimed body of work across several disciplines, has called this the single most important technological invention of the twentieth century. It has brought about a revolution in agriculture that has, in turn, triggered a population explosion. From 1.6 billion people at the beginning of the twentieth century, there are well over 7.5 billion humans today. Artificial nitrogen not only transformed the weaponry of war, it turned food production into the greatest weapon human beings have possessed.

The post-war boom established the new technological order, bringing a new prosperity. The US and the Soviet Union emerged as the two bastions of technological innovation, surpassing traditional European colonial powers. It is after attaining this prosperity that the countries of the 'North' confronted the environmental consequences of industrialization. The after-effects began to emerge in the 1960s, one of its greatest symbols being Rachel Carson's 1962 book, *Silent Spring*. The nuclear holocaust was now a clear danger, given the nature of the US–Soviet arms race. European powers that had expanded across the world to colonize distant continents were now facing a reality they did not consider before: the earth has a limited capacity for industrial growth.

This is when poor countries of the 'South' began to industrialize. Most of these countries had attained independence from European colonial powers after the world wars. Before a majority of the poor masses in these countries could benefit from the fruits of industrial progress, the environmental consequences of industrialization became clear. The North had already consumed the low-hanging fruits of industrialization. It could commit resources—technological and financial—to clean up the environmental fallout of industrialization. The South was going to have to divide its severely limited resources between efforts to industrialize *and* dealing with its negative outcome—simultaneously.

The newly independent Indian state's top priority was industrialization. It wasn't merely promoting modern industry in the private sector by awarding permits; the government was itself a 'player'. It promoted industrialization through public sector companies. Before a bulk of the country could industrialize, environmental degradation was becoming rampant. The state apparatus was required to regulate—if not curtail—industrial activity. Cutting down environmental pollution is not only very expensive, it requires large investments in technological innovation, which in turn depends on investments in scientific research. More than anything else, it requires the state apparatus to balance its priorities between industry and the environment. It is worth remembering here that 'Right to Life' does bear upon environmental conditions but does not have a direct relationship with industrial growth. But a clean and habitable environment does not comprise a political asset. Elections can be contested and won on the promise of greater employment and industrial progress; good environmental conditions do not win elections; not in India, not yet in any case.

Which is why environmentalism is sometimes viewed as a luxury, not just in India but across the global South. Sure, the rich countries can pay the price of cleaning up; but the needs of the poor are more basic, it is contended, they need industrialization. Such arguments are ill informed. The ordinary people of the global South depend on healthy environmental conditions for livelihood, not for luxury. A majority of poor people depend on occupations directly affected by environmental conditions like agriculture, forestry, and fishery; their production feeds several tertiary sectors. In the industrialized North, a very small percentage of the population depends on such sectors. Moreover, the South harbours far greater biodiversity than the North. Its major economic resources are directly linked to nature. The collection of non-timber forest produce, for example, gives several Scheduled Tribes of India steady income; moreover, this produce feeds several tertiary sectors that use, for example, bamboo and herbal extracts. Degradation of forests hits them directly. This majority lives in rural areas that are scattered. It struggles to make its voice heard in the cities where the leaders, policymakers, and regulators sit. The governing elite has little time for this majority; its priorities—and its imagination—are urban and industrial.

A state apparatus hardwired to promote industry lacks regulatory nous. A regulator must not shy away from punishing violators when need be, sometimes to set an example. It must have a strong carrot-and-stick approach to deter violations and promote compliance. Its job depends on maintaining a distance from those it regulates, much like an umpire or a referee is expected to be neutral in interpreting the laws of a game on the pitch. Across the world, a regulator's role is difficult and controversial because it walks a thin line. Not in India, though, because the match here is fixed in favour of industrialization. Most regulatory bodies in India are toothless. There is an elaborate legal framework for environmental regulations, the high point of which is the Environment (Protection) Act, 1986, and the all-powerful 'Right to Life' enshrined in our Constitution. The enforcement of all these laws and regulations lies in the hands of the executive, the government. The executive in India is committed to promoting industry and economic growth at all costs.

Consequently, public sector corporations have been among the largest polluters in India. The private sector has followed their cue. Factories using dangerous industrial chemicals and processes find it much cheaper to bribe the regulators than follow the norms for pollution control. Even the norms for setting up of industrial units are routinely flouted. Report after independent report has shown that the socio-environmental safeguards, such as 'Public Hearing' and 'Environmental Impact Assessment' required before setting up mining or industrial units, are actually not taken seriously.

There exists an elaborate bureaucratic mechanism to obtain these clearances without any real assessment; the game is rigged in favour of industry. Besides, the location of large industrial units is critical for their efficiency; proximity to mines of raw materials like coal and bauxite is important. India's mineral resources are situated below its richest natural forests; this is also where several forest-dwelling Scheduled Tribes live. The Constitution has protected these traditional societies with special status and protection.

India's Constitution blazed a new trail in recognizing the traditional customs and lifestyles of indigenous people. The Fifth and Sixth Schedules of our Constitution were created by reinterpreting the 'Partially Excluded Areas' and the 'Excluded Areas' under British colonial rule. The Constitution gave them a new kind of protection built around the principle that tribal societies had a special bond with their lands; hence special laws were devised to prevent their alienation from their lands. The history of independent India, though, is strewn with violations of the spirit of those provisions. The safeguards are routinely violated to favour industrial growth, especially for mining. The protection of Scheduled Areas has become an ideal that is iterated in policy statements and violated in action. In the meantime, countries like Canada and New Zealand have done a much better job in recent decades of recognizing indigenous societies and their customs; they have given them legal protection and made it mandatory to seek their participation in the political process on their terms.

This pattern of decay has been repeated in the environmental sphere. India commanded a position of stewardship in international environmental politics in the 1990s. The rise of environmental concerns across the world in the 1980s resulted in the 1992 Earth Summit in Rio de Janeiro, Brazil. The rich countries arrived in Rio ready to blame poor countries for environmental degradation; the then US President George Bush made it clear that he was not there to negotiate the 'American way of life'. This unjust proposition was contested by India, which emerged as the voice of the global South. Poor countries rallied behind India as it stood up to Europe and North America; India's intervention not only prevented the industrialized North from blaming the poor countries for climate change, it actually held industrialized countries accountable for using up most of the planet's ecological space for their industrial growth. 'Common but differentiated responsibility', a maxim that guides action against climate change, is a term that owes its existence to India's leadership at Rio 1992. It put the primary onus of corrective action upon those who were responsible for the problem in the first place, in accordance with the 'polluter pays' principle. International environmental treaties became an instrument for justice and equity.

Since then, India's role in negotiations to address climate change has petered out. Today, the industrialized North has managed to club India with China into the spotlight of climate-change culprits. Several reasons have contributed to this. There's no doubt that this is a strategic failure of Indian diplomacy. Successive governments have lost the strategic fight in favour of tactical convenience, failing to rally support among poor countries. This has turned the UN Framework Convention on Climate Change (FCCC) into a free-for-all circus.

The Rio Summit produced two other international accords of note, apart from the treaty on climate change: the Convention on Biodiversity (CBD) and the Convention to Combat Desertification (CCD). The earth's biodiversity is concentrated towards the warmer countries of the tropics and sub-tropics. This region, close to the equator, is also where most of the poor countries are situated. It is also where the world's largest hot deserts occur. Apart from addressing large planetary concerns, both these treaties were critical to the health of poor nations—economic, ecological, and environmental health. The rich countries, mostly located in the temperate regions, are not interested in these matters. These two treaties are often called 'Rio's stepchildren'. Because addressing climate change has large-scale economic ramifications for the North, UNFCCC has dominated international attention. As a leader of the South, it was up to India to press the importance of CBD and CCD. It has failed to do so. Even on climate change, it has failed to mount pressure on the US to hold it accountable for its historic emissions and its blatant refusal to act.

Most studies agree that India will be hit particularly badly by climate change; perhaps more so than any other country. Our hydrological regime is peculiar and entirely reliant on the monsoon. Most projections from climate models say climate change will introduce new variabilities in the monsoon regime. Extreme rainfall will increase—it already has—and the number of rainy days will decline. This will subject us to more intense floods and more devastating drought. Our modern hydrological systems aim for the control of water supply, relying on predictable water availability; this seems increasingly unlikely.

It's obvious that we will not be able to command and control nature. We will have to find ways to live with it, adapt to it. We will have to adjust our ambitions according to reality. If we do not do so now out of wisdom, we'll be forced to do it by unprecedented changes in the natural world. This is the time to remember that our traditional systems of managing land and water were designed to deal with variability and unpredictability. Their wisdom was not laid down in policy documents, engineering tomes, or in knowledge and facts. Because these systems were built and managed by ordinary people, they did not have access to such expensive pedagogical methods. They conveyed their values through stories, through songs, festivals, and rituals that even children could understand and practise. A famous evolutionary biologist once said humans are primates who tell stories.

One of the most popular and feted mythical stories dealing with this subject involves a seven-year old Krishna; it appears in the *Bhagavata Purana*. In this, the boy Krishna persuades his father to not conduct puja for Indra, the god of rain, but to worship the Govardhan Mountain, which is the real provider for the pastoral people of the region. Indra gets upset about getting upstaged and visits his vengeance upon them in the form of a week-long downpour. Krishna and the Govardhan Mountain rescue the residents. Indra is humiliated. Krishna proves that attending to the natural world and its culture is better than praying to capricious gods. The story is said to contain an early explanation of Karma Yoga. Some people have called Krishna a revolutionary, who upturned the power of an older, tyrannical Vedic god.

We have no way to tell whether the story is based on real events or not. What we do know for sure is that Krishna is the most popular deity, not just of the Braj region in which he was born, but also in the desert state of Rajasthan, which has the lowest rainfall in India, especially in its western half. Indra is baited in Rajasthani folklore, at times even insulted; the erratic nature of his rainfall is not lamented because people were prepared for the worst. The same region has created perhaps India's most sophisticated water management systems. Kings have worked for it, rich traders have worked for it, artisans, pastoralists, nomads…there wasn't a demographic that did not invest in water management. They did not complain about the vagaries of the monsoon or the rain god. They were ready to face the worst and prepared to do their best to harvest every drop.

Today, climate change is real. We face unpredictable environmental conditions. Scientists have been debating whether to call time on the unique climatic stability of the geological era, called the Holocene, and calling our age the Anthropocene, or the age of man. It's not a compliment to our species but a description of the wide-ranging impact, mostly deleterious, we have had on our biosphere. It's an age of disillusionment. Before we come to terms with it, we must find the language in which environmental matters are discussed without gloom-and-doom or feel-good slogans; in which we are not unsettled by the complexity of the natural world and can appreciate it for what it actually is; one that helps us relate to the outcome of the empirical method in a way that is comprehensible for the storytelling ape that is Homo sapiens. It's not enough to just use terminology that lets go of the old, tyrannical gods; tyrannical ideas of centralized engineering must also go. We need to look for fresh ways of engaging with the natural world. Without affectation, without the self-aggrandizing rhetoric of 'saving the planet'. We have to find a way to save ourselves from ourselves. That's the environmental challenge.

# 17

## A MESSAGE FROM VERSOVA

### ERIK SOLHEIM

In 2016, an unusual movement was born in Mumbai. Afroz Shah, a young lawyer practising at the Bombay High Court, had returned to his childhood district. One day he looked out of his window from the tenth floor in his modern, yet slightly rundown apartment building. He wanted to enjoy the beautiful Versova Beach. Afroz was filled with horror, revulsion, and anger. The once fantastic beach was gone. There were no youngsters playing cricket or soccer, no young couples going for a walk to enjoy the sunset, no one bathing or simply relaxing on the beach. Turtles were nowhere to be seen. The vibrant beach life had been replaced with plastic waste, turning Versova into a dead beach. Half a metre of hard-packed plastic had destroyed the incredible beach of Afroz's youth. Life was gone. Plastic was the king of Versova.

In that moment, Afroz made a decision: he could not live that way any longer. He and others like him would need to restore the glory of the beach. They had to bring back the playing children, the loving couples, the beach traders, the turtles.

I doubt Afroz thought of the Mahatma while clearing out the Versova Beach. But he acted in a truly Gandhian manner. His first reaction was not to fire off a letter to the chief minister of Maharashtra or a tweet to the prime minister condemning the state of the beach and demanding action. Nor did he assemble a picket line or write a piece in the Mumbai newspapers. He simply spoke to a neighbour and together they went down to the beach and started removing the plastic. Year after year, plastic washed up on the beach by the forces of nature and currents had forced the plastic deep down into the sand, making its removal extremely complicated.

No one on that day had any idea that a Gandhian movement had been born. Afroz just thought they had done their duty as citizens, as Indians, and as human beings growing up by and with the sea. But slowly everything changed. The neighbours saw what the pioneers did and came to offer their support. Soon they were in the tens, then in hundreds, then in thousands. When citizens engage with a cause, so do businesses and politics. Political leaders joined in and offered support as participants in the clean-up and as agents for the wider change needed. The prime minister heralded Afroz as a hero to people of India in his talk with the nation. Business executives rolled up their sleeves, joined the clean-up, and offered to bring in more heavy equipment which could dig up the plastic and make the clean-up more efficient. The actions of one had become the movement of many.

What started at Versova Beach in 2016 continues today. Over more than 200 consecutive weekends, the people of Mumbai cleaned up the Versova Beach, the other beaches, and then moved on to the horribly polluted Mithi River.

After a modest start, the movement gradually transformed from a local beach clean-up to a broader political movement. People cleaning the beaches soon understood that the work would continue indefinitely unless the pollution was curbed at its source. They started demanding extended producer responsibility for the companies producing the plastic waste. They held discussions on which plastic products can easily be banned like straws or cutlery. They were delighted when the prime minister declared a ban on single-use plastic on the 150th birth anniversary of Mahatma Gandhi to reduce plastic waste and avoid unnecessary products. What started as a practical clean-up project by a few turned into a political movement of thousands.

Similar movements started in different parts of the world. Working at the United Nations Environment Programme, I saw plastic waste moving fast to the top of the global environment agenda. Beach clean-ups became fashionable. An issue that had been at the fringe of the environment agenda became the primary agenda of prime ministers, presidents, and business executives all over the world. The European Union passed a directive banning several plastic products we can live well without. Led by Rwanda, one by one, governments in Africa prohibited plastic bags and many other products. In Kenya you were threatened with severe punishment if you produced or marketed plastic bags. TV channels like the BBC and Sky News ran programmes which focused on the beauty of the ocean and the threat to marine life posed by plastic waste. Millions of viewers watched reports on whales, turtles, and sea birds perishing after eating plastic, mistaking it for delicious sea food.

The global mass movement adopted a three-pronged programme. First, it advocated avoiding and banning of unnecessary plastic products. Then, it encouraged business innovation through the use of non-plastic products, which can degrade naturally in the environment, made from, for instance, potatoes or sugar cane. Finally, the movement put pressure on governments and businesses to move to a circular economy where used plastic serves as raw material for new products.

In three years' time plastic pollution has moved from a non-issue to a key global concern. The chances of it disappearing from our horizons before the issue is resolved are zero. The plastic menace is usually of local origin. Nearly all the plastic on Indian beaches is Indian. In China, it is Chinese and in the US, it is American. This means it is meaningful for any government to attack the problem to protect its own inhabitants and the beauty of its own land. Global treaties may be helpful, but they are not a precondition for action.

There are three components of nearly all societal change: a strong citizens' movement, visionary politicians leading the charge, and the forces of business innovating, making new and better products and taking solutions to scale. This was how we solved the problem of the hole in the ozone layer. This is how acid rain was removed from the atmosphere in America and Europe. Acid rain and the ozone hole were considered the prime environment issues a generation ago. Now the discussions are gone, because the issues are resolved. I am convinced if these forces are combined, we will solve the plastic issue too.

It all started in Mumbai even if activists moved in parallel in many corners of the world. And the movement had some prominent Gandhian aspects.

It started in the spirit of the Mahatma believing that changes in society are not only a matter of laws, the Constitution, and political decisions, but of societal change from below. Citizens need to change their behaviour for society to change.

The movement can be seen to be Gandhian in its integration of personal behaviour and political action. The activists started avoiding unnecessary plastics in their own life, thereby setting an example for the society at large and thus driving decisions at the top level of the governments of Maharashtra and at the center. Private life and society life are not separate. We need to be and to act the change we want to see. But we also need the change to be coded in laws only governments can bring about as also in business practice which will need action from the big chemical and consumer companies.

Unwittingly, the movement is Gandhian in yet another way that was important to the Mahatma himself. The movement has become an embodiment of Hindu–Muslim unity, of religious tolerance, and cooperation. Afroz, of course, is a Muslim but has been working closely with local politicians from the Hindu nationalist camp. A memorable moment was when Afroz and hundreds of dedicated theology students gathered at Aljamea-tus-Saifiyah in the old city of Surat. The Dawoodi Bohra community of Islam supported cleaning the Mithi River in Mumbai as well as the Tapti River in Surat. The wider clean-up and anti-plastic waste movement has benefited from strong support from a number of religious leaders and gurus.

I see the Versova Beach movement as a harbinger of something new: India's promise to lead the world on the issue of the environment. But then, it may not be a completely new idea. Mahatma Gandhi, of course, advocated a worldview of harmony between humans and nature and among humans. He spoke on the need for frugality and against a wasteful way of living. In many ways, Indira Gandhi was also a strong environmentalist as Jairam Ramesh has described in his 2017 book, *Indira Gandhi: A Life in Nature*. She was the founding mother of the United Nations Environment Programme in 1972, with the Swedish prime minister Olof Palme taking the role as the father. Indira at the time wanted to establish the United Nations Environment Programme's headquarters in Delhi, but lost out to Kenya, perhaps because the Americans wanted to retaliate after her successful and righteous intervention in the Bangladesh crisis.

Environment is established deep in the Indian soul. The indigenous Indian religions may put a higher premium on the environment than those originating in the Middle East. The Bible starts and ends with nature and protecting Mother Earth is a strong green thread in Islam. Hinduism adds another dimension of respect for our fellow-beings in nature with its emphasis on vegetarianism, with Gods that are part-human and part-animal like Ganesha and with the past and future of humans embodied in life forms other than human. Jainism takes this further, emphasizing that we have no right to destroy other living beings.

Indian history is also different from other major global cultures in important aspects that may help India lead on the issue of the environment. For instance, while China has always emphasized the state as the main vehicle for human happiness, India has put society and religion above state. India is home to an extremely dynamic and diverse civil society, without any comparison in the developing world, hardly anywhere.

Historically, Indians have lived in a circular economy. That's not different from other pre-modern societies where people had nothing to waste. My grandmother in Norway also hardly threw away any item. There was a use for everything. But practical experience with a no-waste economy is more recent in India and may, therefore, be more relevant for other developing countries.

As late as 2009, at the Climate Conference in Copenhagen, the overriding perspective of Western environmentalists was arrogant. Westerners wanted to teach India and China the importance of climate so they could understand what the West had already learned. Ideas and practice and teaching were a one-way street leading from the Western centres to the Indian and Chinese periphery. At the Bali climate talks in 2007, a backroom deal was struck without even involving India or China. It flopped spectacularly.

How much has the world changed in the past ten years? During the Trump years there was no American government leadership on environment issues. The global leadership passed on to Europe, China, and India. China is now moving as fast in the green direction as it did on poverty after the opening of its economy in 1978. By 2021, there is no person who is extremely poor in China. At the same time, China has moved to become the world leader in solar and wind energy, in high speed rail, electric buses and cars, and metro construction. China has halved its air pollution and is introducing new concepts to clean up rivers, green deserts, and protect nature.

The domestic Indian debate has also been completely turned on its head. For decades it tended to be a debate between poverty and protection of nature. The questions were normally framed on whether India should focus on development or on protecting the planet. Should India promote growth or conservation? Not surprisingly, except for a few hardcore environmentalists, the majority went for growth. When brilliant climate negotiators like Jairam Ramesh came back home from global climate talks, they were normally accused of selling out. Whatever climate measure they had agreed to in the United Nations was tantamount to a sell-out of Indian interests as a developing nation.

Thankfully, the debate is now being reframed. Nearly everyone understands that India is not engaging in climate protection for someone else. Instead, it is in the deepest interests of Indians to do so. India is indeed more vulnerable to global warming than the US or China.

Even more importantly, technology has provided India with a generous opportunity. For the first time in history, triple-win policies are available in most areas—policies which are good for the planet, for businesses and jobs, and for social welfare all at the same time. It's probably true that historically there was a choice to be made between environment and development. The historical process that started with the Industrial Revolution in England in the 1780s and spread to Europe, North America, and to Japan, Korea, and, finally, China was based on a total commitment to growth and very little concern for the environment. First, nations became rich and then they started worrying about the environment. They polluted first and then they cleaned up. After the fall of the prices of renewables, there is no such choice to be made any longer. Solar and wind are not only better for health and environment than coal, they are also cheaper. A new development paradigm is born. India can be the first nation taking this to scale.

India is now home to the first all-solar airport in the world—in Kochi, Kerala. The first all-solar rail station can be found in Assam. The Delhi Metro is expected to go solar from 2021, powered from Madhya Pradesh. Planned coal plants have been shelved. Globally, India has initiated the International Solar Alliance with France.

It is not just the movement against plastic usage started by Afroz Shah. Many ministers, business leaders, and activists all over the developing world will seek India's advice, best practices, and leadership. They are very comfortable with India taking the lead because Indian experiences are closer to theirs and more recent in time. The era of a dominant Western leadership is gone. Environment and environmental activists are part of India's soft power in the twenty-first century.

The success in the conservation of tigers is a happy story for the conservation movement. The tiger population is, of course, still minuscule compared to a hundred years ago. But the number of tigers is increasing, bringing them back from the brink of extinction. Nepal became the first country to double its tiger population. The highest number overall is in India owing to tireless conservation efforts. I saw this happening in the Nagpur area. Activists and authorities are connecting parks and establishing causeways for animals to pass railroads and roads. This conservation work can be an example for the developed and developing nations to learn from.

As we, in this festschrift, honour Gopal Gandhi, few proposals would be more worthy than promoting Indian leadership for a world more in harmony with nature. Whenever I met Gopalji it was hard not to think of his grandfather. They are similar in so many respects. This may be natural since Gopal is the son of Gandhi's favourite son, Devadas. Gopal simply radiates kindness. Bringing this kindness to the wider society means taking better care of all living beings, of humans, and of nature. I believe that we, in the twenty-first century, will see India leading the world towards a brighter and greener future.

# 18

## 'CAPITALISM' THROUGH AN ASIAN LENS

### AMITAV GHOSH

Mahatma Gandhi once said, famously, that Western civilization would be a good idea: he might as well have said the same about 'capitalism'. Viewed with an Eastern eye, capitalism as the 'invisible hand of the market' was never anything but a fiction, a ballroom mask for empires and imperialism.

It is strange to think that the fall of the Berlin Wall is still widely read as a vindication of 'capitalism'. The truth is that the world's experience over these last decades could more accurately be read as proof that untrammelled capitalism inevitably leads to imperial wars and the expansion of empires. If that was not the case, then surely the almost-uncontested reign of a single system would prove to be an epoch, if not of universal peace, then certainly one in which there would be a broad agreement on the means of ensuring peace?

Yet what we see is exactly the opposite. We find ourselves in a period of extraordinary instability and fear, faced with the prospect of an endless proliferation of thinly veiled colonial wars. In fact there is less agreement on the means of ensuring peace today than there was at the time of the founding of the United Nations in 1945.

Today, especially in the Anglo-American world, capitalism and empire are once again being packaged together, in a bundle that is scarcely distinguishable from the old 'civilizing mission'. Not having been around in the centuries when it was first marketed, I am only now beginning to appreciate the full extent of the package's appeal, especially among the ingenuous and the well-meaning.

In 2003, just before the war in Iraq, an eminent New York

editor, a man of wide experience and generally liberal views, summed up for me what he thought to be the difference between the United States of today and the empires of the past: unlike the great powers of old, the United States was not acting primarily in its own self-interest. My objection to this was that he was being unfair, not to the US, but rather to the empires of the past. For it is a fact that the ideals of empires are often noble: the problem lies with their methods, which are invariably such as to subvert their stated aims and ends. This is because the processes of conquest, occupation, and domination create realities that become alibis for the permanent deferral of their professed ideals. Thus did some Jacobins argue for the necessity of slavery in France's colonies; thus did the author of *On Liberty* preside over hundreds of millions of conquered Indians; thus does torture come to be reconciled to the promise of liberty. None of this is new. Let us recall that the slave trade in the eighteenth century—arguably the foundational commerce of speculative capitalism—was long justified on the grounds that it bestowed freedom on Africans by removing them from the tyrannies of their native continent.

The packaging of capital+empire is still beribboned with these processes of double-think. Thus the ideologues of 'globalization' often make the argument that the market economy will universalize the standards of living of today's developed economies; the promise, in other words, is that given free rein, capitalism will make the American dream available to the whole world. This is an interesting thought, so let's try to follow it through? Let us, for a moment, think of the details: for example, the two-car family. How many cars would this bestow upon India? Perhaps 400 million? What if we were to add another 400 million cars in China and perhaps another 300 million in other neighbouring countries? Let us extend the analogy and consider similar figures for household consumption of detergents, pesticides, and other chemicals. Let us ask then what would happen to the planet if India and China were to reproduce the Western patterns of consumption. Fortunately, we need spend no time scaring ourselves with this prospect for, as we all know at heart, it is not even a remote possibility. The truth is that the major powers would intervene forcibly to prevent such an outcome; they would have to, simply for reasons of collective survival.

It is plain then that the packaging of the American economy as a model for the world is a thinly disguised hoax: this isn't because the American life is not rewarding or enviable. It is because the world would asphyxiate. It doesn't take much to see this so we can be sure that the hucksters selling the package know that their version of capitalism+empire will result in a dual system: it may well be that the standards of living in India and China will improve substantially, but under the terms of this model, they can never be the same as those of the 'West'.

For the time being Asians are content to be grateful for the comparative rise in their living standards—a great improvement on the conditions that prevailed through the twentieth century. But there was a time, before the eighteenth century, when most of the world's trade and commerce originated in China, India, and Southeast Asia. What if this were to happen again, as it well might: would Asians still be willing to accept a system of perpetual inequality? However, it doesn't really matter whether they accept it or not, for either way the dual system will still be a model for permanent conflict. This is because the very gap will be an affront to the universalizing impulses of empire. Those who set out to stamp their image on the world will not be satisfied with an imperfect portrait; for them, the flaws in the depiction will be an invitation to rip up the old copy and start again. And since no copy will ever be as good as the original, the process will repeat itself again and again. Capitalism+empire is, in other words, a programme for permanent war—the prospect once beloved of Trotskyists, and now embraced afresh by the neo-conservatives who conceived of the 'Project for the New American Century'.

# SECTION IV

# POLITICS AND PUBLIC AFFAIRS

# 19

# THE ROOTS OF 'HYPER-NATIONALISM'

PRABHAT PATNAIK

The term 'nationalism' is often used as a homogeneous, undesirable category in much of the discussions in the West. But 'nationalism' is not a homogeneous category. The anti-imperialist nationalism that informed the struggles of the oppressed colonial peoples must be distinguished from the aggrandizing 'nationalism' of those who oppressed them: for instance, Gandhi's or Ho Chi Minh's nationalism must be distinguished from Churchill's.

The concept of 'nationalism' that developed in seventeenth-century Europe in the wake of the Westphalian peace treaties was of the aggrandizing variety: it was majoritarian (which located an enemy 'within'); it was imperialist (each European 'nation' vied with other European 'nations' for overseas territory); and it apotheosized the 'nation' by placing it above the people, meaning that the 'nation's' interest was not synonymous with a better life for the people. Rather, it demanded that the people should make sacrifices for the sake of the 'nation'. It was an era of what Marx had termed the 'primitive accumulation of capital'[1], which an emerging bourgeoisie in each European country was busy carrying out.[2]

The broad characteristics of this bourgeois nationalism remained unchanged over time, though the specific class configuration that

---

[1] See Karl Marx, *Capital*, Vol. 1, Part 8, Moscow: Progress Publishers, 1978.
[2] Even John Maynard Keynes, an avowed anti-Marxist, traced the beginnings of capitalism in Europe to the inflow of Spanish gold in the seventeenth century which Marx considered an instance of primitive accumulation of capital. See J. M. Keynes, *A Treatise on Money: The Applied Theory of Money* in *Collected Writings of John Maynard Keynes*, Vol. VI, London: Macmillan and Cambridge University Press, 1978.

sustained it kept changing. The finance capitals that developed in Europe at the end of the nineteenth century, and caused intense rivalry among European powers for imperial possessions (or for a 'repartitioning of the world' as Lenin had put it)[3], aggressively promoted the aggrandizing kind of 'nationalism'. In fact, Rudolf Hilferding would identify a 'glorification of the national idea' as the ideology of finance capital.[4] This intense inter-imperialist rivalry eventually culminated in the First World War which saw 'nationalism' as the rallying cry for the war effort—a phenomenon captured, among others, by Erich Maria Remarque in his classic novel, *All Quiet on the Western Front.*

The Bolshevik Revolution was the first major blow against this concept of 'nationalism', but the defeat of proletarian revolutions elsewhere in Europe, followed by the Great Depression and the subsequent massive unemployment, reinforced this 'nationalism' in the horrendous form of fascism. It is only with the defeat of fascism that this form of 'nationalism' retreated from Europe (of which the formation of the European Union was a symptom); though lately, signs of its recrudescence have erupted once again, causing deep concern among the European Left.

The nationalism that developed over much of the third world in the twentieth century, and that informed their anti-imperialist struggles, was altogether different. It was inclusive, drawing all segments of the people into the anti-imperialist struggle; indeed it had to be so, since in each country it faced a mighty imperial power. There was, therefore, no question of any particular religious or ethnic group being considered the 'enemy within', though the imperial powers made concerted efforts to promote ethnic and communal divisions among the people to weaken the struggle against them. Secondly, this nationalism was not itself imperialist, but rather built bridges with other oppressed people to fortify its

---

[3] V. I. Lenin, *Imperialism: The Highest Stage of Capitalism* in *Selected Works* (3 volumes), Vol. 1, Moscow: Progress Publishers, 1976.
[4] R. Hilferding, *Das Finanzkapital,* Vienna: Wiener Volksbuchhandlung, 1910.

struggle against its overwhelmingly powerful adversary. Finally, it envisioned 'national interest' as synonymous with the interest of the people, with an improvement in their condition of life; the question of people making only sacrifices for a metaphysical entity called the 'nation' standing above them did not arise. The purpose of the nation, to borrow Gandhi's words in the Indian context, was to 'wipe away the tears from the eyes of every Indian'.

The question may be raised: if the class roots of the 'nationalism' that came to the fore in Europe lay, in the late nineteenth and early twentieth centuries at any rate, in the ascendancy of finance capital, or monopoly capital as some would put it, then why didn't monopoly capital in countries like India, where it had developed considerably even before Independence, promote a similar aggrandizing nationalism? Why did it go along with a different concept of nationalism?

The answer is twofold: first, even monopoly capital in pre-independence India was constrained by the colonial regime and suffered from not having access to state power, unlike its counterparts in Europe; hence, it had to join the anti-colonial struggle. Second, the anti-colonial struggle was a multi-class struggle, over which the monopoly bourgeoisie, even when it was in a leading position, did not have exclusive control. Even if it had wished to exercise control and to use such control to promote an aggrandizing nationalism, it could not have done so.

Building a 'nation' in the newly independent countries, in keeping with the vision projected during the anti-imperialist struggles, was a novel and arduous task, the like of which had never been attempted before. (In this task, as it turned out, much of the third world failed eventually.) In India, the first-ever articulation of this vision was in the Karachi Congress Resolution in 1931, which painted a picture of what an independent India would look like.

Though capitalism itself, given its immanent tendency to generate wealth at one pole and poverty at another, was recognized as being subversive of the project of realizing this vision, it was felt by the nation's leadership at Independence that if capitalism was controlled and made to fit into a wider framework of a mixed economy, with the public sector occupying the 'commanding heights', then it could still serve a useful purpose.

Accordingly, a unique regime, which blended public and private sectors, was developed after Independence in the realm of the economy, while in the realm of the polity, a government formed through universal adult franchise was to wield executive powers within a constitutional framework that guaranteed everyone a set of fundamental rights (the way the Karachi Congress Resolution had envisaged).

What is important for our present discussion is that notwithstanding obvious failures on the economic front, and many questionable actions of the state that often violated the premises of our anti-imperialist nationalism, the nation did not for a very long time repudiate the basic ideological framework of our nationhood, defined by this inclusive, non-imperialist, and people-centric nationalism, which was totally different from its European counterpart. The official commitment to this nationalism, whose concrete expression was a secular, democratic, and egalitarian order, remained unimpaired.

All this, however, has changed now. The 'nationalism' that is being promoted currently is akin to the aggrandizing European variety. It emphasizes the presence of an 'enemy within' comprising the Muslims, and the intelligentsia that remains committed to the inclusive, people-centric, and non-hegemonic 'nationalism'. It places a metaphysical notion of a 'nation' above the people, with 'national interest' having little to do with an improvement in the material condition of people's lives. And it believes in exercising hegemony, if not over the outside world as yet (that would be difficult in today's setting), then at least over the regions of the country itself whose autonomy it believes in undermining in a manner suggestive of internal colonialism.[5] It is instructive that Articles 370 and

---

[5] P. Chatterjee, 'Kashmir is the Test-Bed for Internal Colonialism', *The Wire,* 28 August 2019.

371 of the Constitution, which had been incorporated precisely to accommodate different regions with their specificities within the Indian union by providing a certain flexibility to our federal structure, are being summarily and unilaterally repudiated through a mere resolution of the parliament passed by a simple majority.

The question arises: how did we move from one notion of 'nationalism' to another that essentially is its very opposite. What was the process of this movement and its class basis?

## II

The first step in this shift was the introduction of economic 'liberalization' in the country, in particular after 1991. The shift to a neoliberal regime did not just mean a change in economic policies. It brought about a change in the class configuration in the country. It hitched the country to a global scenario which had been marked by the hegemony of international finance capital.

Starting from the 1970s, the globalization of capital flows, including, above all, of financial flows, had led to a situation where the world, instead of being divided into separate spheres, each dominated by a particular country's finance capital, had now become open for the more or less unrestricted movement of a new entity, an international finance capital whose country of origin hardly mattered. Since the state remained a nation state, the openness of any country to cross-border capital flows, including financial flows, meant that the state had to act willy-nilly according to the demands of this globalized or international finance capital, for fear that not doing so would frighten finance into leaving the country en masse causing a financial crisis. Retaining the confidence of globalized finance became the overriding concern of the nation state. And this finance was not just what originated abroad; it also included domestic capital which was now integrated with globalized finance.

This meant that the state, which had earlier claimed to be standing above all classes associated with the anti-imperialist struggle and protecting the interests of each—a claim not altogether without justification despite the fact of capitalist development—now worked almost exclusively in the interests of international capital and the domestic big bourgeoisie that was integrated with it (together with the rich landed interests who managed to retain their position in the countryside by *diversifying out of agriculture*).

There now developed, therefore, a hiatus: the big capitalists, integrated with international finance capital and themselves going global (together with the rich landed interests) stood on one side of the divide, the millions of peasants, petty producers, workers, and agricultural labourers stood on the other side of the divide. Not that such a divide did not exist before, but it changed in crucial ways; first of all, it got greatly accentuated; secondly, there was a fundamental shift in the nation state's attitude towards foreign capital; thirdly, the formulation of state policy did not even pretend now that it protected the interests of all classes. (Prime Minister Narendra Modi's recent remark that the capitalists are the 'wealth creators' of the nation, a remark that no earlier prime minister of India would have dreamt of making, is symptomatic of this change.) And, fourthly, and most importantly, there was a palpable withdrawal of state support and state protection from the petty production sector leaving that sector increasingly vulnerable to encroachment by the corporate sector. Thus there was, in effect, a fracturing of the old 'nation'.

The economic consequences of this 'fracturing' are obvious: peasant suicides (over 3 lakh in the last two and a half decades); acute distress in the countryside; a crisis of the petty production sector afflicting artisans, craftsmen, fishermen, traditional household industry, and even small capitalists; an exodus from the country to the city where the rate of job creation under the neoliberal regime has declined drastically compared even to the earlier period of dirigiste development, despite a much higher growth rate in the Gross Domestic Product in the neoliberal period; and so on. At the same time, however, professional middle classes have done well because of the outsourcing of a range of service sector activities from the advanced capitalist countries to our shores.

This new dispensation has brought poverty to large masses of people: the percentage of rural population not able to access 2,200 calories per person per day, the earlier official benchmark of rural poverty, has increased from 58 to 68 between 1993–94 and 2011–12; the percentage of the urban population not able to access 2,100 calories per person per day, the similar benchmark for urban poverty, has increased from 57 to 65 over the same period.[6] Simultaneously, the share of the top 1 per cent of the population in total income has climbed up to 22 per cent in 2013–14, the highest since 1922 when income tax data from which these calculations are made first became available;[7] their share in total wealth, according to Credit Suisse, was 58 per cent at the end of 2016. But while greatly concentrating wealth and income in the hands of the top 1 per cent, the neoliberal regime has also improved the conditions of a segment of the urban middle class.

This new dispensation requires an ideological prop to sustain itself. The old ideological prop of an inclusive 'nationalism' cannot obviously work any longer because of the fracturing of the old class alliance that had constituted its class basis. In the beginning, there were references to the prospects of a 'trickle down' of the benefits of growth to all classes. When this lost credibility, the idea was presented that a rise in GDP created the *potential* for the state to effect a redistribution of incomes in favour of the deprived sections *at a future date*, so that no bars should be placed in the way of raising GDP. And since in a neoliberal economy it is the capitalists whose investment played a crucial role in ushering in GDP growth, the state had to promote their interests, even at the expense of the interests of other sections, such as workers and peasants, for the sake of higher growth that was in the interests of *all* in the long-run. This GDP-fetishism played an interim role as

---

[6] These figures are taken from Utsa Patnaik, 'Exploring the Poverty Question: Inequality and Poverty in India 1973–74 to 2011–12' (unpublished report).
[7] T. Piketty and L. Chancel, 'Indian Income Inequality 1922-2014: From British Raj to Billionaire Raj?', CEPR Discussion Paper No DP 12409.

an ideological prop for the neoliberal regime, as the old concept of the 'nation' got fractured under this regime.

But this could not be sustained for long. In any case, if GDP growth continued for some time without any *actual* redistribution taking place in favour of the working people, the myth of its potential benefit for all would have got exploded. Besides, the economic crisis increasingly engulfing the world economy under neoliberal capitalism and spreading to countries like India, put even greater burdens on the working people. A stronger ideological prop was required in the new situation to prevent the working people from demanding a shift away from the regime of neoliberal capitalism. This is where the adoption of an aggrandizing nationalism became useful.

The Hindutva forces, long-time votaries of an aggrandizing 'Hindu nationalism', had kept themselves away scrupulously from the anti-imperialist struggle, some of their members having even hatched the conspiracy that led to the assassination of Mahatma Gandhi (a feat which some of their current-day acolytes celebrate unashamedly). The corporate-financial oligarchy now formed an alliance with the Hindutva forces to propagate this brand of aggrandizing 'nationalism'.

The class support behind the 'hyper-nationalism' of today therefore comes from the corporate-financial oligarchy, the rich landed interests who in any case were always opposed to the idea of Dalits and 'other backward classes' getting socially and economically empowered in post-independence India, and the upper segment of professional middle classes who have done well out of the neoliberal regime and are afraid of any move away from it.

What this 'hyper-nationalism' does is to give maximum priority to establishing the country's status as a superpower and to link GDP growth to it. The case for GDP growth in other words is no longer argued on the grounds of its being *potentially welfare-augmenting for all*; it is argued on the grounds that it would enable India to emerge as a superpower. If the GDP growth slackens, as it is doing, then that becomes an even more pressing reason to demand sacrifices from the people: to push through 'labour law reform' (a euphemism for unrestricted freedom on the part of capitalists to 'hire and fire' workers), and to demand ease of land acquisition for various projects (almost all of which including industrial ones have a real estate component). If defence expenditure is threatened due to slackening revenue collections then it is sought to be kept up at the expense of transfers to states from the centre (a proposal now made to the 15th Finance Commission).

The curtailment of civil liberties is also sought to be justified by invoking this 'hyper-nationalism'. Since any criticism of the civil rights situation, say in Jammu and Kashmir, can be made use of by the country's 'enemies', such criticism must be suppressed. Since the United Nations would be able to 'interfere' if there is open domestic discussion of the repression in Jammu and Kashmir, such discussion must not be allowed. In other words, criticism of any authoritarian measure, no matter how ruthless, becomes an anti-national act; likewise, any resistance to the so-called 'wealth-creators' (the capitalists), becomes a hurdle in the process of growth and hence in the process of the country's emergence as a super-power; it needs, accordingly, to be curbed in the 'national interest'.

The interests of the Hindutva elements, who are eager to establish a Hindu Rashtra, which is necessarily authoritarian and represents a counter-revolution against India's long march to modernity, democracy, and egalitarianism, and those of the corporate-financial oligarchy, which also wants a suppression of the working people, thus come together. 'Hyper-nationalism' provides the means for cementing the corporate-Hindutva alliance and giving it ideological ammunition for ushering in an authoritarian order.

It is because of this corporate-Hindutva alliance that the BJP has been by far the biggest beneficiary of the Electoral Bonds Scheme. The fact that it managed to spend, according to the Centre for Media Studies, ₹27,000 crores in the 2019 general elections can only be explained in terms of such an alliance, which poured copious amounts of corporate money into the BJP's coffers. Little wonder then that the stock market witnessed a huge upsurge when it became clear that the NDA government would come back to power at the centre for a second term.

### III

The 'hyper-nationalism' being pushed today is different from, and the very opposite of, the anti-imperialist nationalism that underlay India's emergence to nationhood, though it seeks to cash in on the popularity of the latter. 'Hyper-nationalism' seeks domination; its tendencies are authoritarian; and its predilections are against the basic structure of the Constitution, which upholds democracy, secularism, socialism, and federalism. 'Hyper-nationalism' is an instrument for centralizing power, for whittling down the rights of states (of which the bifurcation of the state of Jammu and Kashmir and the conversion of each part into a union territory without consulting the people of the state is a classic example). It is also a means of subverting the secular nature of our polity (an obvious example of which is the Citizenship Amendment Bill, 2019, that explicitly discriminates against the Muslims).

The retreat from anti-imperialist nationalism to Hindutva 'nationalism' has been seen by many as inherent within the religious symbolisms often used during the anti-imperialist struggle. Perry Anderson, for instance, sees the emergence of Hindutva as having descended directly from the anti-imperialist nationalism as practised by the Congress Party.[8]

This, in my view, is erroneous. The emergence of Hindutva 'hyper-nationalism' is not a continuation or a descent from the anti-imperialist nationalism of the Congress party; it represents the ideological *accoutrement* of a neoliberal capitalist regime in a period of decline of neoliberalism. Transcending it accordingly requires a return to the basic tenets of anti-imperialist nationalism; but this return cannot simply be a going back, it must entail carrying *forward* the agenda of the Karachi Congress Resolution,

---

[8] P. Anderson, *The Indian Ideology*, New Delhi: Three Essays Collective, 2012.

by incorporating into it new features, such as a set of fundamental, justiciable, and universal social and economic rights. To resume India's social revolution, the Karachi agenda has to be carried forward.

# 20

## WITH BORROWED EYES
## A VIEW OF INDIA'S FUTURE

### RAJMOHAN GANDHI

What will India's future be like? Disinclined to trust astrologers and incurious about astrology, I will not try to imagine, in any clear shape, the probable future of our land and people. Of course, I have my hopes, fears, and prayers. But I won't try to awaken my predicting self. That is best left asleep.

Nor will I walk up a slope to an edge from where I might see what India *should* be like. There are times for everyone to sketch the India of their dreams, but I am not sure this is one of those moments for me. Fantasizing holds no appeal for me just now.

But I will ask myself what I would want to do in the future, and for India's future, were I a young man today. After all, born ten years after me, Gopu to me is and always will be very young. He may be one of contemporary India's ablest individuals, a public figure who is creative and scholarly from his private space, but to me he remains childlike. In his honour, I turn myself into a twenty-one-year-old.

I don't want to return to 1956. I want to be useful for India's future from today, that is, from 2019. Though only twenty-one, I am aware of what an eighty-four-year-old knows; my life experiences are part of who I am. This may seem a form of cheating. Still, pretending to be twenty-one years old is easier than banishing everything I've absorbed.

◆

Knowing what I do, I would, for a start, *mourn* the India we have lost: the India where the weak, the helpless, and the outnumbered asked for justice without being shouted down by the strong, the armed, and the voice of the majority.

Not that the victim always obtained justice or protection in the India we have lost; she was lucky when she got it. But at least the leaders of society and the state were on her side. In May 2019, drumbeats announced the departure of the old India, which had already started to slip away since 2014.

Many young and old compatriots of mine celebrate this loss. To them, India's 'Hindu majority', to which they assume they belong, feels 'on top' today as it has not done for centuries, not since the late 1190s, when the Sultanate began to rule in Delhi.

How they know how people felt over the centuries, who exactly felt 'on top' before the 1190s, how those 'on top' were different from those below, and whether the 'Hindu majority' is indeed a clear and homogeneous category, are all questions for another time. But I don't begrudge their celebration.

Say the celebrators: 'The Sultans, the Mughals, the British, the Congress—none of them permitted the Hindus to come into their own. After nearly 800 years, festivals are in order. But we will be generous.

'As long as the others do what we tell them, shout the slogans we want, eat what we prescribe, wear the clothes we permit—in other words, if culturally they become Hindus, which they must, for Indian equals Hindu and vice versa, their lives will be safe. We won't kill or torture them the way their forebears killed and tortured our forebears centuries ago.'

Putting aside the questionable logic, ethics, or history in all this, I will recognize the achievement and acknowledge what lies behind it. Part of the credit goes to the sweat, patience, resolve, and resilience of the leaders and workers of the RSS and its parivaar for almost a hundred years.

Perhaps the accomplishment is not very different from the feats of Muslim organizations in Turkey, Iran, Pakistan, Afghanistan, and elsewhere, or of their Jewish counterparts in Israel—all countries where committed outfits have captured the state, or large swathes of it, by systematically drilling a mix of nationalism, militarism, and religion into their politics and societies.

Not essentially different, either, from the feats of political organizations in countries like Russia, China, Hungary, and Poland that have captured or consolidated state power using the same methods.

Nonetheless, as a twenty-one-year-old Indian, I recognize the triumph of the three-pillared majoritarian project in my land. Knowing what I do, I am troubled as well.

For the project's nationalist pillar seems to rest not on an Indian's warmth for fellow-Indians, but on his/her dislike for certain Indians and dislike for a flawed neighbour. Its religious pillar fosters not compassion but contempt. In its zeal to wave the flag, the military pillar forgets the vulnerable who need its shade.

These pillars leave me cold. I would aim to join or enlist every young compatriot, including any RSS worker or sympathizer, in a bid to make India a land where nationalism means love for the nation's poor, disabled, and deprived, but not frenzied dislike for a neighouring nation. A land in which a religious or altruistic spirit turns its people—be they Hindus, Muslims, Christians, Sikhs, Buddhists, rationalists, or atheists—into listening, caring, and understanding citizens. And where a martial or fighting spirit springs forward to protect the threatened and the oppressed.

Two politically promising projects were launched in India in the last four or five decades. One sought to unite all Hindus against the 'dangerous' and 'un-Indian' Muslims and Christians and their alleged foreign supporters. The other offered to unite all the nation's under-privileged (counted as the great majority) against Hinduism's 'oppressive' high-castes (reckoned a small minority).

The former project has clearly triumphed over the latter. Its promoters are entitled to kudos.

◆

But it is time now, in 2019, for India to begin to witness, and offer to the world, a greater project, uniting people of all faiths or no faith against every form of suffering. I would give my life for such a project, or for a tiny part of it in one corner of our land.

Can gigantic fireworks of celebration hide India's tragic record in dignity and care for our disabled, who make up a vast number? Pointing out that 'of the 70 million persons with disabilities in India, only about 100,000 have succeeded in obtaining employment in industry,' a UN document adds: 'A small 2004 survey in Orissa, India, found that virtually all of the women and girls with disabilities were beaten at home, 25 per cent of women with intellectual disabilities had been raped, and 6 per cent of women with disabilities had been forcibly sterilized.'[1]

In 1947, we won a full political independence. More than seven decades later, I would join any effort to ensure that our disabled gain a modicum of dignity. As also any bid to confront the cruel reality in most of our 'institutions' and 'homes' for the disabled, and in our 'corrective' jails and prisons.

I would also support any sincere effort to restore life to opposition politics. Thus, notwithstanding the downs in bids by persons like Mayawati, Akhilesh Yadav, and Tejashwi Yadav for Dalit–OBC–Muslim unity, I had welcomed the not-very successful attempt by Prakash Ambedkar and Asaduddin Owaisi to unite Dalits, OBCs, and Muslims in Maharashtra. Yet I would ask persons like them: why not partner also with Marathas? And with Brahmins?

Why exclude anyone?

As for the Congress, I would endorse my brother Gopal's practical suggestion: let its parliamentary wing fight in legislatures, national or state, and let an ideological wing of the Congress instil ideas of liberty, equality, and fraternity into Indian society.

◆

---

[1] "Factsheet on Persons with Disabilities', United Nations available at <https://www.un.org/development/desa/disabilities/resources/factsheet-on-persons-with-disabilities.html>

India belongs to all who reside in it. This was the precious idea the INC brought to our people. That idea will *never* lose relevance, even though many have a hard time accepting it.

To Rahul Gandhi, I would say, you have played a gallant part, in the teeth of slander and persecution, in preserving that idea. Now identify, train, and empower a dozen men and women to champion that idea across the land, and help them to remain united as they go about it.

Can a Congress team underlining the liberty, equality, and fraternity of all Indians stay united in that task, in fair or foul weather, in office or out of office, for a decent number of years? If Rahul and others in the party can create that miracle, the Congress has a great future.

If I were a twenty-one-year-old in West Bengal, I would firmly back Mamata Banerjee's fighting spirit, and also ask her to identify a dozen or more young women and men who would take care of her party in the years to come.

Didi, I would say to her, if I got a chance, I want history to remember you not only as the fearless and artistic woman who stood up like a tigress, first, to powerful Left parties, and then to the mighty BJP, but also as the builder of a democratic party that allows capable and committed persons to gain influence.

This twenty-one-year-old may also say something above his grade to the Left: even a big defeat may be a stepping stone for future success, if lessons are learnt. Let your concern for the deprived overcome your disappointment with colleagues, allies, and partners. Let that concern grow into goodwill for all human beings, beyond class, and beyond Kerala and Bengal. Elsewhere in the world, many ardent leftists turned into dangerous fascists. Don't let that happen in India.

◆

Indian society beyond politics would, however, be my karmabhoomi. I would marvel at most of my compatriots, young and old: their skills, bustle and energy; their giving spirit; their ability to put aside personal setbacks to help others in need; their coping with inconveniences; their smiles on difficult days; and more.

But I would also hold a clear mirror before fellow Indians and ask them to confront unpleasant truths, one of which is that we possess a strong imperialist strain. There are few parts of the world where people tell one another what they should do as readily as we do in India. Parents do this to children, children to parents, siblings to siblings, aunts and uncles to nephews and nieces, A to B, and Z to Y. I've just done some of it in this essay.

Advice can easily become dictation. John Bull quickly became a bully. It is not hard for Indians to become bullies. The urge to dictate has found its ugliest form in the mob which surrounds and coerces a helpless individual to surrender her dignity or swallow his conscience, and which kills when resistance is offered. As a twenty-one-year-old, I would want to be part of a bid to help Indian society face its coercive side, be ashamed of it, and expel it.

Shouldn't dissenters, no matter how few or solitary, be able to walk about freely in all parts of India, with heads held high, receiving the respect of those they dissent from? Be able to think, speak, believe, eat, dress, and marry as they choose?

Punishing bullies and extortioners, even when what they extort are 'nationalist' slogans, would help. Even more effective would be acknowledgement and repentance by a coercer. I would want to be part of an effort to obtain such admission and repentance.

Valmiki was a bully before he changed and gave us the Ramayana. When the slave-trafficker John Newton faced his sins in the eighteenth century, he wrote 'Amazing Grace', the song that continues, three centuries later, to stir Americans towards honesty and solidarity.

There's a chink in the Hindutva armour: the Hindu nationalists clamour for the world's praise. They want the world to think of India as a democracy. Moreover, their friends and relatives live in countries such as the US, where too there is a clash between tolerance and intolerance, and where Hindus and Sikhs, along with Muslims, Hispanics, and African Americans, may on occasion be told to 'Go back where you came from', even when they are second-generation Americans. Bullying is much less attractive when you're at the receiving end.

More than that, many supporters of Hindu nationalism sincerely believe that Hinduism can offer something precious to the world. They are right. A Hindu who is sensitive to his neighbour's pain and who respects the rights of others to their beliefs and practices has what the world needs. I would join all those striving to become or encourage such Hindus. Or such Muslims, Christians, Buddhists, or rationalists.

◆

As a twenty-one-year-old facing the future, I would look at India's large and varied countryside, much of it overrun by swelling towns, parts of it almost vacant now. Villages have gone into history, their young into the cities, and thousands of peasants into the world beyond, flung there by debt and suicide.

I ask, how will life be restored to rural India? In future decades, who will produce the nation's food? Then I look at our overcrowded cities, many of them unable to pump water, all of them pushing noxious fumes into the atmosphere. Not possessing solutions, but certain that innovation, ingenuity, teamwork, and willpower can create them, I will join the search.

Much would need to emerge: economic policies and perhaps tax differentials that re-route investment and humans into villages and agriculture; rural roads, schools, and hospitals that make life in villages easier and appealing; all this and more.

I would want discussion and inspired ideas for such outcomes. I might also take the option of settling in a village, along with (if I am lucky) three or four comrades, to make it an attractive place of manufacture, craft, art, theatre, and employment.

For India's survival and sanity, the drain of humans and wealth from village to city has to be reversed. In places elsewhere in the world, people living in a village are seen as fortunate, enjoying enviable lives. City life is considered poor in comparison. It can happen in India too. Why not, to all-round relief, a sustained movement from city to village?

At the heart of my chosen village would be a neat, clean, and aesthetic space where, bar none, anyone and everyone who respects the space would be welcome, and also invited to join everyone else in looking after it. This village heart or centre would be a place of friendship, quiet listening, warmth, hospitality, conversation, and creativity.

There people would listen to one another, also to the submerged, wounded voice of our planet, and, God willing, to their own, oft-ignored, inner voice. From listening, art might emerge, as would honesty, sympathy, healing, mutual forgiveness, and solidarity.

◆

As a youngster who will soon run past a milestone that says, '75 years ago: Independence,' I would utter, while running, two missing words, 'and Partition'.

A far-seeing man, who was killed in January 1948, had said that Partition would hurt everyone and leave lasting wounds. Impatience with the Brits and with one another combined with the desire—in both the Hindustani and Pakistani areas—to have ministers, prime ministers, and presidents of *our own kind* (what a problematic phrase!) forced the issue. Dismissing the far-seeing man's warnings, the price for Independence was paid for with Partition.

With fears and hates unaddressed, Partition has among other things led, on both sides of the border, to the Big Bomb that ticks away in basements, the diversion of scarce resources to arsenals of war, communal polarization, and the persecution of minorities.

Even if you run at a furious pace, you cannot go back in time. You cannot undo Partition. You may, in certain unlikely but not impossible circumstances, for example, at the end of a nuclear or non-nuclear war, find a 'victorious' government 'gaining' charge over an entire subcontinent in flames, but who would want that kind of charge?

Undoing Partition is a mad thought. Reconciling neighbours is a project of sanity. As a twenty-one-year-old, I would seek to enlist partners everywhere—in India, Pakistan, Bangladesh, and elsewhere—for the thankless, unpopular, discredited yet inescapable goal of turning enemies into friends in our subcontinent.

It's a goal that would transform the daily cynical show at the Wagah–Attari border into a fable for Christmas, Eid, or Diwali. It would also enable Muslims in India, and Hindus, Sikhs, and Christians in Pakistan and Bangladesh, to breathe freely again. And it would rocket trade, travel, and friendships to unimaginable heights.

Even as I strive for harmony between India, Pakistan, and Bangladesh, I would not forget Nepal, Sri Lanka, Afghanistan, Bhutan, or the Maldives. Or Myanmar. Or Tibet and its wonderful people, even if, following the Dalai Lama, I see it as part of China.

And I would focus on China. Despite oft-heated rhetoric, India–China trade grows steadily. Though the number is still pitifully small, more and more Indians learn Mandarin in some of our colleges. There's a sharp rise in Indians working in China, whether for Indian or non-Indian companies.

Nevertheless, no irony is greater than the fact that the world's two most populous neighbours remain in near-total ignorance of life on the other side of their Himalayan divide. Until recent times, that divide was impassable for all but the most intrepid. Now the mountains are comfortably crossed by air or road. Before too long, even train travel between the countries may become normal.

Is there anything which the Indians and the Chinese acting together—and along with their Nepalese, Pakistani, Afghan, Bangladeshi, and Bhutanese fellow-neighbours—cannot do? For the environment, for mutual respect and friendship among the world's peoples; for the health of future generations, and more?

But we must begin to know one another as individuals, beyond race or nationality. It is not sufficient that Chinese food is known in most parts of India. Whatever their first language, Indian youngsters should get to know China's Shakespeares, Wodehouses, Agatha Christies, and Rowlings.

And China's youngsters should get to know our Valluvars, Vemanas, Kabirs, Tukarams, Tagores, Nazrul Islams, Ghalibs, Mantos, and others.

This, then, is my final thought, or prayer: as India's present blends into its future, may Indians and their neighbours commingle with one another.

# 21

## BENGAL: A SHORT HISTORY OF A LONG DECLINE

### RUDRANGSHU MUKHERJEE

'The times of happiness are past and times of trouble lie ahead. The days grow worse every new tomorrow.... A dreadful time is at hand, confounded by much trickery, beset by many vices, when all conduct and acts of dharma shall be soiled.'—Vyasa to his mother Satyavati, in the Adi Parva of the Mahabharata.

Like most things related to Bengal, its culture, and its politics, the story of the region's decline begins in the nineteenth century. Already in the middle of that century, contemporary journals were writing on the themes of crisis and decline. The decline is like a chronicle foretold. In the very recent past, especially in the grim present, the perception of decline has become a palpable reality. Why this haunting sense of despair? Why is there an overwhelming sense that Bengal is not being governed, and the growing fear that perhaps Bengal cannot be governed at all?

Without going back to the nineteenth century, when the people of Bengal, for obvious historical reasons, could not govern themselves, it is more convenient to begin with the post-independence years. Up till 1967, the government and the official machinery of the state remained in the hands of the Congress party. The latter considered itself the torch bearer of the national movement and, therefore, the natural and obvious party of governance. It presented itself as the party of order. It not only dominated politics and the government, but, at a more informal level, it also wielded enormous influence over many of the institutions of civil society—the universities, the newspapers, and some of the cultural fora.

Away from the seats of governance and civil society, a different mode of politics was emerging and gaining momentum. This was the politics of agitation and protest growing out of several social and economic factors. One was the problem of rising population caused by the influx of refugees from East Pakistan. The Bengal economy became one of shortages especially that of food grains and housing. The departure of the managing agencies, the pivot of industrial and commercial activities in the state, and the overall conditions adversely affecting the Indian economy resulted in industrial stagnation. Unemployment spiraled. In Bengal, the dreams that Independence had conjured turned into nightmares.

The middle of the 1950s witnessed strikes, hartals, and mammoth rallies at the forefront of which were tram workers, bank employees, and students—all organized by the Communist Party of India (CPI). The politics of protest eroded the basis of the politics of order that the Congress party represented. The mass agitations and opposition to the government led to the emergence of alternative centres of power that challenged the existing structures of governance. As the social scientist Partha Chatterjee has observed:

> If Writers' Building, Raj Bhavan and the Assembly House were the centres from which the destiny of the State was being controlled by those who had the mandate to rule, then Esplanade East, the Monument and the Brigade Parade grounds, lying outside the protective cordon thrown around the citadels of power, were the new rallying points of mass protest.

There are two features of this kind of politics that should be underlined since they have kept on recurring in the politics of Bengal. One is the large-scale destruction of public property by the protestors and the other are the repressive measures—arrests and police firing—of the administration. The momentum of this kind of politics led to the victory of the United Front in 1967— the first non-Congress government in Bengal. Two other factors contributed to the success: the growing radicalization of politics, which, in turn, was the result of the influx of refugees and the influence of the CPI (which split in 1964 to form the CPI and the CPI (M)); and the growing perception that the Congress was no longer the party of the people but of the propertied—a party that ruled through machinations and the manipulation of privilege.

The radicalization of politics was intensified by objective conditions: food shortages, rising prices, and increasing income disparities. Even sections of the population not usually associated with agitational politics joined bandhs and various forms of work stoppages. Protests frequently turned violent and common targets were markets, rice mills, procurement offices, railway stations, trams, and buses. The period also witnessed the emergence among the urban population of a new note of social criticism and radical activism. At the vanguard of all this was a cosmopolitan intelligentsia with the dream of socialism in its eyes.

In this kind of heady atmosphere, in 1967, an electoral victory—the product of a united opposition to the Congress—was seen and celebrated as a socialist seizure of power. This made the United Front forget the responsibilities of running a government. Antonio Gramsci, the most important Marxist thinker after Karl Marx, had written about such a situation: 'What is needed for the revolution are men of sober mind, men who don't cause an absence of bread in the bakeries, who make trains run, who provide the factories with raw materials and know how to turn the produce of the country into industrial produce, who ensure the safety and freedom of the people against the attack of criminals, who enable the network of collective services to function and who do not reduce the people to despair and to a horrible carnage. Verbal enthusiasm and reckless phraseology make one laugh (or cry) when a single one of these problems has to be resolved even in a village of a hundred inhabitants.' Under the United Front from 1967 to 1969, and subsequently from 1977 for the next thirty-four years, not to speak of the interregnum between 1971 and 1976, what Bengal got from the ruling dispensation was exactly the opposite of Gramsci's explicit expectations. Bengal ceased to be governed.

Immediately after being voted to power, the United Front government announced that its policies would be directed towards 'recognizing the rights of workers and peasants to voice their just demands and grievances'; and it pledged itself 'not to suppress the democratic and legitimate struggles of the people'. Calcutta and its industrial suburbs were the first to feel the impact of these policies. These years set the pattern of politics in Bengal: attack against capital and gheraos were seen as a legitimate weapon in settling labour-management disputes. There was a drive, led by the CPI (M), to unionize the workers, and promises were held out to the workers that all their demands would be met even if they did not perform their duties. Workers were guaranteed that their wages would rise irrespective of performance. The immediate result was that between March and August 1967, 583 establishments were subjected to 1,018 gheraos. The police, under orders from the government, did nothing. Capital fled and smaller businesses shut down. More importantly, work culture came to be eroded.

Violence escalated across the state from the late 1960s to the early 1970s because of the activities of the CPI (Marxist-Leninist) and its brutal suppression by the police, who often acted with the full cooperation of the Congress cadre. The repression was masterminded by Siddhartha Shankar Ray (who became chief minister in 1972 after the United Front had been displaced by a Congress ministry) and it spilled over to the killing of CPI (M) activists.

These years set the pattern of politics in Bengal: attack against capital, open violence by party cadre, the police and the administration acting only at the behest of the ruling dispensation, irresponsible trade unionism, and the collapse of work culture. The people of West Bengal came to learn from political parties that they could always collect their pay packets without performing their duties. Agitation replaced governance, and the unemployed and the unemployable were given the assurance that they could always depend on the patronage of political parties. Governance became synonymous with populism.

Agitation and populism have made Bengal ungovernable. These two facets of politics also initiated a vicious cycle. They encouraged investment to flee, and this created the conditions of economic stagnation and unemployment, and these, in turn, intensified the politics of protest and populism. The only attempt to bring back investment to the state happened at the beginning of the twenty-first century when Buddhadeb Bhattacharya, the communist chief minister, persuaded the Tatas to set up a factory in Singur to produce the Nano, the small car. The project was destroyed by an agitation led by Mamata Banerjee, who, when she eventually became the chief minister, abandoned even the pretence of governing.

Mamata Banerjee's political career has been meteoric. She fashioned herself as the sole spokesperson and leader against the rule of the CPI (M). The latter's misgovernance and the use of state- and cadre-sponsored violence allowed her the space and the opportunity to position herself as the harbinger of change and of hope. She walked into power with a massive mandate from the people. This overwhelming popular support added substance to her call for change. She had the support and the political goodwill to bring about change. In the euphoria of success and the relief of removing the CPI (M) from political power, very few pointed to the dark side of the moon. Within a short time of her being voted to power as a harbinger of change, it is the dark side that has grown more prominent, so much so that many people in West Bengal and elsewhere have begun to doubt if ever there was an illuminated side. The lack of governance, the abuse of power, the complete intolerance of dissent, rise in violence, the use of foul and abusive language, the pampering of minorities to cultivate a vote bank, the open disregard of the rule of law and an escalating scale of corruption—these are the hallmarks of the regime of Mamata Banerjee. And the regime is bolstered by supine ministers, bureaucrats, and police officers.

Many people, especially those outside of Bengal, find it difficult to believe that the Bengalis, who are so proud of their culture and their political consciousness, could actually invest someone like

Mamata Banerjee with power in two successive elections. They point to the fact that Mamata Banerjee possesses none of the virtues of which Bengalis are so self-consciously proud—education, culture, refinement, and sophistication. Yet, she is the leader of Bengal, elected by the people who live in Bengal. People outside Bengal, and even some Bengalis, cannot quite work out this riddle. Is it an accident, a coincidence produced by the unpredictable character of electoral arithmetic and majority preference?

Coincidence is only part of an answer, perhaps only a superficial part. The time has come to ask some more fundamental questions that relate to Bengal's past and the self-image of the Bengalis as a cultured and refined group of people. This image does not have a long lineage. It dates to the nineteenth century—the period often described as the epoch of the Bengal Renaissance. Stretching across the nineteenth century, from Raja Rammohun Roy to Rabindranath Tagore, this era was marked by the work of outstanding individuals in the fields of literature, social and religious reform, education, institution building, and so on. This remarkable and inexplicable coming together of so many talented individuals has given that era a unique aura and has prompted comparisons to a similar coming together of outstanding individuals in Italy in the fourteenth and fifteenth centuries. To the Bengalis, the nineteenth century has become a kind of benchmark—the high-water mark of cultural achievements. Even individuals born in the twentieth century have their achievements measured by the standards and influences of the nineteenth century stalwarts. A Satyajit Ray and an Amartya Sen are often spoken about as renaissance figures or as torchbearers of that rich and awe-inspiring legacy.

This justified homage to the achievements of the nineteenth century and the galaxy of great men has had the consequence of distorting perspective: it views only the great peaks of achievement and thereby ignores the less-elevating aspects of the past. Even the enlightened nineteenth century had its sordid underbelly. That unforgettable description of life in Calcutta in the second half of the nineteenth century in Kaliprasanna Sinha's satirical *Hootum*

*Pyanchar Naksha* reveals how shallow, how wasteful, and how vulgar and tasteless the daily life of the city actually was once the focus is shifted from the activities of the literati to the level of the popular and the ordinary.

It is salutary to remember that in their own times, men like Rammohun Roy, Vidyasagar, and Rabindranath were vilified, lampooned, and attacked and not always by the uneducated. In the case of Vidyasagar, the intimidation was physical. The responses and reactions of Bengalis have not always been refined and sophisticated. The Bengalis, in the past as in the present, have abused and threatened opponents and, on occasion, even killed them. These are also parts of the 'culture' of Bengal, and they tend to get obscured by the works of great men. The temptation is to see such episodes as aberrations. The question that needs to be asked is, are they aberrations or should they be seen as integral parts of the history of Bengal, and thus the glorification of the Bengalis as a cultured and refined people be brought down a notch or two? There has always existed a subterranean undertow to Bengal's history, and this should not be obscured by the light that inevitably falls on the great peaks of achievement.

The experience of the recent past bears testimony to the strong pull of the undertow. The descent is unmistakable and begins at the top. Having said this, it needs to be emphasized that the precipitous decline is the continuation of a process. Much of what is deplorable today had its beginnings under the rule of the CPI (M)—the use of cadre to intimidate, the abuse of state power, the use of violence and the language of violence, and the scant regard for governance. Mamata Banerjee promised a change from all this; she represents a breach of promise, a betrayal of hope. Under her, Bengal continues on a slope of decline that began, arguably, under a man called Pramod Das Gupta, who revelled in the populist and the mediocre. Mamata Banerjee is the vulgate edition of the gospel of Pramod Das Gupta.

People get the leader they deserve, or in a democracy, the leader they elect. In Bengal, the collective hopes of the people are now bereft of enchantment. The result of the last general election has proved beyond any reasonable doubt that Mamata Banerjee's popularity is nowhere near what it was a few years ago. She now has a new challenger that is gaining ground in large parts of Bengal. This is the Bharatiya Janata Party (BJP) which, even a year back, did not have a prominent presence in Bengal's electoral politics. It is now clear that the BJP has not only won a significant number of seats in the new Lok Sabha after the 2019 polls but its ideology of Hindutva and hatred of Muslims has created a strong and growing support base in Bengal even among the educated middle class. One factor in the rise of the BJP, and the ideas associated with it in Bengal, is the open pampering of the Muslims by Mamata Banerjee. It is a powerful vote bank that she assiduously nurtures. There is, of course, also the impact of the overwhelming trend of national politics which Bengal cannot avoid.

But all this should not deflect attention from the methods that the BJP and its other wings have adopted to win Bengal. The methods are similar to what the CPI (M) and Mamata Banerjee used to come to power: confrontation, incitement of violence, hate speech, disruption, and use of cadre power. In the case of the BJP, all this is spiced up by its own ideology of Hindu majoritarianism. In these successive political battles—Congress vs CPI (M), Trinamool Congress (TMC) vs CPI (M), and now BJP vs TMC—the central problems affecting the decline of Bengal—absence of investment, the consequent lack of employment opportunities, the collapse of governance and law and order, the pitiable state of the infrastructure, the disappearance of the dividing line between political parties and state administration, and so on—are never addressed. The path of violence and confrontation is now seen to be the proven path to electoral and even cultural and social success.

To add to Bengal's plight, politics and society have now become sharply polarized along communal lines. To echo the epic, 'A dreadful time is at hand' as the rough beast of communal violence slouches around Bengal to haunt all those who live there.

# 22

# NORWAY'S ROLE IN PEACEBUILDING AND CONFLICT RESOLUTION

JON WESTBORG

**Introduction**

It is an unquestionable reality that Norway has been, and is, actively engaged in peacebuilding and conflict resolution. But, most generally well-informed individuals tend to view such involvement as a recent phenomenon—linked to negotiations prior to the Oslo Accord of 1993 between Israel and the Palestine Liberation Organization. It is often explained as a consequence of Norway's new-found oil wealth; however, this is a misconception.

In the early Middle Ages, Norway was an independent kingdom with an active foreign policy. During 1380 to 1814, while legally a separate kingdom under the Danish king, Norway effectively lost its independence. It regained significant self-determination when it was transferred from Denmark to Sweden as part of the Kiel Treaty in 1814. But it was only after the country broke out of the union with Sweden in 1905 that it could handle its own foreign policy.

Despite being a newly independent nation and one of the poorest countries in Europe, Norway was enthusiastic in its support for the establishment of the League of Nations. Owing to several issues related to the Charter for the League, as well as its own domestic politics, Norway was unable to participate wholeheartedly. Yet, as a small nation, Norway was quite successful in advocating the peaceful resolution of conflicts and the development of an 'international rule of law'. Norway, therefore, supported both the creation of a structure for peaceful bilateral conflict resolution under the League of Nation's mediation, and the establishment of the International Arbitration Tribunal in The Hague. Norway also advocated and supported the League's work in rehabilitating prisoners of war and refugees after World War I. The famous Norwegian explorer, Fridtjof Nansen, was one of the country's representatives to the League of Nations. He later led the League's work as the High Commissioner for Refugees, and was awarded the Nobel Peace Prize for his efforts.

After World War II, Norway supported the establishment of the United Nations (UN). This stemmed from the country's experience of wartime occupation over five years, and its realization of the vulnerability of small, disarmed, and neutral nations in a world without respect for the rule of law. In the following years, Norway contributed soldiers to UN observer and peacekeeping forces in Kashmir, Cyprus, the Middle East, Congo, and worked with the UN in peacebuilding and conflict resolution.

This tradition of Norwegian internationalism was the precursor to Norway's efforts in support of peacebuilding and peaceful conflict resolution in regions and countries like Guatemala, Israel/Palestine, Aceh, Burma, Sri Lanka, Ethiopia–Eritrea, the Philippines, Balkans, Sudan, Colombia, and Mali.

Consequently, the more interesting questions related to Norwegian involvement in peacebuilding and conflict resolution are not about its origins, but why, with what objectives, and how Norway sees its future engagement.

## Why Norwegian Involvement?

For the sake of clarity, it is useful to look at this question at two levels: first, the issue of involvement at the level of principles, and second, at the level of individual conflicts.

## Principles of Involvement: Altruism and Realism

In the late 1980s and early 90s, Norway framed the concept of 'Policies of Involvement' (PoI) to describe the sum of Norwegian engagements in development cooperation, humanitarian assistance, peacebuilding, and conflict resolution. This enabled the government to distinguish these activities from other elements in the diplomatic 'toolbox'.

The Norwegian Governmental Development Fund, the forerunner to the Norwegian Development Cooperation (NORAD) was established by an Act of Parliament in 1952, while Norway was still in the throes of reconstruction after five years of occupation and ravaging by war. In spite of a strained economy, the decision met with popular support and public enthusiasm. The popular approval of this step has generally been credited to the influence of strong mission societies in Norway. In addition to spreading the gospel, they have worked on education, health, and livelihood programmes—several from the beginning of the nineteenth century. Support of the Labour Party and the unions, which viewed development assistance in the light of international solidarity, also proved important. In both cases, the support for external engagement stemmed from an altruistic rationale. Emergency assistance, support to freedom movements, conflict resolution, and peacebuilding—all followed naturally in the eighties and nineties.

Around 2005, the foreign policy experiences of various governments over the past decade came under scrutiny and there followed a broad public discussion of Norwegian interests in a changing world. Following these debates, the foreign minister tabled a White Paper in Parliament in March 2009. The Policy of Involvement was given a prominent position, and therein peacebuilding and conflict resolution. The rationale for this policy was stated as altruistic. And so it was, as far as the objective was to contribute towards a better life for those less fortunate around the world. However, the White Paper and subsequent discussions noted that in a globalized world, Norway too would benefit from the successful pursuit of this policy, while a failure to engage could result in problems knocking at its doorstep.

Likewise, it was recognized that in widening the Norwegian foreign policy perspective, the PoI could also contribute towards a greater acceptance of the need for stronger international structures, and maintaining the 'international rule of law'. As a small nation with insignificant hard power, strengthening this element has been, and always will be, central to Norwegian foreign policy.

Finally, the White Paper recognized—admittedly without great emphasis—that an active and consistent implementation of the PoI also had the ability to open the doors to the echelons of the big and powerful nations. Not only within the areas related to the PoI, but also for other Norwegian interests. If the White Paper, after nearly two decades of experience in implementing this policy, had failed to recognize these beneficial effects, it would have been construed as an attempt to project the policy as completely altruistic.

As the ambassador to Sri Lanka (1996–2003) and later to India (2003–2007), I was actively engaged in the Norwegian efforts to facilitate the Sri Lankan government and the LTTE in finding a negotiated settlement to the ethnic conflict on the island. From personal experience, I can, therefore, affirm that this engagement improved Norway's access to relevant big powers when this was needed in order to explain the background to a situation in Sri Lanka, or to build an understanding that could be important for the ongoing process. In addition, the goodwill emanating from Norway's involvement created space to lobby for Norwegian positions on other issues of international concern. At times, this even enabled the country to raise issues of pure self-interest—whether this was in Washington, DC, New Delhi, London, or Tokyo.

This experience clearly showed that Norway's attempt to facilitate the Sri Lankan peace process raised Norway's profile and status—even if the parties to the conflict eventually opted for a return to hostilities.

Researchers who have critically studied the PoI process from the early 1980s to 2008, however, tend to agree that the process did not proceed on a plan to secure Norwegian self-interest. There was no grand design, but more of trial and error, which gradually made both bureaucrats and politicians, realize that this involvement also benefited Norway.

In his speech at the Ambassador's Annual Conference in 2001, Foreign Minister Thorbjorn Jagland might have caught sentiments correctly with the following statement:

> While we show solidarity and lend a helping hand to fellow human beings in misery, we become a more central actor in the international polities than what our natural conditions would have made us, something which makes us an experienced contributor and interesting conversation partner, and opens doors which otherwise would have been shut.

Whether Jagland recognized it or not, this was an excellent manner of stating the Norwegian reality. The effort is, and is meant to be, altruistic, but that is no reason why Norway should not benefit from it.

However, given the benefits of peacebuilding and conflict resolution activities, it is somewhat surprising that this was not actively pursued and 'marketed' among the Norwegian population. In explaining this, it might be worth looking at the connections between the government's restraint and public opinion. Opinion polls over the last thirty years have consistently shown that more than 72 per cent of the voters were in favour of providing aid to deserving countries or population groups. A majority have also supported the level of assistance provided. As late as in 2017, the level of aid was approximately US$ 4 billion, and 87 per cent expressed their support for aid generally. Further, a comfortable majority continues to believe that allocating 1 per cent of Norway's GDP to aid should remain the annual goal for humanitarian assistance. A majority was also of the opinion that the aid provided was useful. Further, it should be noted that the majority of the opposition to this policy was found in one political party.

Therefore, a substantial majority of the politicians did not have to make a case for self-interest in order to defend the financing of the PoI. On the contrary, many politicians could expect to be questioned if some ulterior motives, rather than altruism, were shown to be the main reason for a given engagement. This suggests that up to a point, ethical principles and values, rather than pure self-interest, will continue to guide Norwegian policy in this regard.

## Some Experiences to be Considered

Using the 'door opener' for self-serving purposes can create useful shortcuts. However, in the Sri Lankan case an individual used this 'door', but, in the rush, overstepped the boundary of hospitality, thereby jeopardizing a solution, rather than solving the problem.

Similarly, the facilitator in developing a 'door opener' has shared information provided in confidence by one of the parties to the conflict—only to find that this information was fed back to the party in question. Breach of trust can prove to be irreparable. Beware: 'Nations have no permanent friends or allies, they only have permanent interests.'

Similar reactions have also been the result when a facilitator has used such access to create alliances to pressurize the parties to accept solutions that the facilitator or big power finds advantageous, without having cleared these solutions with parties to the conflict. Such actions can often become 'deal breakers'.

## Involvement in Individual Conflicts—Norwegian Branding

### Issues Influencing Choice of Norwegian Involvement

Experience indicates that the type of conflict is of little consequence for Norway's choice of involvement. Whether it is cross-border or internal, majority/minority, ethnic, religious, territorial, peacebuilding or conflict resolution, or both, experience has shown that each conflict has to be handled based on its own reality, merits or lack thereof.

## Influence of Territorial Interests

Since the Viking Era, Norway has not engaged in colonization of inhabited territory.

On the contrary, for nearly 500 years, Norway was either a colony of Denmark or Sweden and had lost significant territories to these two countries. It has, therefore, no inhabited geographical area where it could be expected to 'look after' inhabited territories outside its own domain. Nor has it invested state or private capital in such a manner that they need to be 'protected' through force or negotiations. Norwegian engagements in peacebuilding and conflict resolution cover conflicts in Eastern Africa, South and Southeast Asia, the Middle East, Latin America, and even Europe. Geography is clearly not a determinant of where Norway gets involved. Nor do internal politics, ideology, or religion play any significant role in the choice of conflicts in which to intervene. Finally, to the best of this writer's knowledge, Norway has never made its assistance conditional on any form of return.

## Evaluating Probability of Impact

Norway is generally open to considering requests for assistance from any of the conflicting parties. However, the last thirty years' experience has taught Norway that in each case it must evaluate if it has the necessary wherewithal to make a positive difference. One significant consideration will always be whether Norway has or can secure human resources with sufficient background to understand the setting in which it will have to operate. For a small country like Norway, this remains a challenge.

This consideration, rather than conscious design, is perhaps the reason why around half of Norwegian engagements are in countries where Norway has experience and networks from prior engagements in development cooperation and humanitarian assistance. Similarly, the paucity of Norwegians with competence in French language and culture has meant that Norwegian initiatives to support peace initiatives in Francophone Africa are few and far apart.

## Financial Implication of Engagement

Another obvious issue to consider is if financial backing can be secured. Norway has a significant budget for humanitarian and development assistance. It also tends to view the issue of sustainable peace and development as interdependent realities. With considerable resources, Norway can place them at the disposal of its peace and reconciliation engagements. However, the country also takes pride in pledging that if it accepts a request for assistance, it will be in for the long haul. Clearing the question of financial support prior to an engagement is always important.

Heavily dependent on its exports, Norway rates high on per capita income, but it is a small economy. A seldom talked about but nevertheless important consideration is the financial impact of the country's involvement in a given conflict especially for Norwegian companies and national trade. The impact can be both positive and negative, and often depends on the impact of Norway's involvement.

## The Ownership of a Process

Drawing on other experiences, quite early on, Norway concluded that for facilitation efforts to be useful, the conflicting parties must take ownership of the process. They can assist the parties in finding peaceful solutions; but the overriding responsibility for a process can only rest with the parties to the conflict. Sustainable peace is dependent on the parties' genuine interest in finding political solutions. Norway cannot, and should not, pressure the parties into solutions that the parties have difficulty in seeing as useful. Without a clear understanding of these parameters, it ought not to enter into a conflict resolution process. Nor can it continue its efforts if one or both parties no longer, for whatever reason, see the people they represent benefitting from a peaceful solution. However, each conflict is in this respect unique, and as Norway has experienced in several cases, it can be appropriate to come back and assist the parties in restarting processes when the parties have changed their mind.

In the case of Colombia, both parties and facilitators recognized that the situation had changed. Therefore, despite the failure of the earlier two attempts, they felt it imperative to try again—and have so far succeeded.

In the Sri Lankan case, a time came when the infighting between the president and the prime minister made it unclear about who was in charge of the peace process. The Norwegian foreign minister, Jan Petersen, and the state secretary, Vidar Helgesen, publicly stated that it was necessary for Norway 'to go home and wait', probably for better weather. After a snap election that bolstered the Sri Lankan president's position, they came back and continued their attempt at facilitation for several years. In the end, following a change of president, the parties to the conflict were unwilling to make further efforts—not even to save the lives of thousands of combatants and civilians. A bloodbath followed and the war ended. Whether it was constructive for Norway to continue as long as it did remains a question.

*Importance of International and Regional Powers*

In my experience, Norway also needs to ensure that its involvement has the backing of the relevant global/regional powers, or at least that these do not have significant objections to Norway's facilitation process.

Without close contact and acceptance from the United States, the Norwegian involvement in the Israel–Palestine conflict was unlikely to have had any impact.

Similarly, in the case of Sri Lanka, in my opinion, Norway would have been unable to operate in these difficult waters without India's understanding. Nor would it have been possible to convince the LTTE to enter into negotiations. Anton Balasingham, LTTE's chief negotiator, was adamant that without India's acceptance, no solution could become reality. In addition, President Chandrika Bandaranaike Kumaratunga, Foreign Minister Lakshman Kadirgamar, and, later, Prime Minister Ranil Wickremesinghe, shared this view.

For the Norwegian side, the Indian connections started with the then High Commissioner Gopalkrishna Gandhi in Colombo and National Security Advisor Brajesh Mishra in New Delhi. Shortly thereafter, this extended to the Ministry of External Affairs and Foreign Minister Jaswant Singh. The Norwegian contact with New Delhi on the Sri Lankan issue continued with their successors. From 2006, when the LTTE opted to return to arms, the Sri Lankan parties effectively abandoned the ceasefire, and the need for continuing the contact on the Sri Lankan issue became moot. Contact naturally continued, but cooperation and relations gradually moved to other areas, affirming the value of the engagement as a door opener—one that benefited Norway in the following years.

## Other Characteristics of Norwegian Engagement

In an article published in November 2018, the Norwegian Ministry of Foreign Affairs sought to present to its own citizens, as well as to potential conflicting parties, the key characteristics of Norwegian involvement in peace and reconciliation efforts. These had been identified and developed gradually through experiences and research. In addition to the issues that supposedly influenced Norway's choice of involvement, the article highlights several important issues. First, Norway emphasizes the importance of talking with all stakeholders—even when this might not be to the liking of their opponents. Such an approach builds confidence and develops an understanding of the underlying interests. Second, Norway does not operate in a vacuum, but recognizes the importance of building networks related to peacebuilding and conflict resolution. The annual 'Oslo Forum' is an example. Indeed, several of the conflict resolution processes in which Norway is engaged were initiated by NGOs, the UN, and other countries. Most of the processes in which Norway is involved seek the cooperation of other state and non-state actors. Norway's experience also underscores the importance of researching and sharing information as well as making it available to the parties in a conflict situation and to other institutions working in similar situations.

Third, Norway strives at all times to be an impartial facilitator. Being impartial does not, however, imply that Norway will be value-neutral. In negotiations, Norway actively encourages the parties to abide by international law and human rights—even if it meets resistance from one or both the parties. Similarly, Norway aims to encourage processes where the parties also include the civilian population including women, children, and those directly suffering the consequences of the conflict. Last, and not least important, Norway recognizes and accepts that the risk of the parties not succeeding in finding a solution are considerable, but also that what initially is viewed as failure can later prove to be necessary preparation for successful solutions.

These statements by the ministry make it amply clear that the current Norwegian government continues in the footsteps of past governments in its commitments—not only to provide altruistic support to peacebuilding and conflict resolutions, but also to 'punch above its weight in the international community' as former US President Bill Clinton so aptly put it.

# 23

# THINKING ABOUT POLITICS IN INDIA

## GOPAL GURU

Politics in transition is arguably a process that involves shifts which can be negative or affirmative, regressive or progressive. Transition can also be defined in terms of the shift in the language used for expressing politics. On the affirmative or progressive side, transition involves morality as a motivating force to detect the political errors committed in the past and their rectification in the present and complete elimination in the future. Thus, politics in transition underscores the need on the part of political activists and leaders to develop the moral capacity to reflect on mistakes and correct them in favour of the process of purifying and enriching the humane aspects of democracy, polity, and civil society. Similarly, the language that is needed to express the moral foundation of politics has to be normative and hence conceptual or theoretical. Such a conception of politics thus assumes a teleological thrust that is internal to affirmative or egalitarian modes of transition.

In such understanding of politics, those who are engaged in it, are thus expected to move from facts to truth, from fake news to truth and being imposture to becoming genuine representatives of the people. Or, politics in transition has to be taken as a sphere of opportunity where moving away from historical errors to their rectification in the present should not be treated as a strategic or pragmatic move but one that should be integrated into everyday political practice. Political leaders are expected to put themselves on probation, meaning they are supposed to submit themselves to the continuous ethical scrutiny through engaging in dialogue with the self and with the Other. For truth, both relative as well as absolute, resides in such a dialogue and it acquires ethical purity through dialogue with the self. Is it not closer to the Gandhian conception of relative truth which is to be realized by bringing oneself in harmony with peace and non-violence? This could be interpreted as a noble truth which is discovered in normalizing the self and the Other in the essence of dignity. This notion of truth would necessarily arrest the authoritarian ambition to become supreme by duping or terrorizing the fellow citizens. On the other hand, tragic truth associates with atrocities and violence which does not have any regard for the language of the soul and, hence, holds no place in Gandhi's ideals. Similarly, in B. R. Ambedkar's idea of politics, the life of the mind plays an important role in shaping and orienting political transition in accordance with egalitarian principles. Coercive truth, which, for its self-definition, finds the politics of hate quite favourable, therefore, has no place for the life of the mind either; and so leaves no place for Ambedkar.

In the above context and perhaps the ideal conception of politics, the current essay seeks to assess contemporary politics by raising the following questions. First, do social forces in Indian politics actively work as a transitional process; a process with affirmative thrust? Do the forces respond to transition by eliminating or repeating the historical errors? Finally, does the concept of transition provide the teleological purpose for choosing means that are necessary to move forward in achieving purity in politics?

This essay, in the first section, will focus on the nature of contemporary politics. In this section, the essay will try and discuss the nature of political means that suggests the repetition of errors rather than their decisive elimination. Secondly, the essay will address questions on the nature of oppositional intervention in politics in transition. The essay argues that the oppositional exclusive focus on facts tends to limit the access to truth. Facts, data, and information seem to have become the main plank of political intervention and mobilization against the government which is alleged to have withheld data on crucial aspects of the society, economy, and polity. In the second section, the essay will argue that while holding the government accountable is important, the focus of facts may not open up access to truths that are buried deep beneath the structures of which facts are merely manifestations. As a corollary to this point, the exclusive focus on disputing data or facts gives rise to a language of accusation and counter-accusation. In the third section, therefore, we shall discuss the need for conceptual language that plays a crucial role in the formulation of truth.

In the final section, we need to account for the emergence of the category of 'imposture'. This category, as the essay would argue, exists outside the ruling party and the Opposition but performs the function of disorienting people from accessing the truth. The essay will address the issue of how exactly this category negotiates with the question of truth. Does it curtail access to the truth? The essay argues that it effectively thwarts political as well as moral mobilization of people towards the truth by rhetorically and deceptively using the very notion of truth.

## Regressive Nature of Political Transition

As mentioned at the beginning of this essay, political transitions in a certain progressive sense are desirable in as much as they offer an opportunity to the political or social forces so that they can eliminate past errors through continuous and sincere rectification. As the political developments of the past few years indicate, instead of being characterized by the reflective rectification of historical errors, the present is replete with the repetition of such mistakes. The most prominent of which is the ongoing political project that wishes to move towards an authoritarian regime by gaining domination over fellow men, application of violence, fraud, fake news, manipulation, and even competition. The transition in regression is much more serious inasmuch as it does not allow any space for democratic dissent.

A more serious aspect of the politics of suppressing truth is the collateral suppression of the way the conditions of truth are expressed. The governing class seeks to silence the voice of truth through excommunicating from the public fora those who try and communicate the truth of caste structures that produce atrocities and the truth of communalism that produces lynching. However, the attempts to silence truth expression not only result in the loss of freedom of those who speak the truth but it also underlies the loss of freedom of those who perpetrate caste and gender violence. Those who unleash violence on the weaker sections of society do not seem to exercise their freedom that is necessary to expose the pernicious consequences of the caste system. This inability to acknowledge one's limits, according to Ambedkar, is another kind of unfreedom.[1] Indians have today developed the fear of being fearless[2]. Accessing truth, therefore, lies in being fearless[3].

## Facts and Truth

Contemporary politics is an enterprise that seems to be located in a continuous area of dispute. Similarly, the Enforcement Directorate has also underpinned the politics of vendetta. But let us take simpler facts that will help us establish their incongruence with truth. Simply put, facts are the outer manifestation of the larger truth that resides in the moral and material framework of a society and polity. The emergence of facts suggests the truth conditions. Let us explain this with one prominent illustration: a political party crossing the 300 mark is a matter of fact. But is it the truth or its outer manifestation? The truth resides in the conditions and processes of arriving at such 'truth'. It lies in the buried conditions or moral material. So, truth will be in the kind of means used to gather votes in the general elections. The pursuit of truth would make it imperative to ask the following question: have the political parties

---

[1] B. R. Ambedkar, *Annihilation of Caste*, BAWS, 1979, p. 36.
[2] Judith N. Shklar, *Political Thought and Political Thinkers,* Chicago: University of Chicago Press, 1989, pp. 3–20.
[3] Karuna Mantena, 'Another Realism: Politics of Gandhi's Non-violence', *American Political Science Review*, Vol. 106, No. 2, May 2012.

secured the votes by making sincere, transparent appeals? Did the political parties use the element of rationality while making election promises to people? Have they made promises which can never be fulfilled? Have they sought votes on the basis of the inherent limits in the empty appeal or in the limitlessness of such appeal? The second is often the case. There is a lack of rationality in such appeal and, hence, there is a corresponding lack of truth in such electoral mobilization. And yet some parties which shop in the limitlessness of such appeal end up winning more than 300 Assembly seats. The election studies, however, stop at stating, comparing, and calculating votes and such efforts do not aid us in accessing the truth at the bottom of such appeal. Securing the majority of seats may not suggest proximity to truth, but political outcomes, both tantalizing and tragic, suggest their proximity to the truth. Thus, those losing in the elections may also suggest proximity to the truth. This is made strikingly evident in a perceptive observation made by a legendary Hindi lyricist, Gulzar, who said 'that he is always voting for a candidate who is likely to lose the election.' In fact, he suggested that he votes in favour of the truth.

Many social vigilante groups focus on the need to get factual information from the governmental agencies and authorities. The Right to Information (RTI) is important inasmuch as it makes the public aware about the government's politics of concealing the data that impacts their life. However, even RTI has its limits as it does not take you deep into the structure that renews the need for faking data. The question that one needs to address is: do we not require conceptual language for formulating truth? The answer needs to be given in the affirmative.

## Why Do We Require a Conceptual Language?

Conceptual language does not originate from speculation, but from the concrete social and political experience of the people in a given polity and society. Put differently, the organizing principle or norms of politics emerge from the practices of people but they are irreducible to such practices. This means that politics has to be practised in accordance with these normative principles. In this sense, politics is a derivative of principles and norms and vice versa. But principles and norms too need to be moderated in progressively shaping and regulating the human endeavour to achieve emancipation. This kind of integrated approach would help us reduce acute tension between what is to be thought and what is to be done. This perspective, even in a different political context, would help us move away from the invective polemical language rampant in Indian politics and offer us a conceptually more serious and universally applicable language that is necessary for understanding politics. Secondly, we need a universal language—either moral or conceptual—to amplify or elevate facts to truth. Moral vocabulary is universal inasmuch as it demands respect and equality for all human beings in terms of possessing equal moral worth such as respect and human dignity. The equal possession of moral values such as respect and dignity in the ontological sense makes human beings equal over and above their particular locations. Along with a moral language that is expected to be taken seriously by the members of civil society we also require a conceptual language such as of equality and justice which is backed by political institutions and the political community. Equality and justice depend on the political institutions' will power and the capacity to organize the mechanism of redistribution of the fruits of development. While morality depends on the civil society's ethical ability to take initiatives to distribute moral goods such as concern and attention, the state has to provide the condition of freedom within which members of civil society can ensure the minimum human need for morality that has to be universally fulfilled across societies and polities.

It is in this context that it becomes difficult to accept the suggestion that one needs to confront politics on its own terms or rhetorical language and not with the conceptual or theoretical language. Should, therefore, one accept that 'politics be explained in terms of the vocabulary that is in use?' In many ways, this question has already been answered by journalists and TV anchors who are often seen contemptuously making the following observation, 'your point is too academic to deserve any attention'. Such public discourse on politics actively discounts the need for any analytical and argumentative language. Conceptual vocabulary that is both thoughtful and thought-provoking usually gets replaced by instantly dished-out language which finds its expression in 'breaking news', bullet-point presentations, and WhatsApp messages.

Theoretical conceptual language has no standing in politics which is expressed in rhetorical language. Serious normative language does not enter the political discourse. It does not find its direct or indirect expression in public speeches.

The people are being moulded to feed into such a political project. Let us then explain in some detail as to how a conundrum of lying can drive the normative language out of politics and seek to infest the latter to the detriment of truth. Such a political transition was couched in the deceptive language of 'garibi hatao' (eradicate poverty) in the past and 'achche din' (happy days) in the present. Arguably, the present-day rhetorics have taken a deeply regressive turn. This regression is much more serious as it does not allow any space for democratic dissent. Dissent is overshadowed by rampant fake news and blatant lies.

Lies find their relevance in the narrow politics of creating a communal majority using the electoral process. It is quite paradoxical, therefore, to observe that lies do not require open-mindedness as they necessarily take the covert route. Lies have no face to be communicated openly and confidently. Hence it takes the deceptive route through fake news as well as the offensive route of trolling. The need to stay in power by means of using fake news has been a common experience in Indian politics. The function of lies is to cover under its deceptive spell both relative as well as absolute truth.

Imposture and fakery are the two manifestations of deception. Imposture uses the failure of the Other to justify his/her own intervention in the politics of the marginalized.

## Imposture as the Manifestation of Deception

The practitioners of politics that protect self-interests, however, do not seem to have any use of conceptual language as a necessary discursive condition for the formulation of truth. They are usually disposed towards using the practical, rhetorical language that is deemed to be adequate for giving expression to their political moves and motives. In the contemporary electoral politics there is something which is fundamentally paradoxical in the political practice of the leaders and activists. These practitioners locate truth in the cause while illusion is produced for dramatic effects alone. In other words, they see truth in the reason while something unreasonable and unfair is produced as a consequence. They see reason in autonomous politics as an initiative to take on the communal forces. The political leaders, particularly those who claim to represent the deprived castes tirelessly, invoke the truth that the 'secular' parties, particularly in recent times, have been unable to prevent the right-wing parties from capturing political power. These leaders go one step further and say that the deprived castes have, in fact, been manipulated by the secular parties on the issue of 'secularism'. Thus, the truth of manipulation provides cause for such leaders to make a case for contesting the elections without allies and rise to power by defeating their rival parties. We have yet to discover the rationale behind the self-assured hubris with which these claims are made by such leaders. But in actual effect, these parties indirectly, help the right-wing parties gain advantage over the 'secular' parties. The truth in the cause gets discredited or overshadowed by the illusion that is evident in miserable failure that these leaders face at the electoral front. The genuine cause loses its moral vitality and its essence tends to diminish at every move that is made by these leaders at every election. The cause is always genuine but the consequences are deceptive. The truth is not in the cause but in the consequences. These leaders' moves and motives are necessarily devoid of truth and are infused by illusion.

Those (imposture) who participate in their self-deception

subordination through objectification settle for relative or differential value rather than for equal value which is a defining criterion of self-respect. One requires an egalitarian political sphere in which every member can be a self-respecting ideal specimen. But for this to manifest into a reality, an egalitarian political sphere must become a precondition which has textually been provided in the Indian Constitution.

It is this commitment to safeguard one's self-respect that makes the 'ideal specimen' irreplaceable. Ethical expectations can be built on a peoples representative who assigns priority to moral good such as self-respect as an intrinsic value and correspondingly shuns the instrumentally seductive value. Instrumental value does acquire universal character inasmuch as it transmutes a person with intrinsic value into a commodity. The person, on account of becoming the object of exchange, for example, through defection or placing price tags on voting, ceases to be an autonomous subject and hence loses his capacity to set high moral standards both for the self, for party politics, and ultimately for an entire polity. Instead, he becomes an exemplar that is replicated throughout the world politically. Ironically, such opportunists also become universal, not in terms of being a moral example, but on account of acquiring a universal identity as the commodity to be bought and sold across parties. Those who look at politics as an advantage to leverage their personal interests effectively become fungible. In such a fungible state of existence these opportunists tend to be reduced to identical items (defectors have no caste, no ideology, no language, and no region-based identity) and hence are to be replaced by another item by a party with the dominant ambition to become authoritarian. It will be unfortunate if the moral quality of democracy is determined more by the political production of fungible rather than by the ideal specimen.

# SECTION V

# MEMOIRS

## 24

## GETTING TO KNOW GOPAL

### RAMACHANDRA GUHA

I cannot remember where and how I first met Gopal Gandhi. But I clearly remember the impression he made on first meeting my wife, Sujata. This was at a party in South Delhi, at the home of a classmate of mine who had joined the Indian Administrative Service (IAS). The year was 1989; Gopal, like our host, was still in the IAS. At some point that evening, Sujata and Gopal struck up a conversation, without either catching the other person's last name. Driving home afterwards, I told her he was the grandson of Mahatma Gandhi. 'That is not possible!' she exclaimed, 'he speaks such good Tamil.' I explained the lineage, adding that he was Rajaji's grandson too, and had served in the Tamil Nadu government.

While Gopal spoke excellent Tamil, it was in fact only his third language. Hindi (or more accurately Hindustani) was the first; and English was the second (he had taken two degrees in English literature). When his parents, Devadas and Lakshmi, got married, they decided that their children would speak neither's mother tongue, but Hindi, which was both the language of their locality, and of the nation. All four siblings grew up effortlessly bilingual; and because of his service in the Tamil country and through his marriage to a Tamil, Gopal spoke that language too. His father had longed to teach at least one of his children Gujarati; the privilege fell on Gopal, the youngest. So he learned to read, write, and speak in this language, as well.

Gopal's lovely wife, Tara, was a wildlife biologist, and we had things in common too. Our families had meals together every other week, and Gopal and I spoke on the phone more or less every day.

This was Delhi in the early 1990s, so our conversations were mostly about the three raging controversies of the day: Mandal, Masjid, and Market, as they were known. But from time to time we also spoke about Gandhi. As the youngest of four children, Gopal saw many associates of the Mahatma visit or stay at his parents' home. He spent his summer holidays with Rajaji in Madras, where he met other freedom fighters.

On my part, I was meeting contemporary Gandhians such as the Chipko leaders, Chandi Prasad Bhatt and Sunderalal Bahuguna, and encountering traces of Gopal's own family in the archives. Thus Gopal had many things to tell me about Gandhi, and I had some things to say to him in return. I would spend the day working in the Manuscripts Division of the Nehru Memorial Museum and Library, and afterwards walk over to his house (a cricket ball's throw away) and tell him of what I had found; for instance, a letter written by Rajaji from Government House in Darjeeling in 1948, describing 'little Gopu', then aged three, as a 'perfect gentleman at the dinner table' (as he still was).

For thirty years now, Gopal Gandhi has been a friend, but also a sounding board. His knowledge of the political history of modern India is staggering, and possibly unsurpassed. I can consult him about caste, religion, and community; Gandhi, Nehru, and Ambedkar. On all these subjects he has fresh information as well as original insights. Nor is his knowledge merely academic. He began life as a lowly civil servant in the districts of Tamil Nadu, before becoming secretary to the president of India, high commissioner in South Africa, Sri Lanka, ambassador to Norway, and governor of West Bengal. He has seen how the Constitution works (or does not work) at all levels of government, and is thus well placed to correct or amplify the perspective of a historian who takes his own clues from the archives.

In 1991, Gopal Gandhi was appointed Founder Director of the Nehru Centre in London. I visited England several times that year, always staying with Gopal and Tara in Mayfair, every morning walking across Green Park and St James's Park and then over the

Blackfriars Bridge to the India Office Library beyond. I would spend the day poring over unpublished letters and documents from the 1920s and 1930s, which I would discuss with Gopal over dinner.

One Sunday, when the archive was closed, I dragged Gopal along to Highgate Cemetery, to see the grave of Karl Marx. To reach our destination we had to change two tubes and walk up (by London standards) a steep hill. En route, we swapped stories. I told Gopal of how, at the insistence of some left-wing Congressmen, Gandhi was compelled to read Marx's *Das Kapital* when in his seventies, but gave up after the daunting first chapter on commodity fetishism. Gopal told me, in turn, about a press conference conducted by Gandhi's so-called spiritual successor, Vinoba Bhave, at the height of his 'Bhoodan' movement. Asked the difference between Gandhism and communism, Vinoba answered: 'Communism is Gandhism plus Violence'. When Vinoba boasted of his witticism to his colleague Jayaprakash Narayan, JP acidly remarked: 'In that case, is Gandhism merely Communism minus Violence?'

At Highgate, I had expected a modest memorial to Marx; what we found instead was a tombstone eight feet high with a polished bust of the revolutionary thinker on top. This had been erected quite recently, paid for by some wealthy Leftists or perhaps via the London Council's Heritage Fund. Finely scrubbed and polished, the stone had etched on it the slogan, 'Workers of the World Unite', followed by a series of names. These were, Jenny von Westphalen, Karl Marx, Helen Demuth, and Eleanor Marx. At the foot of the memorial was a bunch of fresh flowers placed by an earlier visitor of the day.

Gopal asked me to identify the other names. I did. The company Marx kept in death was pretty much the company he kept while he was alive. Jenny was the wife, four years older, aristocratic in background but devoted to her husband. Helen was the housekeeper and sometime mistress, who bore a son by him (adopted, to save everybody's face, by Marx's best friend). Eleanor was the beautiful and gifted daughter, a feminist and socialist who died by her own hand after discovering the truth about her father's relationship with

Helen Demuth. It was a poignant listing, but one name would have made it complete—Friedrich Engels.

After some minutes in silent contemplation, we turned away, heading, I thought, out of the cemetery and on to the tube station. 'There is something I wanted to see,' said Gopal, revealing for the first time why he had agreed so readily to come with me. To the left of Marx's grave was a sort of Comrade's Corner, graves of other communists exiled from other lands. Here were buried revolutionaries who had sought refuge in England after being thrown out of Iraq, Syria, and the like. The gravestone Gopal was looking for was in the extreme right-hand corner. It was in the name of 'Dr Yusuf Dadoo, president of the South African Communist Party'. I asked Gopal for details. 'He worked with Gandhi in India in the 1940s,' he answered, 'and, back in South Africa, was an early influence on Mandela.' An Indian and a Communist, the one direct link between Nelson Mandela and Mahatma Gandhi.[1]

Gopal Gandhi's services to our republic are substantial; yet they could have been even greater had our political class not been so consumed by pettiness. In 2010, Kashmir was gripped by violence and unrest. An outreach from the central government was called for. It was suggested that an interlocutor be appointed by New Delhi to go to the Valley. Gopal's name was proposed. He was, of course, superbly qualified for the task, having worked on conflict resolution in Sri Lanka, South Africa, and West Bengal. He had a winning personality, and spoke Hindustani (shading into Urdu) fluently, while carrying the name and lineage of the greatest modern Indian.

Gopal's name was enthusiastically approved by the National Security Advisor and by several cabinet ministers. But the prime minister, Dr Manmohan Singh, was ambivalent, and the president of the ruling Congress party, Sonia Gandhi, opposed. In the event, a group of three well-intentioned but relatively lightweight

---

[1] Dadoo, like the Arab comrades who lay next to him, had been born a Muslim. Yet he chose to be buried in what was, in effect, a Christian cemetery, albeit in a corner of this English field that would be forever Communist.

writers from Delhi were appointed as interlocutors. The Kashmiri separatists declined to meet them, and the trouble smouldered on. When an even more savage round of violence broke out in the Valley in 2016, Gopal's name once more did the rounds; but, of course, with the hardliner Narendra Modi as the prime minister, the proposal had no chance at all.

Gopal's own closest friend is his fellow former IAS officer, Keshav Desiraju. I first met Keshav in 1989, in Almora, where he was then district magistrate. In later years I have watched him closely at work in the fields of education and health, and can testify that he was an exemplary public servant, admired and respected by those he came in contact with. Keshav is also a scholar, the grandson of the philosopher Sarvepalli Radhakrishnan and the nephew of the historian Sarvepalli Gopal, and with degrees from Cambridge and Harvard himself. His deepest interest, however, is in Indian classical music (a subject on which he has often, and never patronizingly, instructed me over the years). After retirement he spent his time researching the definitive biography of the great singer M. S. Subbulakshmi.

The languages Keshav speaks fluently are English, Telugu, Tamil, and Hindi, in that order (he can also manage with Kannada). The languages Gopal has an absolute command over are Hindi, English, Tamil, and Gujarati, in that order (he can also manage with Bengali and Urdu). When Keshav and Gopal talk, the puns and allusions flow seamlessly in the three languages they share—English, Hindi, and Tamil—and range across culture, history, literature, and much else.

I have spent many hours with Gopal and Keshav, separately, and much time with them together. Speaking excellent English and modest Hindi, I share but one-and-a-half of their languages, but to be with them is entirely pleasurable, nonetheless. I remember with special warmth a bus journey that we took together from Chennai to Tiruvannamalai and back, since Gopal wanted to take the blessings of the sage Ramana Maharishi before a new assignment. En route he told me that I must write a column urging that M. S. Subbulakshmi be awarded India's highest honour, the Bharat Ratna, while Keshav added some details about her musical genius.

We reached Tiruvannamalai, visited the ashram before undertaking the obligatory parikrama of the hill. It was a hot day, and we needed water; but while Keshav and I (as naturalized hillmen of Uttarakhand) could drink from a farmer's hosepipe, Gopal, having lived the past five years in London, had to carry a plastic bottle. We teased him about this, so he returned to the subject of M. S. and why she deserved the country's highest honour. Gopal cannily argued that a recommendation on M. S.'s behalf would be dismissed as elitist, so to make it work I must argue that the popular singer Lata Mangeshkar get the award too.

I wrote the article asked for by my friend, and followed it up with another. Meanwhile, with the proposal out in the open, Gopal lobbied patiently behind the scenes to get the idea approved by the president of the republic. Some two years after that journey to Tiruvannamalai, Keshav travelled with me to the Narmada Valley, where I was in search of the first wife of the anthropologist Verrier Elwin. We found and spoke to the lady, and afterwards repaired for dinner to the Marwari Bhojnalaya in Amarkantak. There, in the Bilaspur edition of the *Dainik Bhaskar*, we discovered that our friend's campaigning had succeeded, and that M. S. Subbulakshmi had, finally and belatedly, been awarded the Bharat Ratna. We raised a toast (with tea) to Gopal; later, on our long train journey back to Delhi, Keshav told me about all the M. S. concerts he had attended.

On one of my visits to London, Gopal and Tara had the Anglican Bishop and anti-apartheid campaigner, Trevor Huddleston, over for dinner. Here Huddleston said, in answer to a question about his health: 'I hope to see apartheid dead before I am.' The regime in South Africa collapsed three years later. Huddleston made a brief trip back, and lived long enough to see his (comparatively) young friend, Gopalkrishna Gandhi, be asked to serve as India's high commissioner to South Africa.

Gopal Gandhi had been appointed for a three-year term, but after eighteen months in the job was asked to return to Delhi, to serve as secretary to the president of India. Gopal made many friends and a major impression in South Africa, and for the sake of both countries one wished he had stayed longer. Fortunately, when we heard he had been asked to return, Keshav Desiraju and I were able to make a quick trip to South Africa, my first trip to the land where Gandhi had become a Mahatma.

With Gopal and Tara, Keshav and I drove along the glorious Garden Route, visited the fabulous Clarke's Bookshop in Cape Town, and saw the shanty towns hidden away from the tree-lined suburbs of Johannesburg. Two memories of Gopal that remain vivid are, first, the care with which he introduced me to the great South African liberal Helen Suzman at a crowded reception in Pretoria (he wanted to make sure a historian met a person who had actually made history); and a moment in a long drive along the coast when we passed a statue of Vasco da Gama. This set Gopal off on a spontaneous show of his own, mimicking his brother Ramu's voice and manner, imagining the philosopher being confronted with the statue, and saying, 'This is an abomination, this cruel and crude triumphalism, this symbol of conquest and pillage and racism', and then giving, as a teacher and Gandhian must, the other side of the picture as well, and so continuing, 'On the other hand, Vasco was a seeker too, an explorer, even if his aims and methods were of his time, not ours'.[2] A third recollection comes to me as I write; of Gopal at a dinner table in Cape Town, conversing in Gujarati to the person seated next to him, the Ugandan–American political theorist, Mahmood Mamdani, each seizing, with equal relish, the chance to go back to a language of their childhood that they so rarely spoke any more.

Gopal's formal training was in literature. He had published a novel, *Refuge*, based on his Sri Lankan experience; a play on the tragic, doomed Mughal prince Dara Shukoh; and translated Vikram Seth's magnum opus, *A Suitable Boy*, into Hindi. He had

---

[2] Gopal's talent for mimicry is one of his lesser-known gifts. He does Nelson Mandela brilliantly, and Atal Bihari Vajpayee too.

also written a few poems, including one on the destruction of the Babri Masjid. Although his services as a public servant have now eclipsed his other contributions, when we first met, in the late 1980s, Gopal was known in the literary circles of New Delhi as the Gandhi brother who wrote or translated novels, as distinct from the Gandhi brother (Ramu) who wrote or spoke about philosophy and the Gandhi brother (Rajmohan) who wrote or spoke about politics and history.

In acknowledgement of my friend's primary training and orientation, I'd like to end with three literary memories. Some years ago, I was sheaving through a bunch of papers in the home of Professor K. Swaminathan, the chief editor of the *Collected Works of Mahatma Gandhi*. I discovered here a letter that he had written to Gopal Gandhi in June 1987. Swaminathan had just read Gopal's novel, *Saranam* (Refuge), which is about the plight of the Tamil-speaking workers in the tea plantations of Sri Lanka. Whereas the Tamils of the north had settled in the island centuries ago, these workers had been brought by the British in the nineteenth century. They were scorned by the Jaffna Tamils, and, even more, by the Sinhala majority. The latter pressured the Indian government to agree to repatriate these people back to a country their ancestors had been forcibly uprooted from.

When Swaminathan read Gopal Gandhi's novel, he was ninety, and ailing. Yet was moved enough to write his friend (now also mine) a long, handwritten letter, where he observed:

Gandhiji says:
    'When someone commits a crime anywhere, I feel I am the culprit.'
    The crime that you and I feel guilty of is the Indo-Ceylon Agreement of 1964, uprooting thousands of families from their habitat and rendering them stateless, vulnerable, and insecure. When the Jaffna Tamils win an election the 'Indian' Tamils in the plantations (held as helpless hostages) are vicariously punished by the fanatic fury of the Sinhalese. By way of

prayaschitta or atonement, you recognize and celebrate the moral outrage, the indefensible humanity, of these poor people who overcome evil by accepting their fate. In the result, aesthetic catharsis transforms an actual tragedy into an act of creation and this 'documentation of an experience' turns out to be a novel of classical quality and moving power which deserves repeated reading and clamours for filming and translation into Tamil.

A second memory is of a book Gopal translated, rather than wrote. In 2006, I was spending a term teaching at Yale. The day after I arrived, I went across to the university's library, and looked at their holdings on Gandhi. I found in the stacks a little pamphlet, not more than sixty pages long, called *The End of an Epoch*. I had it issued and took it to my room. It had been written by Manubehn Gandhi, the Mahatma's grand-niece and companion of his last days. The book was published in 1962, and it said on the title-page that it was 'translated from the Gujarati by Gopalkrishna Gandhi'.

When I found this book in an American library, I had known Gopal for some fifteen years. He was absolutely one of my closest friends. We had discussed, to death, his lineage and mine, his writings and mine. He had all my books; and I thought I had all of his. Gandhi himself had been a pre-eminent subject of our conversations. It was in, of all places, the Sterling Memorial Library of Yale University, that I now discovered that my friend's first literary production had been a translation, undertaken when he was merely seventeen, and from his fourth language, Gujarati, of a first-hand account of Gandhi's last days on earth.[3]

The last memory is of a book Gopal once owned. In 1991, I was in Bombay, and visited the (now sadly extinct) New and Second-hand Bookshop in Kalbadevi. I bought a pile of books,

---

[3] In his youth and early middle age Gopal wrote (and read) novels and plays, but as he grew older he has returned to Gandhi scholarship, editing anthologies on Gandhi and Sri Lanka, Gandhi and Bengal, Gandhi's legacy of constructive work, Gandhi's correspondence with Rajaji, among other works.

among them a little biography of Gandhi, written by a white priest, Joseph Doke, and first published in 1907. Although my copy was a later reprint I was glad to have it, for the author had been a close associate of Gandhi's in South Africa. I asked the shop to post it to me in Delhi, where I then lived. When the book arrived and I opened it again I noticed that the original owner's name was written on the flyleaf: 'Gopalkrishna Gandhi, July 1957'.

In the three decades since he wrote these words, my friend's hand had scarcely changed. I went over to his place, with the book I had bought in Bombay. He had forgotten that he once owned it. However, he remembered that in the summer of 1957 he was in Bombay, for his father was critically ill. He thought that after his father had died, also in Bombay, the book got lost in the turmoil. I suggested that this copy of Doke's biography of Gandhi was rightfully his. 'No, you keep it', said Gopal generously. He then pulled out a volume from his shelf, and remarked: 'I have this, anyway'. 'This' was the first edition of the Doke book, laminated and bound for the owner by the National Archives. On the book's flyleaf Devadas Gandhi—Gopal's father and the Mahatma's son—had written: 'This is the finest biography of Bapu'. Gopal, naturally, was well pleased with his copy of Doke. And I remained more than moderately satisfied with mine.

# 25

## AN ISLAND OF SANITY

### ELINOR SISULU

The idea of a publication dedicated to reflections on the life and times of such a distinguished individual appeals to the biographer and historian in me and I am deeply honoured by the invitation to be part of this wonderful project.

On a personal level, I appreciate the opportunity of reflecting on a friendship that has been surprisingly strong, given the limited time we spent together. When my husband and I were discussing how I could contribute to this festschrift, we reminisced about an evening, sometime in 1996, spent in the company of Gopalkrishna Gandhi and his lovely wife, Tara, at the home of South African activist Mewa Ramgobin, the former husband of Gopal's cousin, Ela Gandhi. Both Ela and Mewa had been the driving forces in the remaking of Phoenix Settlement into an important site of political and cultural activity and a monument to the teachings of Mahatma Gandhi.

It was a time of new beginnings, full of hope and inspiration. South Africa had weathered the last kicks of apartheid's dying horse. The internecine violence of the late 1980s and the early 1990s had subsided and fears that the country would spiral into civil war had been laid to rest. South Africa had miraculously produced a passably free and fair election and had, for the first time in its existence, a democratically elected parliament. All this overseen by the towering figure of Nelson Mandela, a global icon who transcended political, racial, or religious divides to become the much-loved president leading the country into a future in which anything seemed possible and achievable.

South Africa's democracy was like a new cloth, bright with the new colours of Mandela's rainbow; so it was not surprising that the mood at dinner that night was one of optimism and hope. Both Mewa and my husband, Max, were MPs in the first democratic parliament while Gopal was India's newly appointed high commissioner to South Africa. The conversation, centred on the liberation struggle and the historical relationship between India and South Africa, was of great interest to me because at the time I was researching the biography of my mother and father-in-law, Albertina and Walter Sisulu, who had worked closely with the South African Indian Congress in the 1950s.

Gopal was a fount of knowledge on the history of South Africa's liberation struggle in which his illustrious grandfather had played no small part. Max and I were able to boast that our house in the Johannesburg suburb of Kensington was a few doors away from the house in which Mahatma Gandhi lived for a short period in 1906. In fact, there were two houses in the neighbourhood that claimed that distinction and we were never able to establish which claim was accurate.

As we made our way home that night, my husband commented on how appropriate it was that Gopalkrishna Gandhi had been deployed as the high commissioner in the newly democratic South Africa, not only on account of his family connections but also his own interest and extensive knowledge of South African history and politics.

Around the time we met Gopal and Tara, I had become absorbed with the work of two writers, Kazuo Ishiguro and Vikram Seth, who had both published major novels in 1993: *The Remains of the Day* and *A Suitable Boy*. I had read Ishiguro's exquisite 1986 novel, *An Artist of the Floating World*—a haunting tale of the existential crisis of an aging artist in post-World War Japan. It fascinated me that a writer could switch from a Japanese setting to *The Remains of the Day*, whose protagonist is the embodiment of stiff upper-lipped English repression. This reading led me to Junichiro Tanizaki's 1940s novel, *The Makioka Sisters*, another narrative of a family negotiating its way through post-war changes, concerned with its reputation and the marriage prospects of its daughters.

I loved the Jane Austen quality of *The Makioka Sisters* and in keeping with my penchant for long family sagas, with the search for a husband for the daughters of the house being a strong narrative thread, I was delighted to lay my hands on *A Suitable Boy* which I read voraciously. One of Vikram Seth's friends, William Bissell, is quoted as saying of Seth while writing the book: 'He couldn't think about anything else, he couldn't do anything else. Food, sleep, nothing else mattered.'[1]

*A Suitable Boy* had the same effect on me as a reader. Once I entered the world of Lata, Mrs Rupa Mehra, and their family, I was completely captivated by the world I had stepped into and mesmerized by the characters that were so Indian and, at the same time, so universal. At times I felt as if I was meeting members of my own family in disguise. Mrs Rupa Mehra reminded me of some of my aunts who always worried about me finding a husband. As for the cantankerous Dr Kishen Chand Seth, I felt as if Vikram Seth knew my grandmother! I could not put the book down and my eyesight suffered from the physical burden of the unbroken marathon of reading. I resented visitors and housework and was a negligent wife and mother for those 1,488 pages. And when I reached the last page, I still had not had enough.

I recalled my stint as at the Bunting Institute at Radcliffe College when we had to present our projects to other fellows. There was a woman doing a PhD on George Eliot's *Middlemarch*. I thought she was insane. I could not understand how someone could spend years doing a whole PhD on one novel. After reading *A Suitable Boy*, I understood and apologized to her in my mind. If I had the luxury of time and resources, I could easily delve into the world of *A Suitable Boy* for the duration of a PhD. I like to think that Vikram Seth was speaking for himself when he put the following words in the mouth of one of his characters, Amit Chatterjee:

---

[1] 'A suitable joy', *The Guardian*, 27 March 1999.

But I too hate long books: the better, the worse. If they're bad they merely make me pant with the effort of holding them up for a few minutes. But if they're good, I turn into a social moron for days, refusing to go out of my room, scowling and growling at interruptions, ignoring weddings and funerals, and making enemies out of friends. I still bear the scars of *Middlemarch*.[2]

Shortly after my marathon read, I saw Gopal and Tara at a reception. 'I have just been reading a book called *A Suitable Boy*. Have you come across it?' I asked. Gopal responded, in his quiet and unassuming manner: 'I have just translated the book into Hindi.' I was speechless. One of the longest books in the English language, translated into Hindi? And he is not even a full-time translator! How and when did he do it? Sadly, I did not get the opportunity to ask Gopal these questions because his term as high commissioner to South Africa ended prematurely in 1997 when he had to return to India to take up the position of secretary to the president.

We missed Gopal's presence, especially when Walter Sisulu was honoured with the Padma Vibhushan in 1998, at the time only the fourth non-Indian citizen to receive this accolade. By that time our father's health would not allow him to travel to India, so the award was given at a special ceremony in Johannesburg attended by a huge contingent of anti-apartheid veterans. It was a truly special and joyous occasion.

At the end of 1999, I had the good fortune to visit India for the first time as a guest of the Indian Council of Cultural Relations but did not have the opportunity to catch up with Gopal and Tara because they were out of the country at the time. In 2006, I made my second trip to India as a judge of the Commonwealth Writers' Prize. I called Gopal who I think was in Bengal at the time. During our telephone conversation he congratulated me on my biography of Walter and Albertina Sisulu with his characteristically elegant

---

[2]Vikram Seth, *A Suitable Boy*, New Delhi: Aleph Book Company, 2014 (reprint), p. 1,427.

turn of phrase: 'As we speak, I am looking at your book on my shelf, at a slight angle, with a shaft of light shining on it.' I felt so affirmed that the book that I had spent so many years toiling over had a place on Gopalkrishna Gandhi's bookshelf.

I have admired Gopal's writing both for its literary excellence and political integrity and wisdom. By the time I read his article commending the New Zealand prime minister, Jacinda Ardern, for her response to the Christchurch mosque attack in March 2019, the horrific attacks on churches in Sri Lanka had already taken place, underlining the prophetic nature of his warning: 'If extremists practising their macabre method under the name of Islam now wreak vengeance on churches and chapels with Christian congregations at prayer, the world will not have a day of peace, its religions no freedom from tension, fear, hate. No immigrant anywhere outside South Asia, whether Hindu or Muslim or Sikh will then feel secure. Nor Christians, of an ethnicity same or similar to that of Christchurch's mass murderer.'[3]

Voices such as his are islands of sanity in what sometimes feels like a sea of madness. We in South Africa have been experiencing our particular form of madness, smouldering coals of xenophobic resentment that periodically burst into flames of horrific mob violence against migrants. This violence has sometimes been called Afrophobic because it is mainly African migrants who are targeted although Asian migrants are also affected. Others deny that it is xenophobic violence at all and refer to it as a war among the poor. Nevertheless, it is a terrible stain on the fabric of a nation whose freedom struggle was passionately supported by the largest international solidarity campaign in history. I have been profoundly disturbed hearing South Africans who should know better than bemoaning the 'opening of our borders to criminals and undesirable elements'. There seems to be no understanding that closing our borders will mean that borders will be closed against us and South

---

[3]Gopalkrishna Gandhi, 'Leaders must draw from New Zealand PM's courage and wisdom', *Hindustan Times*, 18 March 2019.

Africa could revert to the isolation of the apartheid era.

The difference in the latest outbreak of attacks in September 2019—xenophobic, Afrophobic or whatever we may choose to call it—is that for the first time there has been a strong response from the African continent. Images of the attacks, looting, and assaults flooded social media across Africa in a way that had not been possible in 2008. Enraged citizens and their governments alike made clear that the continent would no longer tolerate the brutality against fellow Africans. Zambia cancelled a friendly soccer match with South Africa's national team; shock waves rippled through the nation when the Madagascan team, which was hastily roped in as a stand-in, cancelled as well. For the first time, South Africans of the post-apartheid generation had a glimpse of what isolation from the rest of the continent could look like.

In Nigeria, the fallout took the dramatic form of retaliatory attacks on South African businesses. The South African government moved swiftly to manage the situation, sending envoys to African capitals to apologize and clarify that this was not the policy of the government. President Cyril Ramaphosa was booed and jeered at the start of his address at former Zimbabwean President Mugabe's memorial service in mid-September 2019. To his eternal credit, President Ramaphosa apologized, saying that what happened goes against the unity of the African people. As welcome as the apology was, it was just one step in addressing a complex problem with a multitude of causes.

Reflecting on why people should suddenly turn against the next man or woman with sticks and machetes, Nigerian commentator, Azu Ishiekwene, argued in his brilliant article 'The Death of Civility and the Rise of Rage' that politicians must take a share of the blame:

> It's partly because they believe what their politicians have been telling them: politicians who were either products of mob culture or who paved their way to power by feeding that culture have been telling the mob exactly what it wants to hear—that the immigrant has been stealing their jobs,

polluting their streets with drugs and crime, and violating their women. That the immigrant has infested and compromised their social security systems and is stealing their benefits. That the immigrant has been reaping where he did not sow and it's only a matter of time before he will not only steal the harvest but also steal the seed and the land... In our desperation for a better, more secure future after years of failed expectations and betrayal, we have created the fiction that finding scapegoats will heal our wounds and assuage our pain.[4]

Ishiekwene argued that 'politicians should not pretend they're embarrassed, surprised, or even confused. Why should they be? Lack of compromise and the desperation for power for its own sake—two illegitimate children of politicians—have finally come of age. The result has been a deadly culture of rage and self-help among citizens misdirecting their anger.'

The shimmering rainbow-hued fabric of South African democracy is now tattered and frayed around the edges and we have a new generation of young people born after 1994 who are increasingly frustrated with the African National Congress (ANC) and questioning the old orthodoxies. While it is the condition of youth to question earlier generations, I find it very disturbing that the critique is based on little or no understanding of the past. History was not a compulsory subject in South African schools and the loss of historical knowledge in just one generation is frightening. When I mentioned to my sister-in-law, Sheila Sisulu, that I was surprised that some of our children, coming from a political family, displayed surprising ignorance of some basic historical facts, her response was: 'Who is to blame. If we do not teach them how do we expect them to learn—through a process of osmosis?'

There are brash young political leaders who, in the interests of advancing their own political cause, peddle the notion that Mandela was a sell-out and there was no armed struggle in South Africa.

---

[4]Azu Ishiekwene, 'The Death of Civility and the Rise of Rage', *Daily Maverick*, 12 September 2019.

They instead hold up Robert Mugabe as a beacon of pan-Africanism who achieved liberation through the barrel of the gun while the ANC achieved it by accommodating the whites. And, sadly, young people who are not grounded in historical knowledge believe them.

I started a Twitter debate when I countered this assertion by pointing out that after protracted armed struggle Zimbabwe's independence was negotiated at the Lancaster House Conference in 1979 which paved the way for independence in 1980. Clearly many of the people pontificating about armed struggle knew nothing about the Lancaster House Conference and one of them asked me: 'Why are we debating what happened in 1980? All the people who were at that conference are dead and gone!' Which made me feel like a ghost!

Another young person asked: '[How] will history help us while we are being murdered and raped every day. We are creeping closer to total collapse and revolt of the masses. The cost of living is out of control and you guys suggest we sit and discuss history...?' The old adage that 'those who do not learn from history are doomed to repeat it' is applicable here. This young person could not understand the politicians' manipulation of historical fact for the purposes of manipulating their mainly youthful constituency.

Since my sixtieth birthday in 2018, I have become more conscious of how we have failed to transfer knowledge from one generation to the other, not in the form of unquestionable dogma, but as living history that is textured and nuanced and can be examined through different lenses. If we don't engage in a more intentional inter-generational transfer of knowledge and seriously address issues of reading and literacy, we will have the kind of ignorance that gives rise to electorates that vote for vile, chauvinistic, racist, bombastic, dictatorial, and proto-fascist leaders, the likes of whom I prefer to leave unmentioned in this tribute. The frightening thing is not that these characters exist, but that people would actually vote for them, not once but over and over again.

In his thought-provoking reflection on the 150th birth

anniversary of Mahatma Gandhi, Gopal Gandhi had written about a 'sloughing of values':

> Like the icecaps that are melting and sliding off the Poles, certain time-honoured values are flaking off that globe. These values are human rights, civil liberties and democratic dissent. Where inclusion and accommodation were ideals, exclusion, dispossession, dis-entitlement rule. Names and words like 'outsider', 'infiltrator', 'illegal immigrant' are to be heard now in the same timbre and pitch in the world's most advanced 'liberal' democracies as in its entrenched autocracies. Gandhi's legacy seems pulseless as the world moves from the Universal Declaration of Human Rights to a Global Proclamation of Human Intolerance.[5]

A continent away, Azu Ishiekwene argues:

> We have moved from a time when civility urged us to ask a disagreeable person to go to hell in a way that still made them look forward to the trip to a season when we prepare hell and process the inhabitants even before we get to know them.
>
> If we want to change what is happening on the streets, we must start by taking civility back, the golden measure of which is doing to others as we would like done to us. We must deplore lack of compromise in politics and call out – instead of applauding – politicians who play to our base instincts. We must demand more of ourselves as citizens and, of course, demand more of our leaders.[6]

Demanding more of our leaders means transcending political party divides and asking for a new kind of politics. In his analysis of opposition unity, Gopal writes that 'ultimately, what is as important as, if not more than, a change of the party in power or a change

---

[5]Gopalkrishna Gandhi, 'Gopalkrishna Gandhi on Mahatma Gandhi: The pulse of a legacy in an age of heroics', *The Hindu*, 2 October 2019.
[6]Ishiekwene, 'The Death of Civility and the Rise of Rage'.

of leader is the inauguration of a new political spirit. India is tired of its politics. It needs not new politicians but a new politics. The Opposition must offer not a BJP-free but a fear-free and corruption-free alternative to their voters.'[7]

This argument applies almost universally, from the USA to the UK and from Cape Town to Cairo. It certainly applies to Zimbabwe, the country of my birth and my country of nationality, South Africa, where there is increasing disillusionment with political parties and the feeling that we are faced with 'no-choice' elections in which none of the political parties offers solutions to the greatest challenges of our time. I do not know what the new politics would be. It seems that we do not get satisfactory solutions from either the Left or the Right and that humanity is desperately in need of a new paradigm.

What I do know is that in pursuit of the new paradigms that will address the greatest challenges of our time, we need to continue to struggle for the time-honoured values of human rights, civil liberties, and democratic dissent. We must not look to populist politicians who tell us what we want to hear rather than what we need to know, tricking us into believing in simple solutions to highly complex problems. We need politicians who will stick to their principles and not be swept away by the tide of popular sentiment.

Talking about the courage to stick to one's convictions against the tide of popular sentiment, I have enormous admiration for Gopal's support of the mercy plea of Mumbai attack convict, Yakub Memon. I know that I would not have the courage to do so if I were in his position.

The ANC abolished the death penalty when it came to power in 1994 and firmly maintained that the issue was not negotiable, despite periodic demands for a referendum on the issue. Recent anger and indignation against a spate of horrific acts of violence

---

[7]Gopalkrishna Gandhi, 'The Algebra of Opposition Unity', *The Hindu*, 10 November 2018.

against women and children have turned up the volume of public calls for the re-introduction of the death penalty. In a climate where feelings are charged about the high levels of violence against women and children and communities feel overwhelmed, a vote for the reinstatement of capital punishment is quite likely. Those who oppose the death penalty face criticism of siding with the perpetrators than the victims. I have found the opening lines of Gopal's book *Abolishing the Death Penalty: Why India Should Say No to Capital Punishment* the most powerful I have read on the matter:

> When a man kills, he breaks the law. When the state punishes by death it upholds the law. The man murders, the state executes; one deals death, the other awards it. Murder extinguishes life; the death penalty annuls the right to stay alive. The purposes are different but the result identical—a corpse where a human being was.

Finally, the best part of participating in this festschrift has been the exercise of reading Gopal's writings over the years—reflections of the highest quality—that resonated with me on so many levels. Hopefully, one day I will be able to reminisce with him, over a cup of tea, about the state of the world and the translating of *A Suitable Boy*.

## 26

## MAKING TRUTH POWERFUL

ARUNA ROY

The seeming advantage of being born to particular privilege can be an extraordinary burden to carry in life. Living up to the irrational expectations of an extraordinary legacy can be even more difficult. In India, where heredity and privilege are both glorified and criticized, it can become a baggage that overshadows one's individuality. But Gopal's contributions to public life have come from an evolved and organic way of life that has set him apart. They resonate with the values of the pre- and post-Independence era, while exploring the role of a public intellectual and a worthy citizen in each phase of his working life. His commitment to social justice and ethical and constitutional values, regardless of the political structure, has been a non-negotiable part of that paradigm.

His gentle and persistent presence in the sphere of public expression has placed constitutional values persuasively and unambiguously at the centre of open debate, enriching and deepening the discourse, without seeking popularity or public approval. Through his regular writings, columns, and public speeches, he has brought dignity and humanity to bear on constitutional democracy. Most of the issues he has taken up have been at the forefront of our consciousness. His public articulations reflect on and draw from the best in our national heritage. Yet they relate to topical concerns, with a candid recognition of the passage of time. His interventions are principled and, therefore, touch on what is constant in the life of nations, people, and the resultant polity. He has not been cautious in addressing uncomfortable and unpopular issues or expressing opinions on them. He is respectful of differences and dissent, though firm in his chosen rational beliefs. Heredity and privilege are a mixed blessing. Those outside the charmed circle look at the aura of a famous name with envy. But I wonder how much of a burden it places on those born into it. Gandhiji and C. Rajagopalachari preceded Gopal in all introductions. Walking the tightrope between the weight of inheritance and the awkwardness of constant comparison can daunt sensibilities. However, this responsibility shaped in Gopal and his siblings a need to bring ethics to public life. It also led them to constantly critique privilege and make persistent attempts to live it down.

These issues continue to preoccupy the concerns of contemporary political debates. Newer forms of privilege have taken over but general attitudes have remained unchallenged. In the case of Gopal Gandhi, many of them were challenged in practice and in the ability to espouse unpopular causes through principled and logical responses.

The style and persona of a public figure are often in contradiction with their statements, legitimizing the impunity of power and its claim to privilege. Gopal Gandhi, wearing the burden of public responsibility and accolades with humility, is in striking contrast to the self-proclaimed propaganda, bombast, and the personal aggrandizement of many public figures who people our papers and unfortunately influence young minds.

I met Gopal more than fifty years ago, in July 1968, on a rainy day at the Lal Bahadur Shastri Academy in Mussoorie. Years later, I was in a roomful of amused listeners, when Gopal publicly remarked that 'only medicines and civil servants come in "batches"!' Nevertheless, it was while training as IAS 'batchmates' in Thanjavur that a friendship began, which grew and mellowed over the years. Although, I quit the civil services in a few years, our shared concerns often brought us together, as we struggled in our own spheres of work, to face a polity with diminishing beliefs in ethics and public morality. Despite living in worlds asymmetrical in physical and structural senses, we walked in the same direction, drawing on lessons and support offered by each paradigm.

Even as an IAS officer, Gopal was driven by an innate and powerful impetus to be 'fair' rather than by his status. He must have thought deeply about choosing a career in which an open examination determined his selection. He served as a civil servant should—with a duty to implement the law, and a commitment to the Constitution. He had no fanfare about even being an IAS officer. In fact, he was best placed to demonstrate the potential importance of the 'role'—and not the 'status' of the popularly exalted 'IAS'.

In his post-IAS career of occupying public office, he demonstrated the same dedication to the duty and responsibility of the 'post' he occupied. As India's high commissioner to post-apartheid South Africa, he set the stage for a lasting relationship of mutual respect and shared concerns. In Norway, he played the role of an ideal diplomat and then championed peace in Sri Lanka. As the governor in West Bengal, he quickly built a reputation of choosing principle over state power or popularity, establishing non-partisan ethics in a state, where he was held by all parties and the people in great respect. As the state's governor, he inaugurated the national convention on the right to food—setting a new standard of state engagement with human rights campaigns.

It is in his post-IAS, post-'public office' era that the ordinary Indian has seen the mettle of a person who can stand up against the majority opinion. It is also only after leaving public office that he was able to freely express his personal views, and help develop ideas and contribute to building public ethics in India. This is exemplified in his writings, but his concern with the death penalty and his advocacy for its abolition is a particular example where he voiced his opinion on specific instances, and even compiled his thoughts on the subject in a book.

There is an India that stays silent and does not articulate its deep concerns, in fear of a government that can become belligerent or vindictive. Gopal's serious concerns regarding the death penalty, expressed in the context of Yakub Memon's mercy petition, stand out as a case in point. The issue was unpopular and the vice-presidential elections were round the corner, a time when any other candidate would have kept their own counsel and remained silent. But his concern for justice and ethics went beyond realpolitik. While filing his nomination for the office of the vice president, he explained his actions: 'As a common, independent citizen, it is my duty to fulfil my principles. I believe in that. I have drawn inspiration on the death penalty from two persons—Mahatma Gandhi who was opposed to it and Babasaheb Ambedkar, who said it is only proper to abolish it.... *'Mahatma Gandhi opposed [the] death penalty. He fell to assassins' bullets, but his two sons appealed to the government of the day, saying that Nathuram Godse should not be hanged.'*[8]

His letter to the president stated:

> Yakub Memon submitted to Indian jurisdiction, when he may quite easily have evaded justice. A respected officer of Indian intelligence has spoken of his cooperation with the law, thus rendering the death penalty completely inappropriate in his case. Former Supreme Court judges have openly said that his execution would be unjust. Public protestations of this nature and from such quarters are rare. They must give us pause, for whether or not there was a secret understanding with Memon that is being disregarded, a doubt would irretrievably be cast on India's integrity of process if in the face of this, Yakub Memon is executed.
>
> As many as 300 persons from all walks of life including former judges, lawyers, politicians and others have appealed to Your Excellency.

This extraordinary support did little to change the decision of the president. In *Abolishing the Death Penalty*, his well-researched and erudite arguments place the issue in the public domain for all those who want to be informed and believe in justice. The compulsion to quote from the book emanates from the desire to resist the 'WhatsApp University' culture, in the swift-moving world

---

[8]'Mahatma's sons opposed [the] death penalty for Godse, Apte. I belong to that school of thought: Gopal Gandhi', *Hindu Business Line*, 11 January 2018. [italics added].

of one-liners and 50-second bytes, where judgements are made with little information, and opinions are manufactured to mislead the people. The answer lies in a critical review of our times, not merely to combat the knowledge deficit, but to beat the deficit of humanity. Instead of civilizing us, as we 'progress with technology', such communication seems to be reducing the human response to its most primitive: persuading the ignorant that revenge and violence will settle scores and lead to permanent solutions. Though the death penalty is part of the rape law, for instance, the truth is it barely touches on the conditions that provoke these acts, or reduces the increasing numbers of such cases. The promotion of violence—whether as punishment or as war—raises a question on the linearity of civilizations marching on to a better world. It pushes us back to savagery and inhumanity as essential responses. Among its many fallacious arguments is the claim that in order for humanity to survive, we have to propagate inhumanity.

In Gopal's book, he describes the death penalty as 'judicial or an administrative murder'. He adds further: 'And that has to do with a hinterland of views, predilections and considerations that find their way into, what can be called, the sociology and politics of capital crime. When a man kills he breaks the law. When the state punishes by death it upholds the law. The man murders, the state executes; one deals death, the other awards it. Murder extinguishes life; the death penalty annuls the right to stay alive. The purposes are different but the result identical—a corpse where a human being was.'

Without complicated arguments, or convoluted language, this analysis cuts to the core of the issue. During the Right to Information (RTI) campaign, Gopal was a constant enthusiast, supporter, and participant through his writings, and we found his sharp perception and commonsensical articulation extremely helpful. It was, therefore, appropriate that he wrote the foreword to the book on the movement entitled *The RTI Story: Power to the People* that chronicled the stories of ordinary Indians who contribute unceasingly to keep the spirit of democracy vibrant and alive. The foreword combined scholarship, concern, and wisdom with simplicity and grace. In his simple manner, he wove history with contemporary concerns into an infrangible logic for the readers. To quote:

> India's independence moved us out of the valley of political thralldom and stood us, face to face, overnight, with the realities of our own multiple ills, our enervations and injustices, and the vice-like grip of several hegemonisms which two persons above all others recognized all too well—Mahatma Gandhi and Babasaheb Dr B. R. Ambedkar.

He (as very few others could) connected the thoughts and ideas of two of the most towering figures of the Indian nationalist movement with the role of the ordinary citizen in independent India. He wrote on the two figures:

> Even in the few months that were given to him after 15 August 1947, Gandhi strove, tirelessly, sleeplessly, to make provincial governments and the new central government accountable for assuring human rights to riot victims, especially women, getting administrations to provide shelter and supply minimum rations and clothing to the dispossessed.... Gandhi advised the administration on where and to whom blankets needed to be given and if raincoats were hard to find, to provide them stacks of newspapers to spread on the ground so that the women and children among them would not have to lie on the bare and wet earth. All this nudging of the administration he did as an 'ordinary citizen'.
>
> Babasaheb's detailed and far-seeing crafting of fundamental rights guaranteeing our rights and privileges as citizens, in the Constitution and provisions in it for the accounting and audit of public funds, were designed to open up our newly won freedom to public view, public experiencing. They were to save us from ourselves, help our lungs take in a new breath of our newly free air. The Constitution did not make these

rights absolute or unbridled but it did clothe them with what, speaking in the Constituent Assembly on 4 November 1948, Dr Ambedkar called 'Constitutional morality'. This was a new and novel concept. The authorities of the state, he said, were empowered but their powers derived from the Constitution and the laws and they were open to censure for all their public acts. He thus gave 'morality' a political dimension.

Ambedkar clearly had in mind the possibility that independent India would have and would exercise with verve its political rights, but the common man and woman would lag behind in the claiming of social and economic rights, which are the ethical dividend of citizenship.

Connecting the contemporary RTI movement with the larger questions of justice, while acknowledging the role of the collective struggles of ordinary people, he helped build a clearer perspective, and a comprehensive discourse of the RTI as a robust people's movement. Speaking of the campaign as it forged into a movement, Gopal wrote:

> And yet a connected account of the stages of the campaign gathering momentum, catalysing other campaigns, and then culminating in 2005 in the RTI Act, eluded us.... But the book is more, much more than a chronicle of successive events. It is a testament of the willpower, determination and resolve that comes from a people knowing that their cause is true and just, that it is not just about their 'claims' as individuals but about the veracity and indeed the necessity, in terms of social justice, of claiming that which is legitimate. It is a manifesto of truth-seeking, truth-telling and truth-living. Its author is no individual, no institution. Its author is the true word.
>
> The RTI Act has been true to its mandate, faithful to its promise. From a ration shop in a hamlet to the president's residence in Delhi, it has done what it should be doing. Like any other law, it has had its saboteurs, abusers. A redemptive law should be judged by its successes, but be

ready to be questioned for its failings. An Act that brings about accountability should not be coy when it is itself called to account. The Act has come, like all Acts come, from the wisdom of the Indian parliament. Curiously, it is in its birthplace, its own cradle, the Hon'ble Parliament, that the Act seems to have found some of its most vociferous detractors. They have their reasons. Sections of the political class and of the bureaucracy have also developed methods to tiptoe round provisions of the Act. They have their skills. This weakens the impact of the Act. There is another 'problem'. The Act's workforce, namely, the personnel in the information commissions, reflect all the diversity of our population. Our information commissions and their secretariats have had in their personnel from the many active to not-a-few slothful, from the many dedicated to the not-so-few sceptical. And they include, one might add, some fearful and some rather compromised. 'Compromise' does not need explaining. But all this does not dishearten the true harbingers of the Act who remain prepared to test its working against its experience....

His concerns with violence—and another kind of 'execution', or power-based murder, continued into his relationship with the RTI Act:

Behind the RTI story lies one hugely dismaying fact: the lives of RTI activists and campaigners are at risk. As many as sixty of them have lost their lives. They are martyrs to the cause of the good state, of public accountability, constitutional morality. We honour them. But should such courage be met in our country by murder? It is a national scandal, shame and tragedy that they have been killed. Just as we mourn the loss of brave soldiers protecting our nation's territorial integrity, we mourn the loss of brave soldiers protecting our constitutional integrity. The tragedy is that one is killed by bullets from across the border, and the other by one of our own.

With the imposition of Aadhaar on the entire citizenry and the opposition to making Aadhaar mandatory by many of us from the RTI community, the Aadhaar and the RTI debate have brought in many shades of complex arguments about the use of information, technology, privacy, surveillance, and interpretation of information rights. At a conference in New Delhi, Gopal summed up the core issue by juxtaposing the two concerns and cautioned the government from 'Using Aadhaar as a mechanism by which the state could watch every move of every person all the time. RTI's basic role must be promoted where the citizen can watch every move of the state and government all the time.'

A writer, historian, and scholar, Gopal has emerged out of composite learning—culled from serious reading in many languages, but mainly from life. He is also a popular teacher, writer, researcher, a great public speaker, and an engaged public intellectual. As a meticulous historian looking for evidence and understanding all sides, he would correct misappropriations of Gandhi's words, even if it was a good and powerful statement. His own engagement as a historian and political scientist with Ambedkar, Gandhi, Bhagat Singh, and JP provides some important ways in which we can glean the teachings from all individually and collectively.

I will conclude this short retrospective of fifty years of active life with appreciation of his style of delivery, the crafting of his lectures, and their concise titles, bringing to the fore the student of English literature in him. Delivering a memorial lecture for Justice Krishna Iyer in Trivandrum in 2017, he titled the lecture, 'Who rules India, Parliament, Panchayat or NOTA?' He concluded the memorable evening with, 'Money, fear, and prejudice', actually do so.

Throughout his life, Gopal has championed an India that seeks justice and implementation of constitutional values; a country which upholds progressive and humanitarian values in society. Perhaps for the larger populace, derisive comments about 'liberals' do not hold the stigma that is propagated by their articulators. We share these concerns. But my methods of protesting on the streets and slogan-shouting are not the same as Gopal's ways of registering dissent and difference of opinion; it is propitious that it is so. It is in the plurality of expression and in the tolerance for other forms of communication that we express and acknowledge our respect for India's complex democratic, political, and constitutional plurality.

This remarkable seventy-five-year journey runs parallel with the life of independent India. From a tolerant and mature political milieu, it shifts to contemporary India, where politics has been reduced to its most narrow, restrictive, and often crass form. Integrity has lost to propaganda, and anyone who dares to question the state is turned into a victim. Gopal entered that space fearlessly. It is important to pay tribute to an extraordinary and courageous human being, who used his privileges to 'make truth powerful'. In that lies Gopal Gandhi's true heritage—the tireless commitment and contribution to his country and its people.

# PUBLICATIONS OF GOPALKRISHNA GANDHI

**Play**
*Dara Shukoh: A Play*, Banyan Books, Mumbai,1993; republished by Tranquebar, New Delhi, 2010.

**Novel**
*Saranam* with a foreword by Kamaladevi Chattopadhyay, Affiliated East-West, Madras, 1985; republished as *Refuge*, Ravi Dayal, New Delhi, 1989; Penguin Books India, New Delhi, 2010.

**Translations**
Manubahen Gandhi, *Ba Bapuni Antim Jhankhi*
Translated from Gujarati into English as *The End of An Epoch*, Navajivan Publishing House, Ahmedabad, 1962.

Vikram Seth, *A Suitable Boy*
Translated from English into Hindustani as *Koi Achchha Sa Ladka*, Vani Prakashan, New Delhi, 1997.

Tiruvalluvar, *Tirukkural*
Translated from Tamil into English as *The Tirukkural*, Aleph Book Company, New Delhi, 2016.

**Anthologies and Edited Volumes**
*Gandhi and South Africa: 1914-1948*, edited with E. S. Reddy, Navajivan Publishing House, Ahmedabad, 1993.

*Gandhi and Sri Lanka*, Visva-Lekha, Colombo, 2002.

*Nehru and Sri Lanka*, Visva-Lekha, Colombo, 2002.

*India House, Colombo*, Visva-Lekha, Colombo, 2002.

*The Oxford India Gandhi: Essential Writings*, Oxford University Press, New Delhi, 2007.

*A Frank Friendship: Gandhi and Bengal A Descriptive Chronology*, with a foreword by Amartya Sen, Seagull Books, Calcutta, 2007.

*Gandhi is Gone: Who will Guide us now?* Permanent Black, New Delhi, 2007.

*My Dear Bapu...: Letters from C. Rajagopalachari to Mohandas Karamchand Gandhi, Devadas Gandhi and Gopalkrishna* Gandhi, Penguin, New Delhi, 2012.

*Restless as Mercury: My Life as a Young Man*, Aleph Book Company, New Delhi, 2021.

**Non-fiction**

*Of a Certain Age: Twenty Life-Sketches,* Penguin India, New Delhi, 2011.

*Abolishing the Death Penalty: Why India Should Say No to Capital Punishment*, Aleph Book Company, New Delhi, 2016.

# NOTES ON THE CONTRIBUTORS

MARIA AURORA COUTO is a writer with interests in literature, culture, and education. Her books include *Goa: A Daughter's Story* and *Filomena's Journey: A Portrait of a Marriage, a Family and a Culture*. She currently lives in the village of Aldona in Goa.

JAYANTHA DHANAPALA is a distinguished Sri Lankan diplomat who has made significant contribution in the fields of nuclear disarmament and human rights. He has held ambassadorial appointments at the United Nations and in Washington, D. C., and served as the president of the landmark Nuclear Non-Proliferation Treaty Review and Extension Conference, held in 1995. Between 2007 and 2017, he was the president of the Pugwash Conference on Science and World Affairs.

RAJMOHAN GANDHI's latest book is *Modern South India: A History from the 17th Century to Our Times*. He teaches, writes, and talks, but wishes to learn, read, and listen more than he has done.

AMITAV GHOSH is the author of two books of non-fiction, a collection of essays, and ten novels. His books have won many prizes and his work has been translated into more than thirty languages. In 2018, he became the first English language writer to receive India's highest literary honour, the Jnanpith Award. His most recent publication is *Gun Island*.

VENU MADHAV GOVINDU has co-authored *The Web of Freedom: J. C. Kumarappa and Gandhi's Struggle for Economic Justice* (Oxford University Press, 2016). His professional interests are in computer vision and he is Associate Professor, Department of Electrical Engineering, Indian Institute of Science, Bengaluru.

KESHAVA GUHA is a writer of fiction as well as literary and political journalism. His novel, *Accidental Magic*, was published by HarperCollins in 2019. He lives in Delhi.

RAMACHANDRA GUHA is a historian and biographer based in Bengaluru. His books include *Savaging the Civilized*, *Environmentalism: A Global History*, *Gandhi: The Years that Changed the World*, and *The Commonwealth of Cricket*.

GOPAL GURU is Editor, *Economic and Political Weekly*, and a former Professor at the Centre for Political Studies, Jawaharlal Nehru University, New Delhi.

TISSA JAYATILAKA is a literary critic, writer, and translator. He has taught British and American literature at several universities in Sri Lanka and the US. He also served as the executive director of the United States–Sri Lanka Fulbright Commission.

SOPAN JOSHI is a freelance journalist in Delhi. Travelling widely in India, he has examined a range of social and environmental matters as a researcher, reporter, and editor over the past twenty-five years for several periodicals and publications. He is the author of three books in Hindi.

FEROZ ABBAS KHAN is a theatre and film director and screenwriter. He won three national and numerous international awards for the film *Gandhi, My Father*. He is widely acclaimed for his theatrical work which includes landmark productions such as *Tumhari Amrita*, *Mahatma vs Gandhi*, and the musical play, *Mughal-e-Azam*. He was the first artistic and festival director of Prithvi Theatre.

ISAAC KRAMNICK was Richard J. Schwartz Professor of Government Emeritus at Cornell University. Among his many publications on the history of political thought was *Harold Laski: A Life on the Left* (1993) that he wrote with Barry Sheerman.

# NOTES ON THE CONTRIBUTORS

T. M. KRISHNA is a vocalist in the Carnatic tradition and a public intellectual. His latest book, *Sebastian and Sons: A Brief History of Mrdangam Makers*, traces the history of mrdangam makers and the mrdangam over the past century. He received the Ramon Magsaysay Award in 2016 and the Indira Gandhi Award for National Integration in 2017.

NAYANJYOT LAHIRI is Professor of History at Ashoka University. She is the author of *Pre-Ahom Assam* (1991), *The Archaeology of Indian Trade Routes* (1992), *Finding Forgotten Cities: How the Indus Civilization was Discovered* (2005), *Marshalling the Past: Ancient India and its Modern Histories* (2012), *Ashoka in Ancient India* (2015), *Monuments Matter: India's Archaeological Heritage Since Independence* (2017), *Time Pieces: A Whistle-stop Tour of Ancient India* (2018), and *Archaeology and the Public Purpose: Writings on and by M. N. Deshpande* (2021). She is the co-author of *Copper and its Alloys in Ancient India* (1996), editor of *The Decline and Fall of the Indus Civilization* (2000), *Ancient India: New Research* (2009), and *Buddhism in Asia: Revival and Reinvention* (2016).

JANAKI LENIN is the author of two volumes of *My Husband and Other Animals*. Her latest book is titled *Every Creature Has a Story* and was released in July 2020. She writes on a wide range of wildlife and conservation subjects for newspapers and magazines. She and her partner share their home on the outskirts of Chennai with their pets and free-ranging wild creatures.

VIVEK MENON is an Indian wildlife conservationist, environmental commentator, author, and photographer with a passion for elephants and birds. Founder of five environmental and nature conservation organizations, Menon is Founder and Executive Director of the Wildlife Trust of India. He is the author/editor of ten wildlife books and has written hundreds of articles on natural history.

RUDRANGSHU MUKHERJEE is Chancellor and Professor of History at Ashoka University of which he was the founding Vice Chancellor. He is the author and editor of several books relating to the history of modern India.

DINYAR PATEL is Assistant Professor of History at the S. P. Jain Institute of Management and Research in Mumbai. He is the author of *Naoroji: Pioneer of Indian Nationalism* published by Harvard University Press in 2020.

PRABHAT PATNAIK, an economist, has taught at the University of Cambridge, England, and at Jawaharlal Nehru University, New Delhi, where he is currently Professor Emeritus. His books include *Accumulation and Stability under Capitalism, The Value of Money, Re-envisioning Socialism,* and *Capital and Imperialism* (with Utsa Patnaik, forthcoming).

NIRUPAMA MENON RAO was the Indian Foreign Secretary from 2009–2011. She served as high commissioner of India in Sri Lanka and as ambassador to China and the United States. After retirement, Rao was a Fellow at Brown University and George Ball Adjunct Professor at Columbia University. She is a Global Fellow of The Woodrow Wilson Center, Washington, D. C., and a recipient of the Vanitha Ratna Award of the Government of Kerala. Rao is founder of the South Asian Symphony Orchestra—a peacebuilding project for the region.

ARUNA ROY is a socio-political activist who has campaigned for constitutional rights for the poor, most notably the Right to Information and the Right to Employment. She is a founding member of the Mazdoor Kisan Shakti Sangathan, National Campaign for People's Right to Information, and the School for Democracy. Her awards include the Ramon Magsaysay Award in 2000.

UPINDER SINGH is Professor of History, Ashoka University, India. Her writings range over various aspects of ancient Indian social, economic, religious, and intellectual history. She is the author of *Kings, Brāhmaṇas, and Temples in Orissa: An Epigraphic Study*; *Ancient Delhi*; *The Discovery of Ancient India: Early Archaeologists and the Beginnings of Archaeology*; *A History of Ancient and Early Medieval India: From the Stone Age to the Twelfth Century*; *The Idea of Ancient India: Essays on Religion, Politics*, and *Archaeology; and Political Violence in Ancient India*. She has edited *Delhi: Ancient History and Rethinking Early Medieval India*, and co-edited *Ancient India: New Research, Asian Encounters: Exploring Connected Histories*, and *Buddhism in Asia: Revival and Reinvention*.

ELINOR SISULU is a Zimbabwean-born South African writer and human rights activist and the award-winning author of the children's book, The Day Gogo Went to Vote and the biography of her parents-in-law, Walter and Albertina Sisulu, In Our Lifetime. She is a founder and current director of the Puku Children's Literature Foundation, that runs the multilingual puku.co.za website promoting South African children's books.

ERIK SOLHEIM is a well-known global leader on environment and development as well as an experienced peace negotiator. He served as Norwegian minister of Environment and International Development from 2005–12. He was Chair of the OECD Development Assistance Committee as well as the Executive Director of UN Environment. He led the peace efforts in Sri Lanka and played a vital role in peace efforts in Nepal, Myanmar, and Sudan.

TRIDIP SUHRUD is currently working on the *Diaries of Manu Gandhi* and a volume of letters with Gopalkrishna Gandhi titled *Scorching Love: Letters from Mohandas Karamchand Gandhi to his son, Devadas*. He has previously published critical editions of Gandhi's *Hind Swaraj* and *Autobiography*. He does not spin, neither a charkha nor a tale.

A. R. VENKATACHALAPATHY, historian and Tamil writer, is a Professor at the Madras Institute of Development Studies, Chennai. A winner of the VKRV Rao Prize, his publications in English include *Tamil Characters: Personalities, Politics, Culture, Who Owns That Song? The Battle for Subramania Bharati's Copyright, The Province of the Book: Scholars, Scribes, and Scribblers in Colonial Tamil Nadu,* and *In Those Days There Was No Coffee: Writings in Cultural History.*

JON WESTBORG, born in 1946 in Darjeeling, is a Norwegian and a PIO. He has extensive experience in the fields of humanitarian assistance, development cooperation, and peacebuilding. He also has an M. Phil degree. He served as Norway's ambassador to Sri Lanka, Maldives, India, and Bhutan. He initiated Norway's facilitation of the Sri Lankan peace process with a central role in securing the 2002 ceasefire agreement.